READINGS IN ENGLISH
TRANSFORMATIONAL
GRAMMAR

Readings in English Transformational Grammar /

RODERICK A. JACOBS
University of California, San Diego

PETER S. ROSENBAUM
Teachers College, Columbia University

Ginn and Company
A Xerox Company

Waltham, Massachusetts
Toronto
London

To the children of Vietnam   1945–19??

Contents

PART THREE / Revising the Model

Introduction

The articles contained in this volume are either theoretical or descriptive contributions to the field of linguistic inquiry known as transformational linguistics. The issues considered are general in scope although some area of English syntax is the concern of each writer. The articles, conceived and written between mid-1964 and mid-1968, represent some fundamental reconsideration of the nature and role of deep structure.

By the summer of 1964, the formalization of the distinction between deep and surface levels of sentence representation had been developed by researchers at MIT including Chomsky, Halle, Katz, Postal, and a number of MIT graduate students in linguistics. This theory was presented formally in Chomsky's *Aspects of the Theory of Syntax* in 1965. During the period from 1964 through early 1967, much research was devoted to theoretical extension and descriptive application of the notions proposed in *Aspects*. Toward the end of this period, a phase emerged in which evidence that the *Aspects* model was unsatisfactory began to accumulate. This led to a more serious questioning of that model, and eventually to a third stage where various proposals envisaging relatively fundamental revisions of the model were advanced. The articles in this book have been arranged to reflect each of these three stages in the development of transformational syntax.

The first paper, "Some Lexical Structures and Their Empirical Validity," by Bever and Rosenbaum, is a discussion of the kinds of formal devices which would be required to explain certain semantic phenomena in terms of the version of syntactic theory being developed during 1964. The paper is specifically concerned with the mechanisms of a grammar which are requisite to the classification of words according to their referential properties. The paper moves from a discussion of the hierarchical arrangement of these properties to a proposed descriptive formalism which would permit the prediction of the occurrence of words and their possible interpretation. The analysis proposed offers an interesting explanation of certain types of metaphor.

The second paper, Rosenbaum's "A Principle Governing Deletion in English Sentential Complementation," was written in the fall of 1965. This paper offers evidence from English that the deletion of the initial noun phrase of a noun phrase complement sentence or a verb phrase complement sentence is determined by the proximity of this noun phrase to an identical noun phrase in the main ("matrix") sentence. Rosenbaum proposes a universal condition governing the deletion of one of two identical noun phrases in noun phrase and verb phrase complement constructions. This interest in deletion principles and universal grammar is one pursued further in Ross's article at the end of this collection.

Comparative constructions in any language have proven themselves resistant to satisfactory analysis. Hale's "Conditions on English Comparative Clause Pairings" is an attempt to understand the relation between paired clauses in English comparative constructions. Hale starts with a discussion of the solutions proposed by R. B. Lees and Carlota Smith and then goes on to offer his own analysis of the constraints on well-formed comparative sentences, i.e., what may or may not occur. This analysis, certainly the most complete and acceptable one to date, is very much within the framework proposed in Chomsky's *Aspects*.

Postal's paper "On So-called Pronouns in English," although considered here as within this earlier phase in transformational linguistics, looks forward to Chomsky's later paper, appearing in Part III of this book. Postal presents an unorthodox but very persuasive analysis of the deep structure of personal pronouns and of their transformational derivation. But, more importantly for the student of transformational linguistics, he argues that the notion "part of speech" refers to terminal constituents of phrase structures in their surface manifestation, and shows that a "part of speech" in the surface structure may have a deep structure counterpart possessing fundamentally different syntactic properties.

One topic that has caused some controversy in transformational linguistics is nominalization, here construed as the processes which relate synonymous stems in nouns or noun phrases to those in verbs, adjectives, or verb phrases. The controversy has arisen because of conflicting data on derivational phenomena in English syntax. In particular, certain linguists have argued that verbal elements are basic in deep structure while nouns and noun phrases are derived. Others have suggested that the stems are syntactically neutral and are given syntactic status through the application of lexical rules. These convert some stems to nouns, some to verbs, some to both, and so forth. Chomsky discusses this in a later framework in his paper toward the end of this book. Fraser, in "Some Remarks on the Action Nominalization in English," treats a certain class of nominalizations within Chomsky's 1965 framework. What makes this paper especially important is that it was written in the context of rapidly changing views on the nature of deep structures and their associated lexicons. As such, it stands as a strong attempt to explicate nominalization purely in transformational terms rather than the lexicalist hypotheses preferred later.

Langendoen's article, "The Accessibility of Deep Structures," attempts to understand the meaning of transformational models in cognitive terms. Why should there be deep structures? Why are there transformations? Such questions require answers since a more "ideal" language is conceivable, one eliminating the distinction between deep and surface structure. What is needed is an explanatory theory for such linguistic phenomena. Langendoen suggests lines of investigation which could lead to such a theory.

The next group of three papers, by Perlmutter, Fillmore, and Lees, marks a stage of transition in transformational linguistics. All three are still working within Chomsky's 1965 framework, more or less, but they are becoming aware of data that fit rather uneasily into this framework.

Perlmutter's paper, "The Two Verbs *Begin*," starts with two seemingly incompatible analyses for the verb *begin*. This verb, he argues, occurs in deep structures both as an intransitive verb with an abstract sentential subject, and also as a transitive verb with animate subjects and with object complements. Are there two distinct verbs *begin* in the deep structure — a counterintuitive suggestion surely — or is there simply a single verb with two distinct sets of contextual features? Perlmutter does not attempt an answer at this stage. A third possibility, that *begin* is a simple verb whose occurrence in two different kinds of deep structure is, in some yet unspecified way, predictable, offers a hint as to the future direction of investigation. This paper then provides some suggestions for an informal extension of the notion of deep structure.

Fillmore takes this further in "The Grammar of *Hitting* and *Breaking*." Here he is investigating the nature of the lexicon and of lexical categories. He is especially interested in the properties of the items that must make up the lexicon and in the categories in which these properties can most insightfully be organized. What information must be included in the lexicon in order to account for the properties discussed? Although Fillmore assumes the existence of an abstract deep structure to which generative rules apply, the grammatical model implied by this analysis goes beyond Chomsky's 1965 model. If Fillmore's categories are valid, then the representation of categories in the *Aspects* model must at least be expanded, if not revised.

In "On Very Deep Grammatical Structure" R. B. Lees presents a clear account of these developments, focusing particularly on the work of Fillmore, Ross, Lakoff, and McCawley. He illustrates these developments with reference to his own landmark work on nominalization. Here are summarized the positive developments since his own pioneer work, and here are illustrated the kinds of questions being asked by transformational linguists, questions indicating the need for some revision of the notion of deep structure.

The final group of articles in this collection reveals a more explicit, more strident questioning of the 1965 model. This was particularly noticeable in the latter part of 1966 and early 1967 when the logical possibilities of transformational theory were being explored. Each of the writers examines the earlier theory, notes recalcitrant data, and, in some cases, suggests ways of incorporating the data within a revised and more general grammatical model.

Lakoff's "Pronominalization, Negation, and the Analysis of Adverbs" discusses forms which are synonymous, yet have very different syntactic properties. Do these forms in fact have the same deep structures? Lakoff shows that they cannot have the same deep structures within the *Aspects* model and concludes that deep structures must be much more abstract objects than those in this earlier model of grammar.

McCawley offers a stronger challenge in "Where Do Noun Phrases Come From?" McCawley is primarily interested here in the problem of semantic representation within the framework of a transformational grammar. He suggests a base component consisting entirely of semantic entities. These entities, representable in a notation very close to that of symbolic logic, would replace the syntactic entities of earlier theory. The base component then would be concerned with *propositions* rather than with sentences. McCawley's proposals are primarily relevant to the nature of the base component. Ways to relate these base structures to surface structures would thus require formulation.

However, Chomsky, in "Remarks on Nominalization," comes to very different conclusions. The base component formulated in *Syntactic Structures* was unnecessarily impoverished. It assumed that deep structures were very specific items, that the parts of speech, more or less as traditionally formulated, were in fact deep structure categories. Like Lees and Fraser before him, Chomsky takes up nominalization as a crucial example. In the past, certain kinds of noun phrases had been related to sentence structures bearing the same kinds of semantic relations, by means of transformations which moved strings from a deep structure, through a series of derivations, to a surface structure noun phrase. In the course of this, verbs, for example, were converted into nouns. But, argues Chomsky, there is no a priori way of knowing whether the noun forms underlie the verbs or vice versa. Instead of relating alternative forms through transformations, the base rules should be extended to accommodate the alternative forms directly. This is the *lexicalist* position, in contrast to the transformational position taken earlier by Fraser. However, this lexicalist position, as presented by Chomsky, does not exclude transformational solutions. The base component is an enriched component in which base forms are not specified as nouns, verbs, or adjectives, but have certain stated potentials for becoming one or more of these in the surface structure. Selectional restrictions are thus generated by the particular potentials of a base form. Chomsky ends up with a model still looking rather like that of *Aspects* but so modified as to be more comprehensive. Indeed the ideal of a common base structure for all languages seems much closer.

The final paper, Ross's "On Declarative Sentences," explores the effects on the theory of universal grammar of the assumption of more abstract syntactic representations. With deep structures more abstract and more closely related to semantic representations, the differences between the deep structures of disparate languages get smaller. What we think of as *semantic* "contexts" in English may have important *syntactic* consequences in other languages. If Ross is right, then important steps have been taken towards the formulation of a universal set of base structures. At present it is premature to claim more than the achievement of a few important initial advances in what is after all an infant science, linguistics.

THE "ASPECTS" MODEL

part
one

Some Lexical Structures and Their Empirical Validity

THOMAS G. BEVER

PETER S. ROSENBAUM

1

Discussions of a semantic theory of language can founder on the determination of the data which that theory is intended to describe. In this paper we shall avoid questions of the legitimacy of particular goals for semantic theory. Nor are we concerned primarily with the nature of the computational device used in analyzing the meanings of whole sentences. Rather we report some recent investigations of several kinds of lexical devices which are necessary formal prerequisites for the description of semantic phenomena.

The empirical reality of any descriptive device is initially supported by the facts it describes. It is further supported by the empirical validity of predictions which it justifies. In this presentation we show that the devices proposed for an adequate description of semantic lexical structure also correctly predict the potential occurrence of certain types of words and interpretations and correctly reject the potential occurrence of other types of words and interpretations.

The empirical phenomena and the formal devices which describe them involve the representation of classes of words by features, like "animateness," "plantness," and "livingness." These features are themselves organized hierarchically (e.g., anything that is "living" must be a "plant" or "animate"). Finally, certain hierarchies express relations between particular words rather

SOURCE: This work was supported by the MITRE Corporation, Bedford, Massachusetts, Harvard Society of Fellows, NDEA, A. F. 19(68)–5705 and Grant #SD-187, Rockefeller University and IBM. A preliminary version of this paper was originially written as part of a series of investigations at MITRE Corporation, Summer 1963, and delivered to the Linguistic Society of America, December 1964. We are particularily grateful to Dr. D. Walker for his support of this research and to P. Carey and G. Miller for advice on this manuscript.

3

than between classes of words. At each point linguistic facts force certain formal constraints on these descriptive devices.

Binary Features

Consider first the use of features in semantic description. It is not radical to propose that words are categorized in terms of general classes. Nor is it novel to consider the fact that these classes bear particular relations to each other. Consider, for example, the English words in the matrix presented in (1):

(1)	boy	tree	sheep	carcass	log	water	blood	* "og"	* "triffid"
human	+	—	—	—	—	—	—	—	—
animate	+	—	+	+	—	—	—	—	—
living	+	+	+	—	—	—	+	—	+
plant	—	+	—	—	+	—	—	+	+

On this chart there is a representation of some words in terms of particular binary dimensions. In each case the particular semantic dimension, or "semantic feature," is the marking which specifies particular aspects of the semantic patterning of the lexical item. In (2) the positive value for each feature is associated with some sample sentence frames which indicate the kind of systematic restrictions each feature imposes. Thus in (2a) any noun marked [+human], among other things, can appear in the sentence "the *noun* thought the problem over," but any noun marked [—human] cannot appear in the frame "the *noun* sensed the danger"; any noun marked [+living] can appear in the frame "the *noun* died," and any noun marked [+plant] can appear in the frame "the *noun* has damaged chlorophyll." The privileges of occurrence in these kinds of frames of the different nouns in the figure are indicated by the placement of the "+" and "—" markings on the separate features.

(2) a. [+human]:   The _____ thought the problem over.
                     answered slowly.
                     was a beautiful actor.

  b. [+animate]:   The _____ sensed the danger.
                   ate the food.
                   ran away.

  c. [+living]:   The _____ died.

  d. [+plant]:   The _____ has damaged chlorophyll.
                   needed to be watered.
                   grew from the seed.

That such classifications play a role in natural language has rarely been questioned.[1] But the problem has been to decide which of the many possible aspects of classification are to be treated as systematically pertinent to a semantic theory. We cannot claim to have discovered all and only the semantic features of natural language. However, it is absolutely necessary to assume that there is some universal set from which particular languages draw their individual stock.

Furthermore, if the semantic analysis of natural language is to achieve explanatory adequacy, there must be a precise manner of deciding among competing semantic analyses. In this way the semantic analysis which is ultimately chosen can be said to be the result of a formal device, and not the result of the luck of a formal linguist. If the particular analysis is chosen on the basis of precise, formal criteria, then the reality of the predictions made by the device constitutes a confirmation of the general linguistic theory itself.

Lexical analysis of single words includes a specification in terms of a set of semantic features. We propose furthermore that the most highly valued semantic analysis which meets these constraints be the one which utilizes the smallest number of symbols in a particular form of semantic analysis. For a given natural language this will direct the choice of which features are drawn from the universal set as well as the assignment of predictable features in the lexicon itself.

A Hierarchy of Semantic Features

For instance, the features in the matrix in (1) are specified with some redundancy. We can see from inspection of the frames in (2a) and (2b) that if a noun can act as [+human], then it can occur as [+animate] although the reverse is not necessarily true. For example, if we can say "the man thought it over," we also can say "the man sensed the danger"; but if we can say "the ant ran away," we cannot necessarily say "the ant answered slowly."

Consequently, any word marked [+human] can be predicted as being [+animate]. This prediction, represented in rule (3a), obviates the necessity of lexical entries for "animateness" in nouns which are marked as "human."

(3) a. [+human] → [+animate]
     b. [+animate] → [−plant]

Similarly, it is predictable that if a noun is [+animate], it is [−plant] in English, although the reverse is not true. Then, rule (3b) allows the features [−plant] to be left out of the lexical entry for "ant." Such redundancy rules simply reflect a class-inclusion hierarchy among the semantic features [e.g.,(3c)].

(3) c.

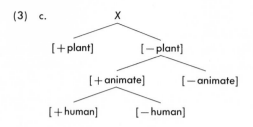

The evaluation criterion requires the simplest acceptable solution to be used. Accordingly, the solution which includes the semantic redundancy rules in (3) is clearly indicated over a solution without these rules, given that the theory allows such rules at all. [Notice that rule (3b), at least, is *not* universal, but is a rule peculiar to English, since there are languages in which at least some plants can be considered animate.]

We now can ask if the predictions made by this analysis about new lexical items are valid or not. Consider the two potential English words, "og" and "triffid," on the right-hand side of (1). "Og" is intended to be a word which signifies the dead remains of an entire plant, in the way which "carcass" indicates the dead remains of an entire animal. "Triffid," on the other hand, indicates a kind of pine tree that moves and communicates.

Neither of these words exist in everyday English, and they may both be classified as semantic lexical gaps — that is, they are combinations of semantic features which are not combined within a single lexical entry. Yet the reasons for their nonoccurrence are radically different according to the analysis in (3). Rule (3b) in principle blocks the appearance of any word like "triffid" which is both plant and animal; but the word "og" is not blocked by anything in the grammar itself. That is, "triffid" is classified by our analysis as a *systematic gap*, while the nonoccurrence of "og" is entirely *accidental*.

This distinction, made as an incidental part of our analysis, appears to be supported by the intuitions of speakers of English. Nobody would be surprised to learn that professional loggers and foresters have some word in their vocabulary which indicates the whole of a dead tree. But everybody would be surprised if they found out that foresters have a single word for trees which they think are animals. (It is that sense of surprise for English speakers which made possible *The Day of the Triffids*, a science-fiction novel in which the discovery of this concept is a primary vehicle for the plot.)

This result represents an independent corroboration of the general form of the semantic lexicon and the evaluation criteria which we proposed above. The rules in (3b) were not introduced to block systematic lexical gaps, but to achieve the highest valued semantic analysis. The fact that the systematic gaps they predict correspond to the intuitive ones is a distinct empirical corroboration of the precise formal characteristics of this form of semantic theory.

We have shown that an explanatory lexical semantic theory is possible, and have indicated some of its characteristics and empirical validations. In the next sections we briefly indicate some other semantic lexical devices, the lexical distinctions which they predict, and the validity of those predictions.

Hierarchies Among Lexical Items

Not all semantic phenomena can be handled by binary features, even if those features are related in a class-inclusion hierarchy. Consider the sentences in (4). Why is it that the sentences on the right are semantically deviant? It is not simply the case that they are counterfactual, since [4e (i)] is counterfactual, but does not involve the same kind of violation as [4e (ii)]. The first doesn't happen to be true; the second couldn't possibly be true.

(4a)	(i) The arm has an elbow.	(ii)	* The elbow has an arm.
(4b)	(i) The elbow is a joint.	(ii)	* The joint is an elbow.
(4c)	(i) The finger has a knuckle.	(ii)	* The knuckle has a finger.
(4d)	(i) The thumb is a finger.	(ii)	* The finger is a thumb.
(4e)	(i) The ant has an arm.	(ii)	* The arm has an ant.

These and other similar facts justify the assumption that lexical entries themselves are arranged in two simultaneous hierarchies: One represents the inalienable inclusion of *Have*, and the other represents the class membership of *Be*. In (5) the solid vertical lines represent the *Have* hierarchy and the dotted horizontal lines represent the *Be* hierarchy. (We use the convention that the subject of an inalienable *Have* sentence must dominate the object in this tree, and that the subject of a generic *Be* must be dominated by the predicate object. Thus we can say, "the body has an arm," "the arm is a limb," but not the reverse.)

(5)

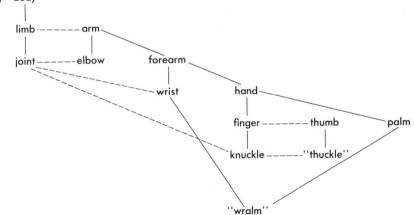

Figure (5) demonstrates why it is the case that semantic features with a limited number of states cannot handle these relations and block the kinds of incorrect sentences on the right in (4). Figure (5) allows the sentences in (6).

(6)   A body has an arm.   An arm is a limb.
        An arm has a forearm.   An elbow is a joint.
        A forearm has a hand.   A thumb is a finger.
        A hand has a finger.   A wrist is a joint.
        A finger has a knuckle.

Any reversal of the nouns in these sentences would produce a deviant sentence, so that just to handle these cases a binary feature analysis would have to use six states.

It is clear that we must distinguish between lexically permanent hierarchies as in (5) and the productive use of "have" and "be" in actual sentences. Thus the fact that we can say "the tree is nice" and "a tree has importance" does not necessarily require a corresponding lexical hierarchy. These cases are "creative" (or alienable) uses of *Have* and *Be* rather than the "lexical" (inalienable) use exemplified in (4).

The Implications of Lexical Hierarchies for Some "Syntactic" Phenomena

Before showing the semantic empirical extensions of the lexical hierarchies, we first indicate certain obvious "syntactic" presences as part of lexical structure. (As could be expected for grammatical structures dependent on the lexicon, the distinction between "semantic" phenomena and the corresponding "syntactic" phenomena is extremely difficult and beside our point.)

Selectional Restrictions

We pointed out above that lexical items are marked as to the binary classes which they share. As demonstrated in (2) these class markings restrict the kinds of noun–verb–noun combinations that may appear within a clause. Such constraints are referred to as "selectional restrictions."

The assumption that lexical entries are organized in several hierarchies makes possible some simplifications of the representation of selectional restrictions. Consider these sentences:

(7)   The firearm shoots bullets.   * The sword shoots bullets.
        The pistol shoots bullets.   * The knife shoots bullets.
        The rifle shoots bullets.   * The dog shoots bullets.
        The revolver shoots bullets.
        The derringer shoots bullets.
        The six-shooter shoots bullets.

In general it is the case that if a lexical item can be selected in a construction, then everything dominated by that lexical item in the *Be* hierarchy (directly or indirectly) can also fit into that construction. For example, the hierarchy

$$\text{firearm} \begin{cases} \text{pistol} \\ \text{rifle} \end{cases}$$

etc., predicts that everything generically true of "firearm" is specifically true of objects subordinate to "firearm." Notice that if a binary feature solution were sought for the above cases, there would be a separate feature (e.g., "$\pm$ shoots-bullets")[2] corresponding to every level in the hierarchy which has a unique set of possible constructions.

A similar simplification is achieved by use of the inalienable *Have* hierarchy.

(8)
car	The venturi mixes gas and air.
engine	The carburetor mixes gas and air.
carburetor	The engine mixes gas and air.
venturi	The car mixes gas and air.

That is, if an item in the *Have* hierarchy is a particular active construction, then the items which dominate it in the *Have* hierarchy also can fit into that construction.[3]

Feature Assimilation

There are independent reasons for postulating the existence of the *Have* and *Be* hierarchies. Consider the following sentences:

(9a) (i)   The boy's knee aches.
      (ii) * The statue's knee aches.
      (iii) The statue's knee broke.

(9b) (i)   The man's neck itches.
      (ii) * The man's idea itches.
      (iii) The man's idea convinced me.

The sentences in (9a) are well formed with respect to the *Have* hierarchy since both "boy" and "statue" stand in the same relation to "knee." But one observes that [9a (i)] has a conceptual status which differs significantly from sentence [9a (ii)]. The difference is a reflection of the fact that a "statue" is normally both inanimate and not living and hence cannot be subject to the set of events in which nouns that are both animate and living can participate. The descriptive problem concerns the fact that the anomalous interpretation of the phrase "knee aches" is dependent upon information which is not included in the lexical entry for the noun "knee." The information that a "knee" belongs to a noun marked either [+animate] [+living] or

[— animate] [— living] is necessarily dependent upon some mechanism which assigns these features to "knee" on the basis of the underlying phrase structure configurations. This mechanism provides a formal object which can be systematically interpreted by the semantic analysis.[4]

The mechanism which assimilates the relevant features in sentences (9a) explicitly refers only to the lexical *Have* hierarchy, rather than to any sentence with "have." This becomes clear on consideration of the fact that such assimilation does not apply in the event that the "head" noun does not stand in an inalienable relation to its modifier, as in [9b (ii)]. Underlying [9b (ii)] is the string "the man has an idea" in which the interpretation of "have" is one of "possession." As was assumed earlier, there are independent reasons for assuming that the nonlexical "have" of "possession" is distinct in certain ways from the lexical "have" of "inalienability." This hypothesis is confirmed with respect to feature assimilation. The hypothesis that feature assimilation involves the lexical *Have* hierarchy is supported further by the fact that sentences in which the *Have* hierarchy is used to its fullest extension have properties identical to those in (9a), as demonstrated in (10).

(10)   a.   The toe of the foot of the leg of the boy aches.
　　　 b.   * The toe of the foot of the leg of the statue aches.

There is a similar additional motivation for the *Be* hierarchy as a necessary component of the grammar.

(11)   a.   A gun which is a cannon fires cannonballs.
　　　 b.   * A gun which is a six-shooter fires cannonballs.

The descriptive problem posed by the sentences in (11) exactly parallels that posed by the sentences in (9a). The peculiarity of (11b) is reflected by the fact that only a gun which has the properties of a cannon can "fire cannonballs." The difference between the two sentences is formally characterized by an assimilation rule which assimilates the features of the modifying noun to the "head" noun: In (11) the features of "cannon" and "six-shooter" are assimilated to "gun." Such a feature assimilation provides the information requisite to the semantic interpretation of the sentences in (11) which is not systematically given by the underlying structure.[5] In particular, it is necessary to know what kind of "gun" is involved in order to determine the semantic well-formedness of the predicate.

Comparatives

There is a set of restrictions on comparative constructions which is characterized exactly in terms of the *Be* hierarchy. Consider, by way of illustration, the following sentences:

(12a)   (i)   A cannon is more deadly than a pistol.
　　　　(ii)   A pistol is more deadly than a cannon.

      (iii) * A cannon is more deadly than a gun.

      (iv) * A pistol is more deadly than a gun.

(12b)   (i) * A gun is more deadly than a cannon.

      (ii) * A gun is more deadly than a pistol.

An examination of the compared nouns in the sentences above in terms of the *Be* hierarchy (13) reveals that the restrictions observed in these sentences can be expressed in terms of the dominance relation obtaining in this hierarchy.

(13)

One observes that the comparative constructions in (12) are grammatical just in case a comparing noun neither dominates nor is dominated by a compared noun in the *Be* hierarchy. Thus, "pistols" and "cannons" may be compared. Furthermore, any item which "pistol" dominates (e.g., "derringer") can be compared with either "cannon" or any other item dominated by "gun" which neither dominates nor is dominated by "pistol" (e.g., "rifle") as in the following examples:

(14)   a. A cannon is more deadly than a derringer.

      b. A rifle is more deadly than both a derringer and a cannon.

Although the derivation of comparative constructions in general has not been fully resolved, it is nonetheless clear that certain restrictions on these constructions require reference to a lexical *Be* hierarchy.

Hierarchies Are Nonconvergent

The examples we have discussed do not involve convergence within one hierarchy. That is, there are no instances of hierarchies like (15)

(15)

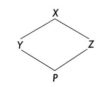

in which the hierarchy branches at *X* and converges at *P*. There are several reasons why convergent hierarchies are not tolerable. First, there are many instances in which a single lexical item is dominated by different words, e.g., (16).

(16)   humans   clocks
         | (excluding intermediates) |
       hands   hands

If convergences were an acceptable part of the formalism, it would be possible to simplify (16) to (17).

(17)   humans   clocks

                hands

But this would transfer to "hands" all the selectional features of both "humans" and "clocks," many of which are mutually incompatible (notably [± animate]). Furthermore, if the senses of "hands" are not distinguished, we could not account for the oddity of sentences like: "The clock's hands look funny, but mine don't."

Maintaining distinct senses of lexical items in distinct lexical hierarchies is motivated independently of the consequences for convergent hierarchies. There are also motivations against convergent hierarchies within the same "lexical tree." Consider the subsection of Figure (5) in (18).

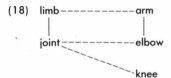

(18)   limb----------arm
         | |
       joint---------elbow

                     knee

"Arm" could dominate "joint" directly (as well as via "limb") since there is a sentence "the arm has a joint." However, this would transfer to "joint" all the properties pertaining to "arm." In turn this would transfer all the features of "arm" to "knee," which is clearly incorrect.

The requirement that there are no convergences in the lexical hierarchy has the result that there are many distinct matrices in the lexicon which utilize the *Have* and *Be* hierarchies.[6] There are many problems about these matrices which require further investigation. We have merely outlined the essential motivations for the hierarchies as lexical structures.

Systematic and Accidental Lexical Gaps Explained by Lexical Hierarchies

The evidence above attests to the general need for lexical hierarchies as one of the structures of grammar. The hierarchies provide mechanisms for the blocking of certain obvious anomalies (e.g., [4a (ii)]) and for the simplification of general selectional processes. The hierarchies also make predictions about the kinds of lexical items which can and cannot occur. That is, they provide a further basis for distinguishing lexical gaps which are systematically explained by the lexical structure of the language from those gaps which have no such explanation and are therefore "accidental."

For example, the combination of the hierarchies as in (5) makes several claims about English lexical structure. The placement of "finger," "thumb," and "knuckle" in the lower right of (5) strongly implies that the single lexical item indicating a "thumb knuckle" would be a regular extension of the present lexical system, since it would fit in the regular slot (labeled "thuckle"). An instance of an irregular extension would be the word which is a unique part of both the wrist and the palm [labeled "wralm" in Figure (5)]. The irregularity of "wralm" is explained by the fact that it would require a convergence of the hierarchy, which is not allowed in our formulation, for independent reasons. Thus, "wralm" would require two separate hierarchies and would involve added complexity.

Surely this result is an intuitive one — the concept "thumb knuckle" seems quite natural, but the concept of "wrist palm" does not. It should be re-emphasized here that it is irrelevant to us whether or not these linguistic properties are reflections of something in the so-called "real world." Our present quest does not include the source for linguistic structure but seeks to define the nature of the structure itself.

The hierarchy may also predict instances in which certain uses of words are dropped from a language. Consider the treatment of the word "sidearm" in the *Be* hierarchy introduced above:

$$A \begin{Bmatrix} \text{pistol} \\ \text{sword} \end{Bmatrix} \text{is a sidearm.}$$

A sidearm is a weapon.

These sentences indicate that "sidearm" would have to be represented with a convergence on "pistol" as in (19), or with two lexical instances of "pistol" as in (20).

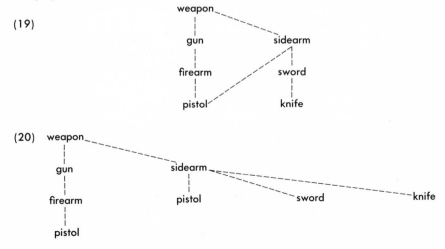

If it were not for the fact that swords (and knives, technically) are sidearms, it would be possible to formulate the hierarchy without any double dominance relations:

(21)

In fact, although we must allow for the possibility of the facts represented in (19), we have set up the formalism such that that type of structure involves a large amount of complexity. Example (20) is represented as two separate hierarchies to avoid the double dominance of "pistol." This offers an explanation of the tendency for the term *sidearm* (meaning "sword" and "knife") to drop out of modern English, since it reduces the complexity of (20) to (21).

As above, we cannot rule out any particular aggregate of features (or possible constructions) on the basis of lexical structure rules, since anything *can* occur as a lexical item. But the theory which we set up to represent lexical structure provides some formal basis for distinctions between lexical items which do occur. For instance, "shotgun" is in an anomalous position in the hierarchy because of these sentences:

(22) a. A shotgun is a firearm.
      b. A firearm shoots bullets.
      c. * A shotgun shoots bullets.

This requires us to mark "shotgun" as an exception to the hierarchy (or to the rule which predicts features on the basis of the hierarchy).

In certain cases the restriction on convergence in the hierarchy is supported directly by intuitions. For example, consider the word "neck:"

(23) a. John's head has a thick neck.
         John's head was frozen, including his neck.

      b. John's torso (body) has a thick neck.
         John's torso (body) was frozen, including his neck.

For some people, sentences (23a) are correct and (23b) are incorrect; for others the reverse is true. From many, both (23a) and (23b) are acceptable at different times, *but not simultaneously:* that is, there is no single lexical hierarchy which includes a structure like (24),

(24)

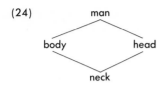

but rather the hierarchy is like (25).

(25)

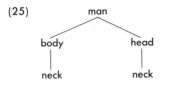

It is tempting to "explain" these facts as an "obvious" reflection of the fact that the neck resides between the body and the head. But there is nothing incompatible with the physical facts in an analysis which would delegate the neck as part of the "head" and simultaneously part of the "body." Thus, it is not "reality" which disallows convergences of lexical hierarchies, but the properties of the lexical system itself.

Metaphor and the Form of Lexical Entry

The final case we shall consider involves what is sometimes called "historical metaphor." For instance, in modern English there is a regular rule [see (26)] which extends surface quality adjectives which are drawn from a restricted set of abstract qualities. Thus, in (27b) the adjective "colorful" is used with the noun "ball" or "idea." Certain adjectives drawn from a restricted set are not affected by rule (26). For example, shapes and colors

(26)

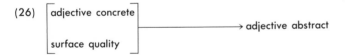

are not regularly applied to ideas, as can be seen in (27d). Whenever shapes are used with abstract nouns, as in (27e), they are defined by our analysis as unique expressions and not as the result of the general rule in (26).

(27) a. The ball is colorful.
      b. The idea is colorful.

      c. The ball is ovoid.
      d. * The idea is ovoid.

      e. The idea is square.
      f. The idea is variegated.

This too seems intuitively correct. In "the idea is square" we know that an interpretation is possible but unique. In this case we happen to know the unique abstract interpretation of "square" but not in "the idea is ovoid." Although we may never have heard the sentence "the idea is variegated" before, we can immediately recognize it as a regular lexical extension of the "literal" meaning of "variegated."

The representation of lexical items in hierarchies facilitates the automatic interpretation of the metaphorical extensions of certain words from their original lexical structure. Consider the analysis of the word "colorful," using the *Be* and *Have* hierarchies simultaneously.

(28)

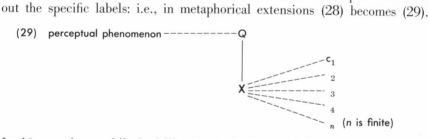

Suppose we use the following metaphorical principle: A metaphorical extension of X includes the hierarchical relations of the literal interpretation without the specific labels: i.e., in metaphorical extensions (28) becomes (29).

(29) perceptual phenomenon ——————————Q

$$X \begin{cases} c_1 \\ 2 \\ 3 \\ 4 \\ n \end{cases} \quad (n \text{ is finite})$$

In this way the word "colorful" as applied to "idea" is interpreted as "having simultaneously a large set of potentially distinguishing characteristics." Similarly for "shape" in "the idea took shape."

(30)

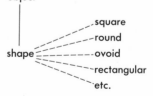

In this usage, "shape" is interpreted as "a particular character out of many (but finite) characters." (Note that although there is an infinite variety of shapes possible, there is a finite number listed in the lexicon; what "the idea has shape" means is that it has one clear, recognizable characteristic, as opposed to an unnameable one.) Consider now the interpretation of "the idea is square." It is "the idea has a specific characteristic out of a finite list of them." But there is no special indication as to which characteristic it is, or how it fits into the abstract realm of ideas. Thus it takes special knowledge to interpret the metaphorical extensions of lexical items at the most subordinate part of the hierarchy, if it takes special knowledge in the original literal interpretation.

For these kinds of cases this principle provides a more general rationale for metaphorical interpretation than does rule (26). It distinguishes cases of metaphor which require no special knowledge ("shape, color") from those which do ("square, green"). It also offers some insight into the nature of the metaphorical extension itself.

There are many metaphors for which this sort of lexical account will not do. Thus, "the secretary of defense was an eagle gripping the arrows of war, but refusing to loose them" is not interpretable in terms of any lexical hierarchy. What we have shown is that the interpretation of "lexical metaphors" can proceed in terms of the original form of the lexical entry, and that this can distinguish between "regular" metaphorical extensions and isolated cases.

Conclusion

The force of the empirical validity of lexical distinctions and the corresponding descriptive mechanisms depends on the extent to which the analyses are arrived at according to a formal evaluation criterion. The exact form of the distinctive features in (1), the feature hierarchy in (3c), the lexical hierarchy in (5), and the metaphor rules will ultimately be determined by the form of universal semantic structures and the complexity of a particular description.

The descriptive devices we have presented do not exhaust what is necessary for semantic theory. What we have shown is that an explanatory semantic theory is possible, and we have indicated some of its features. Primarily, we have tried to show what kinds of empirical considerations must be included in the evaluation of different candidates for an explanatory semantic theory.

NOTES

1. Modern discussions of such features and their integration within grammatical theory can be found in Katz and Fodor (1963); Chomsky (1965); Miller (1967). In this article we will assume that the reader has a basic familiarity with the role of semantic analysis in current transformational linguistic theory.

2. We are not claiming that there are *no* features which are pertinent to particular restricted sets of lexical items — in fact, if one argued that the feature [± shoots

bullets] should be used, then our argument simply is that the feature [+shoots bullets] is predictable for everything below its first occurrence in the *Be* hierarchy. In other words, if other aspects of the formal treatment of the above problem require features for uniformity of notation, this can be accommodated easily. Nevertheless, it remains the case that the hierarchy can be utilized to reduce intuitively the duplication of lexical information.

3. Note that there is something odd about "the car mixes gas and air" although it is technically correct. There are other cases like this: "The electric lamp has tungsten," "The body has fingernails." There are several potential explanations for the oddness of these sentences: (a) Certain words (e.g., "carburetor") are designated as referring to "the whole" of an object and feature assimilation cannot pass through them. (b) We must distinguish between various senses of *Have:* "have *in* it," "have as *part of* it," "have *adjacent to* it." Then a car might be said to have a "carburetor" *in* it but not as *part of* it, while the "venturi" is *part of* the carburetor. It would not be the case that a car and a carburetor "have" a venturi in the same sense of *Have.* (c) There might be a principle of linguistic performance: The more nodes an assimilation of features passes through, the lower the acceptability of the sentence.

4. It is conceivable that the assimilation rules are' to be incorporated into the interpretative semantic cycle itself rather than to provide a derived semantic structure upon which the interpretative component operates. Factors bearing on this decision will not be explored in this paper. At the time when we first proposed the problem raised by sentences like those in (9), several of our friends and teachers argued that a syntactic solution would be forthcoming. This has been incorporated as part of the analysis of adverbs proposed by G. Lakoff. Briefly, [9a(i) and (ii)] would be analyzed as "the boy aches in his leg" and "the statue aches in his leg." The anomaly of the second would be explained as a function of the fact that "the statue aches" is anomalous. Sentence [9b (ii)] would be anomalous because there is no sentence "the man itched in his idea," while there is a sentence corresponding to [9b (i)] "the man itched in his neck." Whether or not one is convinced by this analysis (which we are not), the fact remains that those nouns which can act as agents with verbs, like "ache," "itch," "hurt," etc., are just those which are represented in the lexical *Have* hierarchy as inalienably part of the "head" noun. For example, there is a sentence "I hurt" and "I hurt in my arm," but no "I hurt in my carburetor." Similarly, words like "idea" or "thought" are not entered lexically. So either form of syntactic analysis of these examples presupposes a lexical *Have* hierarchy. (Note that this does not preclude a "creative" grammatical component which would allow for new *ad hoc Have* and *Be* relations to be produced as needed. As we continually emphasize, the ontogenesis of lexical structures is not of concern to us in this paper.)

5. In fact, it might appear that an incorrect result follows from this restriction just in case a particular property or object is shared by many different words. For example, consider the word "electron." Convergent hierarchies would allow this word to appear only once in the lexicon:

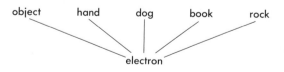

The restriction against convergent hierarchies would appear to force such a word to have multiple representation:

object	hand	dog	book	rock
|	|	|	|	|
electron	electron	electron	electron	electron

However, "electron" does not appear many times, once under each object; rather only once under the word "object" itself. Any other word that *is* an object automatically acquires the property of *having* electrons, by the assimilation rules discussed above.

6. These sentences seem to suggest that sentences like "a gun is a cannon" must be generated in the grammar in order to account for the relative clause formation. In other words, the original motivation for the lexical *Be* hierarchy would seem to disappear. This argument is untenable, however, since it is necessary to postulate that a relativized noun is definite, referring to a *specific* noun: e.g., "A gun fires cannonballs if it (that gun) is a cannon."

A Principle Governing Deletion
in English Sentential Complementation

2

PETER S. ROSENBAUM

A characteristic property of certain types of sentence embedding in English, the general process of which I shall subsequently refer to as complementation, is the deletion of the initial noun phrase of the complement. Exemplifying this phenomenon are such sentences as the following:

(1) John condescended to go.
(2) John defied Bill to go.
(3) Seeing you there caused Bill to wonder.

The infinitival constructions in these three sentences and the gerundial construction in sentence (3) are the residue of more complete sentences which have been embedded and systematically altered. A speaker of English ordinarily will have no difficulty in identifying the implicit initial noun phrase of the embedded sentences. For example, the deleted noun phrase in sentence (1), i.e., the underlying subject of the complement *John go*, must be *John*. The deleted noun phrase in the complement of sentence (2) is *Bill*. Finally, the deleted noun phrase in both the gerundial and infinitival complements of sentence (3) is *Bill*. Two conclusions may be drawn from these observations. First, the identified noun phrases must be present in the structure underlying the example sentences, in the "deep structure" in Chomsky's sense. Second, the identity of these noun phrases with some noun phrase in the main sentence is a necessary condition for deletion. It is also apparent, however, that this identity relation is not a sufficient condition for deletion

SOURCE: The research reported in this paper was sponsored in part by the Air Force Cambridge Research Laboratories, Office of Aerospace Research, under Contract AF19(628)–5127. This paper was originally presented to the Linguistic Society of America in Chicago, Illinois, on December 29, 1965.

20

since the distribution of the relevant noun phrase in the main sentence relative to the complement is variable. Thus, a sufficient condition for determining the deletion must specify which noun phrase in the main sentence must be identical to the initial noun phrase of the complement in order for the deletion to proceed. The purpose of the following discussion is to consider the properties of such a condition.

Sentences (1), (2), and (3) by no means exhaust the constructions which exemplify the phenomenon of initial noun phrase deletion in complementation. Nonetheless, they represent extremely productive distributions and a more detailed analysis just of these cases will prove informative. Sentences (1) and (2) are instances of what I call verb phrase complementation, where a complement S is immediately dominated by VP in the underlying phrase structure. In sentence (1), the verb *condescend* is intransitive and is contiguous with a complement.[1] In sentence (2), the verb *defy* is transitive and an object noun phrase *Bill* intervenes between the verb and the complement. The underlying structure of these two sentences can be represented roughly in terms of the following diagrams:

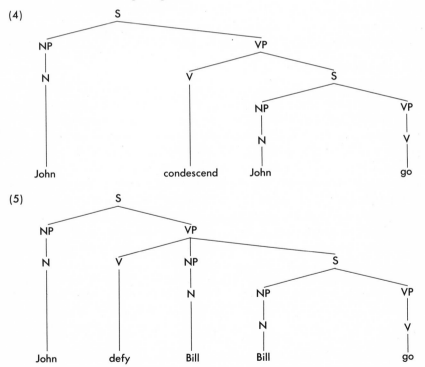

Sentence (3) is but a special case of transitive verb phrase complementation in which the underlying subject of the main sentence is itself an instance of noun phrase complementation. In noun phrase complementation, the constituent NP immediately dominates the complement. Among the reasons for assigning this analysis to the phrase *seeing you there* in sentence (3) are: (a) the fact that this phrase undergoes passivization, and (b) the fact that this phrase participates in the pseudo cleft sentence construction, i.e., *what caused Bill to wonder was seeing you there.* Diagram (6) presents the phrase structure which underlies sentence (3).

(6)

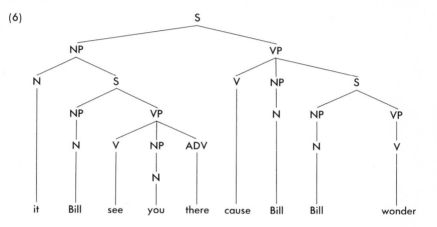

In the light of the structures which underlie sentences (1), (2), and (3), it is possible to observe precisely which noun phrase in the main sentence must be identical to the initial noun phrase of the complement when the deletion of the latter is defined. For sentence (1), the initial noun phrase of the complement must be identical to the underlying subject noun phrase of the main sentence. For sentence (2), the initial noun phrase of the complement must be identical to the underlying object noun phrase of the main sentence. Similarly, for the initial noun phrase of the noun phrase complement and for the initial noun phrase of the verb phrase complement in sentence (3), the relevant noun phrase in the main sentence is the object noun phrase.

As a first approximation to a description of initial noun phrase deletion in the three sentences under study, we might consider three distinct transformational rules of the following form:

(7)   X   NP$_1$ V   [NP$_2$ VP]$_S$ Y
    1   2   3   4   5   6 $\Rightarrow$
    1   2   3   Ø   5   6

This rule applies to the structure presented in diagram (4) and yields the following structure:

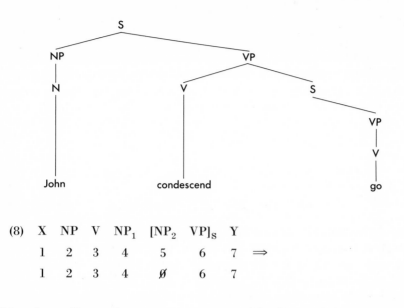

(8)   X   NP   V   NP$_1$ [NP$_2$ VP]$_S$ Y
    1   2   3   4   5   6   7 ⟹
    1   2   3   4   ∅   6   7

This rule applies to the structure represented in diagram (5) and yields the following structure:

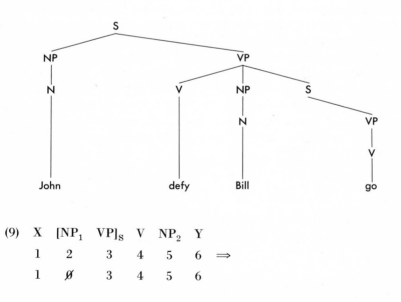

(9)   X   [NP$_1$ VP]$_S$ V   NP$_2$ Y
    1   2   3   4   5   6 ⟹
    1   ∅   3   4   5   6

This rule applies to the structure represented in (6) and, along with rule (8), operates on this structure to yield the following structure:

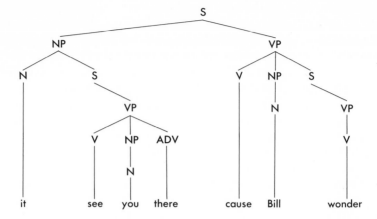

In the event that NP_1 is identical to NP_2 in each of the structures upon which these transformations are defined, the transformation (7) applies to an underlying structure of the form specified in (4) to delete the initial noun phrase of the complement, the transformation (8) applies to an underlying structure of the form given in (5) to delete the same element, and the transformations (8) and (9) apply to the structure (6) to delete the initial noun phrases of both the noun phrase complement [by rule (9)] and the verb phrase complement [by rule (8)].

The transformational rules (7), (8), and (9) are empirically adequate in the sense that they correctly describe the deletion of the initial noun phrase in the complements under study. But it is equally clear that the failure of these rules to describe initial noun phrase deletion as a unified phenomenon in English leaves an important generalization unexpressed. This problem can be seen clearly by comparing the rules (7), (8), and (9) with three distinct, but empirically motivated rules, the pronoun deletion transformation which relates (10a) and (10b), the indirect object inversion transformation which relates (11a) and (11b), and the particle placement transformation which relates (12a) and (12b).

(10)	X	IT	S	Y			a. I guarantee it that
	1	2	3	4	$\Rightarrow$		John is right.
							b. I guarantee that John
	1	Ø	3	4			is right.

(11)	X	V	NP	to + NP	Y		a. I gave the book to John.
	1	2	3	4	5	$\Rightarrow$	b. I gave John the book.
							(assuming the subsequent
	1	2	Ø	4 + 3	5		deletion of *to*)

(12)	X	V	PRT	NP			a. I looked up it in the
	1	2	3	4	5	$\Rightarrow$	dictionary.
							b. I looked it up in the
	1	2	Ø	4 + 3	5		dictionary.

The rules (10), (11), and (12) are quite distinct with respect to the structures upon which they are defined. Furthermore, these rules perform different operations upon the appropriate structures. In these two respects, the transformations (10), (11), and (12), considered as a group, are very much different from the transformations (7), (8), and (9) similarly considered. Not only do the latter rules operate upon very similar structures, in particular upon complement structures; furthermore they perform exactly the same operation upon these structures, namely, these rules delete the initial noun phrase of a complement. In other words, rules (7), (8), and (9) are describing essentially a single syntactic process, whereas rules (10), (11), and (12) are describing three distinct processes. The generalization implicit in rules (7), (8), and (9) is not expressible within the present theoretical framework of transformational grammar since this framework does not value rules (7), (8), and (9) more highly than the rules (10), (11), and (12). This shortcoming is reflected in the impossibility of collapsing rules (7), (8), and (9) into a single rule. Since the theory furthermore provides no evaluative function capable of differentiating between the two groups of rules so as to indicate that rules (7), (8), and (9) involve a linguistically significant generalization whereas rules (10), (11), and (12) do not, the theory is lacking in a crucial respect. [It is interesting that the application of the familiar notational conventions, i.e., simplicity, leads to the false conclusion that the rules (10), (11), and (12) are more general than the rules (7), (8), and (9).] We require, therefore, a new dimension to the theory of grammatical descriptions which will allow an explicit expression of the generalization involved in determining the deletion of initial noun phrases in complements.

Consider now how a more natural and revealing expression of the process of initial noun phrase deletion might be developed. Reviewing the underlying structure represented in (5), the phrase marker which roughly underlies sentence (2), one observes that the main sentence contains two noun phrases, the subject noun phrase *John* and the object noun phrase *Bill*. The problem is to specify which of these noun phrases must be identical to the initial noun phrase of the complement in order for deletion to be defined. In this case at least the facts are clear. The object noun phrase of the main sentence is the only possible candidate. If we were to make the contrary assumption, namely, that the initial noun phrase of the complement must be identical to the subject noun phrase, we should then be led to predict that speakers of English will interpret the implicit initial noun phrase of the complement in sentence (2) as *John*. In other words, this formulation requires that we assume the initial noun phrase of the complement to have been *John*. This prediction is entirely contrary to the facts. The deleted initial noun phrase is uniquely understood to be *Bill*. The identity relation must, therefore, obtain only between the initial noun phrase of the complement and the object noun phrase of the main sentence.

The generalization that determines which of the two noun phrases in the main sentence must be identical to the initial noun phrase of the complement can be expressed in terms of a principle of minimal distance (henceforth PMD). In the underlying phrase structure diagram (5), one observes that the noun phrase in the main sentence which is relevant, i.e., the object noun phrase, is also that noun phrase which is least distant from the initial noun phrase of the complement. Distance here naturally can be defined in terms of the underlying phrase structure itself by making reference to the number of branches in the path which separates the NP nodes in the main sentence from the initial NP node in the complement.[2] Thus, for example, in diagram (5) the number of branches separating the subject noun phrase of the main sentence from the initial noun phrase of the complement is four. The number of branches separating the object noun phrase of the main sentence, the relevant noun phrase, from the initial noun phrase of the complement is three. The principle correctly predicts that the object noun phrase of the main sentence is the noun phrase which must be identical to the initial noun phrase of the complement. Sentence (1) reveals a special case of the principle. In this instance, the subject noun phrase of the main sentence is the only noun phrase in the main sentence and is, therefore, the least distant from the initial noun phrase of the complement.

Apparently there is only one general restriction on the PMD and this restriction becomes clear upon examination of the underlying phrase structure given in (6), which underlies sentence (3). In this structure one observes that the noun phrase in the main sentence which is least distant from the initial noun phrase in the noun phrase complement is a noun phrase which itself dominates the initial noun phrase of the complement. It is a general fact that a noun phrase which dominates an initial noun phrase of a complement is never relevant to the deletion of this initial noun phrase. As further evidence supporting this claim, consider the sentence (13) which has the underlying structure given in (14).

(13)   I want to go.

(14)

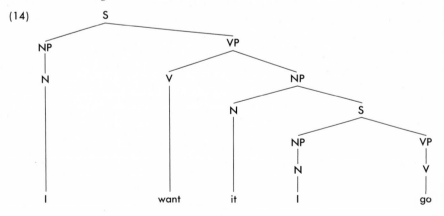

It follows from this observation that a PMD must specifically exclude any noun phrase in a main sentence which dominates the initial noun phrase of a complement.

We thus arrive at a principle which might be semi-formalized as follows [with the phrase-marker (15) providing a model]:

(15)

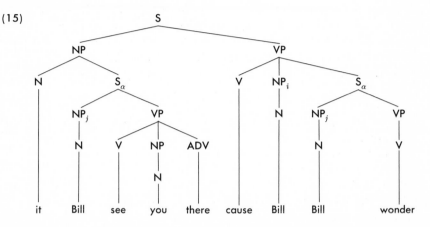

An NP_j [e.g., the initial noun phrase of either embedded S in (15)] is erased by an identical NP_i [e.g., the object noun phrase of the main sentence in (15)] if and only if there is an S_α [e.g., either embedded S in (15)] such that

(i) NP_j is dominated by S_α

(ii) NP_i neither dominates nor is dominated by S_α

(iii) for all NP_k neither dominating nor dominated by S_α [e.g., the subject noun phrase of the main sentence in (15)], the distance between NP_j and NP_k is greater than the distance between NP_j and NP_i where distance between two nodes is defined in terms of the number of branches in the path connecting them.

The PMD expresses the actual generalization that is involved in determining the initial noun phrase deletion under discussion and leads to a grammar of English in which the mechanism required to describe the deletion of initial noun phrases is more highly valued than the group of rules (10), (11), and (12). To put it another way, the principle leads to a direct reflection in the grammar of the significant generalization involved in initial noun phrase deletion by allowing a description of the deletion in terms of a single transformational rule, namely (16).[3] In other words, initial noun phrase deletion in all distributions is treated as a single syntactic process.

(16)   W   (NP)   X $\begin{Bmatrix} \text{for} \\ \text{POSS} \end{Bmatrix}$ NP   Y   (NP)   Z

      1   2   3   4   5   6   7   8 $\Rightarrow$

(i) 5 is erased by 2

(ii) 5 is erased by 7, where a constituent A is erased by a constituent B, e.g., $A \Rightarrow 0$, just in case A and B meet the conditions imposed by the principle of minimal distance.

For illustrative purposes, consider the underlying phrase structure (15). Since the initial noun phrase of the noun phrase complement (Index 5) and the object noun phrase of the main sentence (Index 7) meet the conditions imposed by the PMD, the former is deleted. Since the initial noun phrase of the verb phrase complement (also Index 5) and the object noun phrase of the main sentence (Index 2) meet the necessary conditions, the former is deleted.

It is quite likely that the PMD as stated earlier is but a special case of a general principle of minimal distance. Such a possibility follows from the observation that if the terms of the principle include not only NP, but N, VP, and V, then one discovers that the principle (in its general sense) offers a natural explanation for the identity requirements of relative clause formation and for similar requirements in many instances of verb and verb phrase ellipsis. But the further generalization of the principle is another topic, one which will require careful study. Suffice it to say that a principle of minimal distance, even in its restricted sense, allows a unified syntactic description of initial noun phrase deletion in complement constructions which is empirically adequate for a very wide range of such constructions. There are apparent exceptions to the principle, but it is too early to determine whether the fault lies with the principle or with the analyses ascribed to these exceptions. The important fact is that a principle of minimal distance, even though it may not supply us with a sufficiently broad basis for the theoretical presentation of all identity-deletion phenomena, still must be accorded a considerable measure of "truth," since it provides for a correct description of a great number of cases.[4] Furthermore, and perhaps most important, if such a principle (or something very much like it) is not valid, that is, if a linguistic theory does not include such a principle, the theory predicts, in effect, that the deletion of initial noun phrases in complements will be, for all natural languages, unsystematic, dependent upon distribution at best and upon lexical subcategorization at worst, and essentially random. For English, at least, this prediction is not supported by the facts. This is a strong argument in favor of a principle of minimal distance.

NOTES

1. The reasons for assigning these analyses are discussed in considerable detail in Rosenbaum (1967).

2. It is important to remember that the underlying structures assigned to the sentences under study are motivated quite independently of the principle of minimal

distance. In other words, alternative analyses yield unfortunate empirical consequences which have nothing whatever to do with considerations of deletion.

3. The inclusion of the complementizing morphemes "for" and "POSS" (infinitival and gerundive) is necessary in any adequate formulation, since the deletion of the initial noun phrase of complements is restricted to these distributions.

4. These constructions are documented in Rosenbaum (1967).

Conditions on English Comparative Clause Pairings

AUSTIN HALE

3

One of the key problems that any analysis of the English comparative faces is the manner in which clauses are related to one another in the comparative construction. Lees (1961) and Smith (1961) have provided two opposing answers to that question. Lees held that a constituent clause (i.e., embedded sentence) is related to some constituent in the matrix clause (i.e., main sentence) in the same way as the adverbial *that* is to the adjective *tall* in the sentence

(1)   John is that tall.

Thus, the sentence

(2)   John is taller than Mary is.

is derived from underlying clauses which stand in roughly the following kind of relation to one another:

(3)

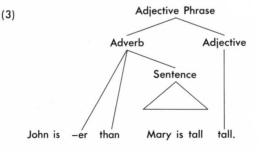

On this view the comparative construction is basically an adverbial modifier of some adjective or adverb in the matrix sentence. Smith, on the other hand, held that *–er than* was a kind of conjunction which formed a complex adjectival (or adverbial) expression. On this view, example (2) is derived from underlying clauses which stand in roughly the following kind of relation to one another:

(4)

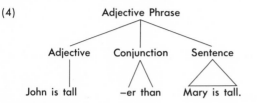

Adjective Phrase

Adjective   Conjunction   Sentence

John is tall   –er than   Mary is tall.

Each of these solutions has much to recommend it, though in view of the fact that we get adverbial comparisons such as:

(5)   John ran faster than Mary.

and nominal comparisons such as:

(6)   More people came than he had expected.

Lees's view appears to some to provide a neater characterization of the notion "comparative."

Another key problem that faces any analysis of the English comparative is that of saying just what can be compared. That is, it faces the problem of making explicit the constraints which distinguish the acceptable pairs of –er clauses and *than* clauses from the nonacceptable pairs. Chomsky (1965, pp. 178–184) and Huddleston (1967) have pointed to the importance of this problem both by the regularities they have uncovered and by the unsolved problems they raise. It is the purpose of this study to take a closer look at the constraints which characterize such pairings. Our concern will be more to determine the different varieties of constraints that are involved than to provide each with an exhaustive description.

The varieties of constraints which will be our concern here perhaps can best be illustrated in terms of sentences which violate them. One of these constraints involves the pairing of identical quantifier elements. If this constraint is violated, we get ungrammatical sentences such as:

(7)   * More came than we accomplished.

Where constraints on the pairing of compared constituents are violated, we get ungrammaticalities such as:

(8)   * Mary bought more records than John is tall.

When the features of the heads of the compared constituents are incompatible, we get oddities such as:

(9)   * The committee meeting was longer than the table.

Where noncompared constituents are paired in violation of constraints, we get ill-formed sentences such as:

    (10)   * Tom steals more money than Bill does to feed his family.

Where *than* occurs in an ungrammatical position, we get pairings which result in sentences such as:

    (11)   * Bill was a bigger man than if Sam were he would have said so.

Where conditions on pairability are violated between the degree constituent and the rest of the comparative construction, we may get monstrosities such as:

    (12)   * Bill was taller than Mary by more than five pounds more than Sam
          ran faster than Pete.

Finally, where derivational constraints are involved, we may get such ungrammaticalities as:

    (13)   * Bill is a taller man than Mary is.

General

The English comparative construction has been the subject of numerous recent studies.[1] Though these studies differ considerably from one another both in the theories they represent and in the conclusions they reach, they do make it relatively easy to give an informal account of the major features of the English comparative construction. These features may be presented in a number of ways. The following is one of them.

    The comparative construction is a modifier of what we will refer to as the *quantifier element*. This element has a number of forms depending upon the environment in which it occurs. In determiner position before plural count nouns it appears as *many* or *few*.

    (14)   Many (few) people came.

Before mass nouns it appears as *much* or *little*.

    (15)   Much (little) butter was lost.[2]

With certain verbs it appears as *much* or *little*.

    (16)   They used it much (little).

With certain adjectives and participles it appears as *much*.[3]

    (17)   He was much afraid.
    (18)   They were much offended.

With most adjectives and adverbs the quantifier elements *much* and *little* appear only under comparison.

(19)   The book was more expensive.

(20)   He drove more recklessly.

There is a special quantifier element that occurs with certain words and constructions which are not normally considered capable of entering a comparison. The sentence

(21)   This block is bigger than that one.

is grammatical, and we assume that the underlying quantifier element (in this case deleted) is *much*. If, however, we substitute *square* for *big*, we must also substitute *much nearly* for *much* as the quantifier element:

(22)   This block is more nearly square than that one.

Other adjectives of this sort include *false, dead, equal, infinite, complete, absolute, expired, void,* and the like. Though apparently restricted to the predicate position, the same kind of quantifier element is required where singular count nouns enter into comparison.

(23)   Bill is more nearly a man than Sam is.

In this position *much of* also appears to be a possible quantifier element.

(24)   Bill is more of a man than Sam is.

Much nearly is also required as quantifier element where prepositional phrases enter into comparison:

(25)   He threw the ball more nearly toward the gate than toward the window.

and consequently it is also required where certain clauses enter into comparison:

(26)   He arrived more nearly (at the time) when Mary left than when Sam did.

It appears with certain verbs as well:

(27)   He more nearly flunked than Bill did.

The comparative construction itself may be viewed as consisting of an optional modifier, which we will refer to as *degree*, a *comparative element*, and a *comparative complement*. Included in the set of comparative elements are the elements *–er, as, too, so, the –est,* and undoubtedly others. The comparative complement may be a reduced clause as in

(28)   John is taller *than Bill* (*is*).

Or, if the comparative element is *–er* or *as*, it may be a noun phrase as in

(29)   John is taller *than six feet.*

The choice of comparative element determines the choice of the element which introduces the complement.

(30)   John is *as* tall *as* Bill is.
(31)   John is tall *–er than* Bill is.
(32)   John is *so* tall *that* he couldn't get in.
(33)   John is *too* tall *to* get in.
(34)   John is *the* tall *–est* boy *that* got in.

If the comparative element is *–er, too,* or *the –est,* the optional modifier, degree, may be present. Degree may consist of a prepositional phrase as in

(35)   John is taller than Bill *by five inches.*

This phrase may be permuted to the front of the comparative construction and *by* may be deleted as in

(36)   John is *five inches* taller than Bill.

Just in case the comparative element is *–er*, degree may consist of *by* followed by a comparative clause:

(37)   John is taller than Bill *by as much as Sally is taller than Joan.*

or by a comparative clause modified by the kind of degree structure exemplified in (36):

(38)   John is taller than Bill *by five inches more than Sally is taller than Joan.*

Pairability and the Quantifier Elements

If the comparative complement is a clause, certain constraints obtain between the complement clause and the clause containing the comparative element. We will restrict our discussion for the remainder of this study to *–er than* type comparison.

Where *–er* and *than* relate two clauses, the quantifier element modified by *–er* must be paralleled by an identical quantifier element in the *than* clause. Thus we get

(39)   Peter ate less than they gave him.

from a source including underlying sentences something like

(39)   a. Peter ate *–er little* N^2
　　　　 b. They gave Peter than *little* N

but we reject

(40)   * Peter ate more than they gave him little.

because the paired quantifier elements are not identical:

(40)   a. Peter ate –er *much* N
        b. They gave Peter than *little* N.

For the same reason we reject

(41)   * Peter was taller than he was nearly a man.
        a. Peter was –er *much* tall
        b. Peter was than *much nearly* a man.

and

(42)   * More came than we accomplished.
        a. –er *many* N came
        b. We accomplished than *much.*[4]

It should be noted here that we are assuming at this point that *–er* and *than* are related to their respective quantifier elements in the same way. The motivations for this as a constraint on pairing will be given in the section below, titled "Pairability and the Position of *Than.*"[5]

Pairability and the Compared Constituents

Not only must the quantifier elements in the two clauses be identical, they must also be constituents of parallel constructions. Huddleston (1967, p. 92) has distinguished six positions in which the comparative element *–er* and its quantifier element may occur. In somewhat revised form they are as follows:

A. Determiner position

    1. Noun head present: Mary bought more records than Peter.
    2. Noun head deleted: Mary achieved more than Peter.

B. Adjective position

    1. In the predicate: Mary is more talkative than Peter.
    2. In a noun phrase: Mary bought a more expensive car than Peter.

C. Adverb position

    1. With an adverb: Mary talks more quickly than Peter.
    2. With a verb: Mary talks more than Peter.

To this list may be added another position which is identical to B(1) for the purposes of this classification, that of adjectival verbal complement.[6]

(43)   John washed the window cleaner than Bill did.

This classification furnishes an approximation to the notion "constituents of parallel constructions." For the compared constituents (i.e., the constructions of which *–er* and *than* are constituents respectively) to be parallel, they must at least be classified in the same way by the above list.[7] Thus while we get

(44)   The window was cleaner than Bill washed it.

we reject

(45)   * The window was cleaner than Peter talks quickly.

since in (44) both quantifier elements belong to B(1) whereas in (45) *–er much clean* belongs to B(1) while *than much quickly* belongs to C(1).

Pairability and the Feature Structure of Compared Constituent Heads

Not only must the two clauses have identical quantifier elements for *–er* and *than*, and not only must these in turn be constituents of parallel constructions; the heads of these parallel constructions also must have compatible sets of syntactic features. We take the following to be the "heads" of their respective compared constituents. Where the comparative element is in determiner position, we take the head of the compared constituent to be the noun immediately dominated by NP.

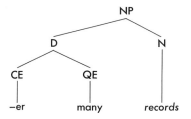

The head of the compared constituent in the adjective phrase of the predicate is the adjective immediately dominated by AP.

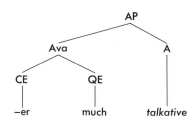

The head of the compared constituent in the adjective position within the noun phrase includes the noun immediately dominated by NP as well as the adjective immediately dominated by AP.

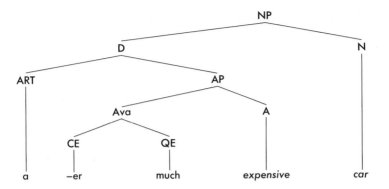

The head of the compared constituent in adverb position within an adverb phrase is the adverb immediately dominated by AvP.

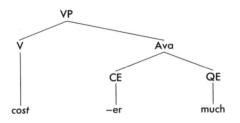

The head of the compared constituent in adverb position within a verb phrase is the verb immediately dominated by VP.

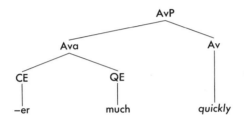

In an *–er much nearly* construction where a prepositional phrase follows *nearly*, the preposition is considered the head of the compared constituent.

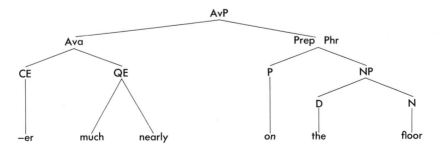

In an *–er much nearly* construction where an adverbial clause follows *nearly*, the subordinator is considered the head of the compared constituent.[8]

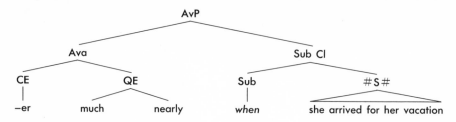

Consider the following sentence:

(46)   * The committee meeting was longer than the table.

from the underlying sentences:

    a. The committee meeting was –er much long.
    b. The table was than much long.

The ungrammaticality of (46) appears to be a result of the fact that in (46a) *long* is an adjective of time and in (46b) *long* is an adjective of dimension. This in turn can be understood as a result of selection between the adjective and a subject which is [−physical object] [+activity] on the one hand and between the adjective and a subject which is [+physical object] [−activity] on the other. Since *long* is what we have termed the head of the comparison, the features of *long* are what concern us here. Note, furthermore, that the features which are apparently needed, [dimension] and [time], are needed for independent reasons in an adequate grammar of English to insure the proper selection of units for quantification. Thus we get

(47)   The table was five inches too long.
(48)   The committee meeting was five hours too long.

but not

(49)   * The table was five hours too long.
(50)   * The committee meeting was five inches too long.

where the unit *inches* co-occurs with adjectives marked [+dimension] and the unit *hours* co-occurs with adjectives marked [+time]. From the ungrammaticality of (46) we may tentatively conclude that adjective compared constituent heads marked [+time] are not pairable with heads marked [+dimension].

The problem of determining which feature specifications block compared constituent pairings is a vast one, and no complete solution is offered here. A few observations will suffice to illustrate some regularities to be found in this area.[9] We wish to allow

(51) The table is longer than it is wide.

but to disallow

(52) * The table is longer than it is short.
(53) * The table is shorter than it is narrow.

and in seeking to do so in some motivated way, we may observe that we get

(54) The table is six feet long.
(55) The table is three feet wide.

but not

(56) * The table is six feet short (narrow).

except in the sense

(57) The table is six feet too short.

We may conclude tentatively that there are two kinds of adjectives marked [+dimension], those marked [+unit], and those marked [−unit]. Only those marked [+unit] may be paired within the domain [+dimension].

The principle that all and only those adjectives within a comparable domain which take measure units can be paired also works correctly for pairs of adjectives and adverbs marked [+time]. Thus we get the adjective pair

(58) He was five minutes earlier than she was late.

but not the adverb pair

(59) * He came five minutes later than she came soon.

as we would predict from the following:

(60) He was five minutes early (late).
(61) He came five minutes early (late).
(62) * He came five minutes soon.

Similarly,

(63) His watch was five minutes faster than hers was slow.

is to be contrasted with the same pair of adjectives in the domain [+rate].

(64) * His car was five miles an hour faster than hers was slow.

In the former case we get units with both *fast* and *slow:*

(65) The watch was five minutes fast (slow).

but in the latter case we get units with neither adjective:

(66) * The car was five miles an hour fast (slow).

There are many other domains which may be defined in terms of quantifier units in this way. The following is a small sample:

[+weight] [−unit]:	heavy, light, . . .
[+cost] [−unit]:	expensive, cheap, costly, . . .
[+temperature] [−unit]:	hot, cold, warm, cool, . . .
[+distance] [−unit]:	far, near, distant, close, . . .
[+duration] [−unit]:	long, short, . . .

From their features we would not expect any of these adjectives to pair.

The principle appears to work correctly in the cases we have been able to examine. It is a perfectly intuitive constraint. Comparison is a kind of quantification, whether numerical or otherwise. Quantification is generally effected in terms of some kind of unit, and the fact that adjectives which take different units in numerical comparison do not pair is an obvious kind of constraint. One can compare the price of eggs in China with the temperature in Chicago, but only in one of the two following ways:

(67)   * It was five dollars a dozen hotter in Chicago than eggs were expensive in China.

(68)   The number of dollars that a dozen eggs costs in China is greater than the number of degrees centigrade the temperature was in Chicago.

Comparison here must rest upon a common unit, and the only one available was that of number.[10]

That only those adjectives within a domain which take units outside the comparative can be paired within a comparative sentence is also an intuitive constraint. Stated differently, only those adjectives with an inherent standard of comparison can be paired within a comparison. The sentence

(69)   * The table is five feet narrow.

is ungrammatical, intuitively speaking, because there is no reference point from which to measure five feet. Obviously, paired adjectives must possess reference points independent of the comparison in which they stand related to one another.

The case of adverbs is similar, except that other than in the domain of [+time] we have failed to turn up any domains with more than one member that takes measure units outside the comparative, and permissible pairings have been correspondingly absent. The following small sample is illustrative:

[+time] [+unit]:	early, late, . . .
[+time] [−unit]:	soon, recently, . . .
[+place] [−unit]:	near, far, close, distant, . . .
[+rate] [−unit]:	fast, slow, . . .
[+frequency] [−unit]:	often, frequently, . . .

There are even similarities among the verbs. Consider the following:

(70)   The tank measures three gallons more than that gauge reads.

where we have

> a. The tank measures five gallons.
> b. The gauge reads five gallons.

We also get

(71)   That book cost five dollars more than Bill paid.

where we have

> a. That book cost five dollars.
> b. Bill paid five dollars.

Verbs from different domains do not pair in this way.

(72)   * That book cost more than it weighed.

The case of mass nouns appears to be rather different. Although certain mass nouns take quantifier units:

(73)   a pound of butter
(74)   five cups of tea

and although there appear to be some domain boundaries across which units and mass nouns cannot combine

(75)   * a loaf of butter

domains in mass nouns do not appear to block pairing.

(76)   He drank three more cups of tea than he ate loaves of bread.

Though other kinds of constraints are also involved, contrasting domains appear to block pairing in the *more nearly* type constructions.

(77)   John lay more nearly on the floor   [+place]
          than in bed   [+place]
      * than in a rage   [+manner]
      * than for a week   [+duration]
      * than a week ago[11]   [+time]

In these kinds of constructions the feature [+unit] appears to play no role.

Pairability and Noncompared Constituents

On intuitive grounds one may say that the *than* clause may contain only those constituents relevant to the establishment of the grounds for comparison. Thus certain constituents other than the compared constituent are allowed in the *than* clause only if they are paired with a like constituent in the *-er* clause. Thus in the sentence

(78)   John ran faster than I did today.

today is understood as belonging to the matrix sentence or possibly to both clauses, but certainly not to the *than* clause alone. In the sentence

(79)   John ran faster yesterday than I did today.[12]

today is understood as belonging to the *than* clause alone. It appears, then, that a fourth kind of constraint on clauses paired in comparison concerns the constituency of *than* clauses. One constraint of this sort is the constraint that a *than* clause cannot contain a *time* adverb unless the matrix *-er* clause also contains one. An analogous constraint appears to hold true for place adverbs:

(80)   John sat longer in the room than I did (in the hall).

for manner adverbs:

(81)   More teenagers drive recklessly than adults (do so cautiously).

for *for* phrase benefactives:

(82)   Bill bought more cars for John than Bob (did so for Tom).

for duration adverbials:

(83)   Bill washed more windows in one hour than Tom did (in three).

for means adverbials:

(84)   We killed more pheasants with spitwads than they did (with slingshots).

for frequency adverbials:

(85)   Tom buys more eggs every day than Sam's whole family does (every week).

for purpose adverbials:

(86)   Tom steals more money to pay his debts than Bill does (to feed his family).

for *sake* adverbials:

(87)   John put more money in the bank for his mother's sake than Paul did (for his son's sake).

for *with* phrases:

(88)   John baked more cakes with Jane than Sally did (with Sam).[13]

This constraint, then, appears to hold true for all adverbial constituents which fall outside the verb phrase on the Lakoff–Ross criterion for verb phrase constituency.[14] Note, furthermore, that it is the function of these adverbials that is important, not their internal structure. Thus the time adverb of the −er clause can be a word, a phrase, or a clause, and the time adverb of the than clause is not constrained to have a similar structure.

(89)   John ran faster when he was being chased by Fido than I did today.
(90)   John ran faster today than Noah did before the flood.

It even appears possible that the temporal function of the auxiliary is adequate in certain cases to allow the deletion of an understood now in the matrix, and the presence of this temporal function still allows the than clause to have an independent time adverb:

(91)   John is running faster (now) than I did yesterday.

Furthermore, time, frequency, and duration all appear to pair interchange- ably. We may suppose that all three are marked [+ time] and that the appearance of one of them in the −er clause makes grammatical the appear- ance of any of them in the than clause:

(92)   Tom just bought more eggs than their whole family does every week.
(93)   Tom just bought more eggs than Sam eats during a whole year.
(94)   Bill washes more windows every day than Sam did in three days last week.

Likewise, direction and place appear to pair interchangeably in the same way:

(95)   More people walked toward the woods than ate their lunch in the bus.

We may suppose that both direction and place are marked [+ place]. The fact that direction but not place is a constituent of VP according to the Lakoff–Ross test corresponds to the fact that direction appears in the than clause independently of any [+ place] element in the −er clause, but place does not occur independently in the than clause.

(96)   More people slept in than walked to church yesterday.
(97)   More people talked than whispered in the library today.

In (96) to church belongs to the than clause alone, whereas in (97) in the library is not peculiar to the than clause, as is also the case with the time adverbs in both examples. These examples also illustrate the fact that time and place are not interchangeably pairable in the way that frequency, duration, and time are interchangeably pairable with one another on the one hand, and in the way that place and direction are interchangeably pairable with one another on the other hand. Note further that other elements which are clearly part of the verb phrase according to the Lakoff–Ross test may be independently expanded in the than clause. Thus we get direct objects independently in the than clause:

(98)   More people were absent than bought tickets to the play.

We get indirect objects independently in the *than* clause:

(99)   **More people were sick than sent him greetings.**

We get adjective and adverb phrases independently in the *than* clause where these are clearly part of VP:

(100)   **More people handed in papers than stayed in the room.**
(101)   **More people came than got sick from eating the food.**

These observations suggest that one principle for limiting the constituency of *than* clauses so as to exclude elements irrelevant to the grounds for comparison might be informally stated as follows: Constituents of VP may be freely expanded in the *than* clause. For any constituent of the *than* clause which is not a constituent of VP, there must be some element in the *–er* clause which contains a feature permitting the occurrence of the function which that constituent represents.[15]

Pairability and the Position of Than

We stated earlier that the position of *–er* and *than* could well be thought of as parallel within their respective constructions. It was further shown that these constructions must themselves be parallel to one another in order to be pairable with *–er* and *than*. It remains to be shown what positions in a sentence a clause can occupy and still accept *than*. The positions of *–er* appear adequately accounted for in terms of constraints already given and will not be further discussed here.

Ross has noted[16] that there are positions that resist relativization. He also notes that these same positions also resist WH attachment and fronting in WH questions. Interesting in connection with the present study is the fact that many of these same positions also resist *than*. Consider the following cases (in each case we will assume the *–er* clause to be: *Bill was a –er much big man.*):

Within *that* nominal subjects:

(102)   **That Sam was a *than much* big man was a false claim.**

→ * **Bill was a bigger man than that Sam was was a false claim.**

Within *for to* nominal subjects:

(103)   **For Sam to be a *than much* big man was surprising.**

→ * **Bill was a bigger man than for Sam to be was surprising.**

Within possessive *–ing* nominal subjects:

(104)   **Sam's acquiring a *than much* big man as slave was a long affair.**

→ * Bill was a bigger man than Sam's acquiring as slave was a long affair.

Within sentential time adverbs:

(105) When Sam was a *than much* big man I was very small.

→ * Bill was a bigger man than when Sam was I was very small.

Within sentential place adverbs:

(106) Where Sam was a *than much* big man he was respected.

→ * Bill was a bigger man than where Sam was he was respected.

Within conditional clauses:

(107) If Sam were a *than much* big man he would have said so.

→ * Bill was a bigger man than if Sam were he would have said so.

Within concessive clauses:

(108) Though Sam was a *than much* big man he didn't say so.

→ * Bill was a bigger man than though Sam was he didn't say so.

Within result clauses:

(109) They fed Sam so that he became a *than much* big man.

→ * Bill was a bigger man than they fed Sam so that he became.

Within purpose clauses:

(110) They fed Sam so as to make him a *than much* big man.

→ * Bill was a bigger man than they fed Sam so as to make him.

Within a nominal complement:

(111) The claim that Sam was a *than much* big man was false.

→ * Bill was a bigger man than the claim that Sam was was false.

Within a relative clause:

(112) I saw one who was a *than much* big man.

→ * Bill was a bigger man than I saw one who was.

Within a conjoined sentence:

(113) I washed dishes and heard that Sam was a *than much* big man.

→ * Bill was a bigger man than I washed the dishes and heard that Sam was.

Observations like these might tempt one to say that subordinate clauses in general resist *than*, but there is at least one exception to this generalization. There is a set of verbs that take *that* #S# complements, some of which also take *to* #S# complements, which includes verbs such as *think, expect, hope, believe, wish, hear, say,* and the like. The complements of these verbs accept *than*.

(114)   My husband's papers are usually –er much long
        My husband expects his papers to be *than much* long

        → My husband's papers are usually longer than he expects them to be.

(115)   He drives –er much fast
        She thinks that he should drive *than much* fast

        → He drives faster than she thinks he should.

There is another set of verbs that take adjectival complements which appear to come from underlying sentences with *become*. This set includes verbs such as *wash, design, dig, draw, paint, scrub, scrape, wedge, pry, nail, cut,* and the like. The sentence

(116)   He washed it clean.

may be a reduction of something like

(117)   He washed it so that it became clean.

Note, however, that while we get

(118)   He cut it shorter than Bill did.

we do not get *than* in the unreduced source:

(119)   * He cut it shorter than Bill did so that it became.

If we accept Ross's rule of tree pruning (Ross, 1966*a*), the complements of these verbs do not constitute an exception to the statement that constituent clauses reject *than*, since the node #S# dominating these complements must be pruned from the tree before they will accept *than*. How our one remaining exception is to be accounted for is not at all clear.[17]

Pairability and Degree

In this section we wish to investigate the constraints that obtain between degree and the remainder of the comparative construction. We will refer to structures parallel to (120a) in the example below as *matrix comparison*, structures in position (120c) as *constituent comparison*, and structures in position (120b) as *linking comparison*. Structures analogous to (120b) and (120c) together comprise degree for matrix comparison. We will speak of *than* in (120a) as *matrix than, than* in (120b) as *linking than* and so forth.

(120)   a. John is taller than Bill.
        b. by five inches more than
        c. Bill is taller than Sam.

Where unit quantifiers are involved in by + NP matrix degree constructions, the choice of unit quantifiers is governed by the domains of the compared heads in the matrix comparison.

(121)   Some men are taller than Mary by as much as five $\begin{cases} \text{inches.} \\ * \text{ hours.} \end{cases}$

There appears to be great freedom in the choice of the comparative element
and the quantifier element of the linking comparison.

(122)   Some men are taller than Mary by $\begin{cases} \textit{less than} \\ \textit{as much as} \\ \textit{more than} \end{cases}$ a foot.

(123)   This car is longer than that one by so much $that$ Mary had a very
        hard time getting used to driving it.

We will limit our discussion in the remainder of this section to constraints
between $-er\ than$ matrix comparison and $-er\ than$ constituent comparison.
Our task is that of characterizing the pairability of matrix comparison with
constituent comparison by way of linking comparison.

In most respects the conditions upon the pairability of matrix and constituent comparisons appear strikingly similar to conditions upon the pairability
of $-er$ and $than$ clauses within matrix comparison. Domain violations block
pairings:

(124)   * John is taller than Mary by as much as Sue is heavier than Sam.

as do nonparallel compared constituents:

(125)   * John is taller than Mary by as much as Bill ran faster than Sam.

and as do noncompared constituents outside VP which occur in the constituent
but not in the matrix comparison:

(126)   * John earned more money than Bill by as much as Sam stole more
        than Pete did to pay his debts.

Constraints on the position of $than$ are identical in the constituent comparison to what they are in the matrix comparison so far as we have been able
to determine. The position of $-er$ and $than$ in the linking comparison, however, is considerably more constrained. Following our assumption that the
position of $than$ is parallel to the position of its corresponding $-er$, the linking
$-er$ occurs only in the degree of the matrix comparison, whereas the linking
$than$ clause always occurs as the only constituent of the degree of the constit-

uent comparison. This assumption provides an explanation of the ungrammaticality of the following two sentences:

(127)   * John is taller than Bill is five feet tall.
(128)   * John is taller than Bill by five inches more than Sam is taller than Pete by three inches.

Just as the matrix *than* exhausts the measure constituent of the *than* clause, excluding the phrase *five feet* from example (127), so also the linking *than* exhausts the degree of the constituent comparison, excluding the phrase *by three inches* from example (128). Thus linking comparison is related to matrix and constituent comparisons as a measure constituent is related to *–er* and *than* clauses.

At first glance it would seem that the feature [– unit] as it occurs in the heads of the compared constituents does not function to block the pairing of matrix and constituent comparisons as it does to block *–er than* pairings within a comparative matrix, since we get:

(129)   John is taller than Mary by as much as Sue is shorter than Sam.

This is, however, not the case. We already have noted that adjectives within quantifiable domains which are marked [– unit] take unit quantifiers when they are part of a compared constituent, but not otherwise. Thus we get

(130)   Sally is five inches shorter than Bill.

but not

(131)   * Sally is five feet short.

How is it, then, that an adjective marked [– unit] comes to accept unit quantification in the comparative? We would suggest that it is by virtue of the fact that *–er* itself is [+ unit] in some sense and that the [+ unit] of *–er* supersedes the [– unit] of *short* so far as the feature specification for the compared constituent is concerned. In this respect *–er* stands in marked contrast to *as* which is [– unit]:

(132)   * John is five inches as tall as Peter.

Here again the feature specification of *as* supersedes that of *tall* in (132) as is apparent from the fact that (133) is grammatical:

(133)   John is five feet tall.

Further evidence that *as* is marked [– unit] may be seen in the following. We get a sentence of the form

(134)   John is taller than Mary by as much as Pete is taller than Gary.

but no grammatical sentence of the form

(135)   *John is taller than Mary by as much as Pete is as tall as Gary.

To say that *as* is [−unit] is another way of saying that a comparison with *as* cannot be paired with any kind of measure, be it a measure expression or a linked comparison. Here again we see that linking comparison is related to matrix and constituent comparisons as a measure constituent is related to compared clauses.

Consider now the following three cases. Where the constituent comparison is replaced by a simple sentence, the feature [−unit] does indeed block pairing as our earlier analysis would predict. Thus we get

(136)   The table was shorter than the desk by as much as the desk was wide.

where *shorter* is [+unit] by virtue of the feature specification for *−er*, and *wide* is inherently [+unit], but we do not get

(137)   * The table was shorter than the desk by as much as the desk was narrow.

where *narrow* is inherently [−unit]. Again, however, we do get

(138)   The table was shorter than the desk by as much as the desk was narrower than the dresser.

where both *shorter* and *narrower* are now [+unit] by virtue of the feature specification for *−er*.

It seems clear, then, that the feature [−unit] blocks pairings of matrix and constituent comparisons just as it blocks unit quantification and pairings of *−er* and *than* clauses. This kind of regularity may account in part for our intuitive feeling that comparison is basically a kind of quantification. The same feature which blocks unit quantification also blocks comparative pairing.

Pairability and Derivation

Chomsky (1965, pp. 180–181, 234) notes that there is a problem with deriving sentences like

(139)   I know several lawyers more successful than Bill.

from underlying sentences like

(140)   I know several lawyers who are more successful than Bill.

since the analogous sentence

(141)   * I know a more clever man than Mary.

has a perfectly good source, but is not itself well formed.

Huddleston (1967, p. 95) follows Pilch (1965) in arguing from similar examples that (139) should not be derived from (140) because this makes it difficult to avoid violations of pairability such as are exemplified by (141).

Consider now the derivation of (141). Sentence (141) may be derived in two different ways. It may be derived from the underlying sentences

(141) a. I know a man.
       b. A man is –er much clever.
       c. * Mary is a man.
       d. A man is than much clever.

in which case the derivation obeys the pairability constraint that predicate adjectives pair only with predicate adjectives in comparison, and attributive adjectives pair only with attributive adjectives. The ungrammaticality of (141) follows directly, in this case, from the ungrammaticality of (141c). Alternatively, (141) may be derived from the underlying sentences

(141) e. I know a man.
       f. A man is –er much clever.
       g. Mary is than much clever.

in which case the ungrammaticality of (141) results from a violation of constraints on pairability.

A problem arises immediately in regard to the ordering of the rules. We assume that the rules will operate cyclically, starting with the most included constituent sentence, and that at the end of the cycle the rules on pairability will apply to determine whether or not the sentence boundaries of this most included structure may be deleted, i.e., whether or not the pairings involved are grammatical. Where the conditions on pairability are met, the boundaries of this most included sentence will be erased, and the cycle will reapply within the next most inclusive sentence. Where these conditions are not met, the sentence boundaries will remain, marking the sentence as ungrammatical.

The problem involved can be illustrated in terms of the derivation of

(142) I know a taller man than Sam.

We wish to allow the derivation of (142) from (143) but not from (144).

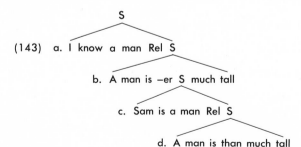

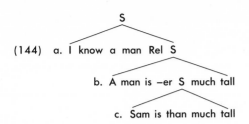

(144) a. I know a man Rel S

b. A man is –er S much tall

c. Sam is than much tall

Consider now the operation of the rules. The rules will apply first to (143d) and to (144c). Presumably no changes relevant to the present discussion will be effected by rules working strictly within the boundaries of these embedded sentences. At the end of the first cycle the pairability rules will compare (143c) with (143d) and (144b) with (144c) to determine pairability. As matters stand we will get the wrong results: (144b) and (144c) are pairable, (143c) and (143d) are not.

Two kinds of solutions could be suggested. One could take the approach that the reason the pairability rules failed to apply correctly here is that the ordering of the rules is wrong. Pairability cannot be determined before the relevant rules either have or have not applied to (143a) or (144a) in each case. It seems, however, that any reordering of this sort sacrifices the notion of transformational cycle.

A second kind of solution is to allow the pairability rules to scan the whole tree and insert rule features as required to insure the eventual pairability of the relevant constructions.[18] Thus in (143) the pairability rules will scan the relevant nodes and their branching relationships and will assign both instances of *tall* the feature [+ adjective move] to indicate that the rule for permuting the adjective to the left of its noun head must in this case apply obligatorily. From (143) we will get

(145)   I know a taller man than Sam.

In (144) the pairability rule will assign the feature [− adjective move] to *tall* in (144b) to indicate that the rule for permuting the adjective around the noun cannot apply in this case. From (144) we will get

(146)   I know a man who is taller than Sam [is (tall)].

and

(147)   I know a man taller than Sam.

but not

(148)   I know a taller man than Sam.

and consequently we will not get

(149)   *I know a taller man than Mary.

from

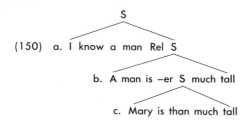

(150) a. I know a man Rel S

b. A man is –er S much tall

c. Mary is than much tall

NOTES

1. Some of the more significant of these studies are Lees (1961); Smith (1961); McCawley (1964); Pilch (1965); Chomsky (1965, pp. 178–184); and Huddleston (1967).

2. The sentences

Many came.
Much was lost.

are here viewed as containing noun phrases reduced from those of the form represented in (14) and (15) by deletion of some uniquely recoverable head noun. *Many* and *much* (and consequently *more* as well) make rather strange heads for a noun phrase. They refuse adjectival modifiers (except where hypostatized)

*I saw a tall much.

as well as determiners

*I saw the much.

As a consequence they reject relative clauses

*I was surprised by a much that sat down beside me.

For an opposing view, see Huddleston (1967, p. 92).

3. *Little* seems much less natural in these cases, though both *much* and *little* occur freely in these positions under comparison:

He was little afraid.
He was less afraid than I was.

4. This sentence may represent more than one violation of constraints on pairability depending upon whether or not *much* in (42b) is viewed as belonging to a noun phrase.

5. Huddleston (1967, pp. 93–94) points out that if we adopt this as a requirement on the position of *than*, we can very easily introduce *than* as an alternative expansion of the quantifier which is mutually exclusive with numerical quantifiers. This would eliminate ungrammaticalities of the following sort:

*Mary bought more records than Peter bought five books.

6. We assume sources like the following for (43):

John washed #S# the window
the window became –er #S# much clean
Bill washed #S# the window
the window became than much clean

7. It seems likely that adverbs and adjectives must share the same function to be parallel. Thus time and place do not constitute parallel constructions.

* John was nearer than Bill was late.

This is not the case with determiners. Subject and object functions are parallel in our sense:

More people came than John could count.
John counted more people than he could give his greetings to.

It seems that the functions of subject and object can be adequately marked by dominance relations between category symbols such as S, NP, and VP within a tree as Chomsky proposes (1965, pp. 68–72) but that the functions of adverbs such as those of time and place cannot be adequately marked by dominance relations between category symbols such as Av, Prep Phr, PP, VP, and the like but require either functional labels such as time and place in the tree as proposed by Fillmore (1966), compound symbols in the tree as proposed by Hale (1966, p. 312), or syntactic features such as [time] and [place] assigned to an element which may be termed the head of the adverbial construction. We take the third option in this study.

8. It may well be that such cases have sources of the sort:

–er much nearly at the time $_S$[she arrived . . . at WH the time]$_S$.

In this case *when* would be a reduction of *at the time at which*.

9. We are not concerned here with cases such as

He is more tall than intelligent.

which represent, as is shown in McCawley (1964), an entirely different kind of construction, one which is not subject to the kinds of constraints on pairability discussed in this section. McCawley notes the following differences between the comparative which concerns us here and the *more than* (in the sense of *rather than*) constructions exemplified by the sentence above:

(1) The *rather than* structure never attaches *–er* to an adjective or an adverb:

John is more sick than depraved.
* John is sicker than depraved.

(2) The *rather than* structure never occupies adjective position in NP:

* John is a more stupid man than ignorant.

(3) The *rather than* structure relates singular predicate nominals to one another in a manner not allowed in comparative constructions:

John is more a philosopher than a linguist.

(4) The *rather than* structure does not answer *how* questions as other comparatives do. Thus the question

How stupid is John?

is not answered by the statement

* He's very stupid: he's more stupid than ignorant.

10. Picturesque speech often gains its spice from the grammatical rules it breaks. Hence:

* The temperature in Chicago today is higher than the price of eggs in China.

is quite acceptable, though ungrammatical.

11. The sentence

John lay more nearly on the floor than a week ago.

is grammatical only as a reduction of

John lay more nearly on the floor than he lay on the floor a week ago.

where [+place] pairs with [+place] and not with [+time].

12. It appears that in certain cases the adverb in the *than* clause may be allowed through pairing with a tense in the auxiliary, or perhaps with a uniquely recoverable, deleted time adverb:

Tom is making more money (*now* understood) than Bill did a year ago.

13. Note that

John baked more cakes alone than Sam did with Sally.

is grammatical, and

John baked more cakes than Sam did, with Sally.

is grammatical only where juncture falls before *with* and is understood as a paraphrase of

John baked more cakes with Sally than Sam did with Sally.

and that

* John baked more cakes than Sam did with Sally.

is ungrammatical.

14. Lakoff and Ross (1966). Other adverbial constituents falling outside VP include *because* clauses, *if* clauses, *without* clauses, and *instead of* clauses.

15. We assume here a hierarchy of features something like the following:

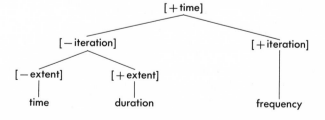

16. Private conversation, December 30, 1965. Some of this material is also found in Ross (1966*a*) and (1966*b*).

17. There are other kinds of constraints upon the distribution of *than* which are frequently referred to in the literature. Negated constituents reject *than*. Thus while we get negation in constituents other than the compared constituents, as in

More frequently than not he failed to hand in his assignments.

where the *than* clause is something like

He did not fail to hand in his assignments than much frequently.

in the underlying structure, and the compared constituent is a frequency adverb, while the negated constituent is the verb phrase, we do not get negation within the compared constituent itself. Thus we reject

* He was taller than she was not.

where the *than* clause is something like

She was not than much tall.

and the compared constituent is negated.

It has also been noted by many that the compared constituent in a *than* clause cannot be quantified. Thus we reject

* He bought more books than she bought five pencils.

Indeed, it was observations such as these that prompted Huddleston (1967, pp. 93–94) to propose the underlying position of *than* that has been used in this study.

18. The general notion "rule feature" used here is taken from Lakoff (1965).

On So-called Pronouns in English

4

PAUL M. POSTAL

Introduction

The following is an informal discussion of certain regularities in the syntactic behavior of forms traditionally called pronouns in discussions of English syntax. By informal I mean that, although the analysis suggested involves a number of highly complex grammatical rules and a very special conception of the theory of grammar, no attempt has been made here to formulate or present any of the rules in their correct form. Nor is very much said about the theoretical assumptions these require. My aim is the much weaker one of trying to suggest that a class of facts requires that English grammar be formulated in such a way that it can contain such rules.

Our traditional lore about English grammar[1] recognizes a class of forms often called pronouns or personal pronouns which includes *I, we, you, he, she, it, they*. At the start, for simplicity, we may ignore the various case forms *us, your, him,* etc., as well as reflexives, although these will become crucial later. Very often it was said that such forms "stand for" or "replace" or "are substitutes for" previously mentioned or understood noun forms. Certain modern students of English such as Robert Allen[2] have noted, essentially correctly, that in many ways such forms actually "replace" whole noun phrases (henceforth NP) rather than nouns, since they cannot occur with articles, relative phrases, and other elements which can occur in the same NP with ordinary nouns. Compare:

(1)   The young girl said that she would go.

SOURCE: This article originally appeared in the *Monograph Series on Languages and Linguistics, 19*, F. P. Dinneen, S. J., ed., Washington, D. C., Georgetown University Press, 1966.

where on one reading *she* can be said to "stand for" the whole NP *the young girl* with:

(2)   The large girl can't stand the small one.

where *one* can only be said to "stand for" the noun *girl*. However, as I argue later, this contrast is a bit misleading, since there is reason to assume that the form *one* or its variants is also relevant at one stage to the "replacement" which occurs in sentences like (1).

Early transformational descriptions of English have shown that the vague and unclear traditional notion of "stand for" can, in its *sentence internal*[3] meaning, be precisely formalized by transformational derivation. Thus, in a transformational grammar a structure like:

(3)   O'Hara is more intelligent than he seems to be.

would be derived from a more abstract structure schematically like:[4]

(4)   O'Hara is more intelligent than O'Hara seems to be.

However, obviously not all pronouns can be so derived, which leads to a differentiation between transformationally introduced pronominal structures and those introduced in the underlying or basic forms, as in:

(5)   He is sick.

The fact that pronouns have two different origins can then be suggested as the explanation for the ambiguity of reference of the pronoun in sequences like:

(6)   Schwartz claims he is sick.

There is a great deal right in all this, and no one who wishes to discuss English pronouns can afford to ignore the insights and observations which underlie the kinds of descriptions just mentioned. It is the thesis of this paper, however, that these analyses ignore some important facts and that there is concomitantly a good deal also wrong in them. Furthermore, what is wrong can be seen to arise from the almost inevitable tendency in grammatical research to assume wrongly that the surface or superficial syntactic forms of sentences provide direct insight into (or are even identical with) their deep syntactic forms.

The "Article" Character of So-called Pronouns

In a transformational grammar, each sentence, and hence, derivatively, each part of each sentence has two distinct syntactic structures as part of its overall grammatical description: a highly abstract deep structure relevant for semantic interpretation and a surface structure relevant for phonetic interpretation.

These two aspects of syntactic form are in general connected by a long and complex chain of transformational rules which, furthermore, derive a sequence of intermediate forms.[5]   In such a grammar it makes no sense to ask such traditional questions as: "Is such and such occurrence of form F a noun?" It makes sense to ask such questions *contextually* only with respect to a specified structure. That is, one can ask whether such and such occurrence of a form F is a noun in the deep structure, a noun in such and such intermediate structure, a noun in the surface structure of the sentence, etc. The answer to some of these questions may be *yes*, to others *no*, without contradiction.   Furthermore, and equally importantly, the fact that an element is present in the surface form does not mean it was present in the deep structure and, conversely, absence from the surface form does not necessarily entail absence from the deeper aspect of grammatical structure.

I mention all this only because it is fundamental to my basic claim which is that the so-called pronouns *I, our, they,* etc. are really "articles," in fact types of "definite" articles.   However, article elements are introduced only as "segments" in intermediate syntactic structures. In the deepest structures they are, I shall suggest, not present segmentally but are represented as syntactic features of nouns, features analogous to [animate], [human], [countable], etc.[6]   Rather deceptively, the articles which have traditionally been called pronouns are, as a result of certain transformational operations, in many cases assigned a derivative noun status in surface structures.

The evidence for this rather extreme set of assertions is complex, fragmentary, and involved with the analysis of a wide variety of different constructions in English. This greatly limits the possibility of providing a full justification here. However, I shall attempt to sketch the reasoning involved and to present those factors which seem most significant. To start, we can determine easily that English NP, that is, the elements which function as subjects, objects, etc., must be categorized into definite versus indefinite in order for their distributional possibilities to be described properly. In large part, but by no means completely, definite or indefinite status is indicated superficially by a particular article. Thus *the, this, that, these, those* are definite, *a/an, some, sm,* and null[7] are indefinite. However, proper nouns are definite even though in general they occur without explicit article. There are exceptions, of course, including *The Hague, the Bronx,* as well as fairly productive instances such as names of ships, names of buildings, etc.[8]

Diagnostic environments for definite NP include special constructions with preposed adjectives illustrated by such sentences as:[9]

(7)   a.   Big as the boy was, he couldn't lift it.
      b.   Big as Harry was, he couldn't lift it.
      c.   Big as that gorilla was, he couldn't lift it.
      d. * Big as some giant was, he couldn't lift it.
      e. * Big as a dog was, he couldn't lift it.

Similarly, only definites occur as subjects in constructions like:

(8)   a.   Fido is John's.
       b.   The house is John's.
       c.   That car is John's.
       d. * Soup is John's.
       e. * Some dog is John's.
       f. * A car is John's.

On the other hand, only indefinites occur in such contexts as:

(9)   a.   It was idiocy for Jack to leave.
       b. * It was the idiocy for Jack to leave.
       c.   It was a scandal that Louis spoke.
       d. * It was that scandal that Louis spoke.

Another diagnostic environment for indefinites is given by constructions with nonlocative, anticipatory *there*:[10]

(10)   a.   There's a book on the table.
        b.   There's some object on the table.
        c. * There's John on the table.
        d. * There's this key on the table.

But investigation shows that all of the so-called pronouns are thereby definite NP:

(11)   a.   Big as I am, I couldn't lift it.
        b.   Big as they were, they couldn't lift it.
(12)   a.   It is Billy's.
        b.   They are Jack's.
(13)   a. * It was it for Jack to leave.
        b. * It was it that Louis spoke.
(14)   a. * There's me on the table.
        b. * There's you in the house.

The definite character of NP containing so-called pronouns[11] is also shown by various prearticle constructions. Although we cannot go into this in detail, notice that such forms as *which of, some of, all of,* etc., occur only with following definites:[12]

(15)   a.   which of the men
        b.   some of the men
        c.   all of those cars
        d. * which of some men
        e. * all of cars

But they also occur with following so-called pronouns if these are plural:

(16)   a. which of you
        b. some of them
        c. all of us

A similar argument holds for superlative phrases like:

(17)   a.   the best of these sheep
       b.   the tallest of the men here
       c.   the fairest of those maidens
       d. * the best of some sheep
       e. * the tallest of men here
       f. * the fairest of sm maidens

which also show the definite character of the pronoun NP:

(18)   a. the best of us
       b. the tallest of you
       c. the fairest of them

An important problem in constructing a grammar of English is, therefore, the following: Granting that in general the definite or indefinite character of an NP is indicated by its article, how is definite status to be assigned formally to NP based on the so-called pronouns? A possibility is to assume simply that the pronouns are a subclass of nouns which occur in deep structures only with the nondemonstrative definite article *the,* which later drops by a transformational rule. Thus the underlying terminal structure of a sentence like *I went* would be schematically (*the I*) *went,* where *I* is a noun and *the* its preceding definite article. This would eliminate the other exceptional fact of no article with pronouns at the cost of the transformational rule to account for the absence of *the* in the surface structures. The apparent advantages increase if a similar analysis is proposed for proper nouns. Not a bad bargain perhaps, but not an especially good one either.

Moreover, further facts strongly suggest that, while it is right to assume that more abstract NP structures of superficial pronoun-containing NP involve definite articles, it is wrong to assume either that the articles are *the* or that at the relevant stage the pronouns are nouns. Most important in this regard are the reflexive forms such as those in:

(19)   a.   Horace washed himself.
       b.   The girl washed herself.
       c.   I washed myself.

As has been argued by Lees and Klima (1963),[13] it is quite clear that reflexive elements must be derived transformationally from underlying NP which are identical to other preceding NP, this identity being subject to certain conditions. These have never been fully or exactly stated, but they concern occurrence of the two NP within the same "simple" sentence structure. This may be ignored here. Thus a sentence like (19a) must be derived from a more abstract, deep structure of the sort schematically indicated: *Horace washed Horace* (subject of course to the remarks of note 4). In previous transformational descriptions, reflexive words such as *myself, themselves,* etc., have been treated as compounds of pronouns and a special suffix, transformationally introduced by the very rule which carries out the reflexivization operation as determined by NP identity within simple sentence structures.

This analysis of reflexive forms will not do, however. The identity and simple sentence constraints are fundamentally correct and unquestioned here although they involve some mysterious and far from fully solved problems.[14] But the treatment of the element *self* as a grammatical formative is untenable. In fact *self* must be taken to be a noun stem as we see clearly in such phrases as *the expression of self in our society, selfish, selfless,* etc. Compare *piggish, brutish, boyish* and *witless, spineless, timeless,* etc. Notice also the *self/selve* plural alternation parallel to that in such unquestioned noun stems as *wife/wive, life/live,* etc. If, however, the stem *self/selve* in reflexive words is a noun stem, what is the preceding element *my, our, him,* etc.? My answer is that they are, of course, articles, definite articles, in fact genitive type definite articles. I view the process of reflexivization as a complex of a number of partially independent operations, some of which are relevant for other grammatical developments such as nonreflexive pronominalization and, most crucially, determination of the surface forms of so-called pronouns. The relevant rules include *Pronominalization, Definitization, Reflexivization, Genitivization,* and *Definite Article Attachment.*

However, it will be impossible to understand these grammatical operations if it is not recognized that the terminal elements of deep syntactic structures, i.e., the morphemes, are not unanalyzable atomic symbols. Rather, they are complexes of syntactic, phonological, and semantic features or properties. Phonology and semantics do not concern us here. But the fact that underlying noun stems have a syntactic feature analysis is crucial. The features involved for English must, apparently, include such as animate, human, masculine, first person (I), second person (II), third person (III), definite, demonstrative, proper, pronoun [PRO], reflexive, genitive, etc. The claim is, then, that, instead of nouns co-occurring with article morphemes in deep structures as in previous transformational and other treatments, superficial structure article differences are represented at the most abstract level by differences in features of nouns, features like definite, demonstrative, and, as we see subsequently, also those involving person and gender properties.

The process of *Pronominalization* is, I assume, a rule which specifies a noun stem as [+PRO] if it is identical to some other noun in the same sentence, subject to appropriate and not entirely understood conditions. The rule of *Reflexivization* is one which specifies a noun stem as [+reflexive] and [+PRO] subject to its identity to another noun stem in the same simple sentence structure (at the point of *Reflexivization*). All nouns start out in the deep structure forms as [−reflexive], i.e., the specification [+reflexive] is only introduced transformationally.[15] However, this is, as we have seen, not true of the feature specification [+PRO] which will be present in some noun bundles in the base, namely, in those underlying such surface NP as *someone, he, I,* etc. in sentences like:

(20)   a. Someone saw Bill.
       b. He is clever.
       c. I don't believe that.

Similarly, *Definitization* involves specifying a noun stem as [+ definite] (and generally but not always [− demonstrative] as well) subject to certain conditions including previous transformational specification of [+ PRO]. Under these assumptions, the overall processes of reflexivization which occur in sentences like:

(21)   A boy hurt himself.

and pronominalization which occur in sentences like:

(22)   A boy said he would help.

are considered to be quite similar. Both involve specification of the repeated noun as [+ PRO, + definite, − demonstrative]. The difference is whether or not the specification [+ reflexive] is also assigned.

A crucial assumption is then that there is a relatively late transformational rule in the grammar which adds certain terminal segments, the traditional articles and now also the definite pronouns *I, him, your,* etc., to NP which previously contained no such segmental elements. The phonological form of the particular article is determined by the features of the head noun stem, these features themselves being partly inherent and determined by the base rules and lexicon which generate deep structures but often partly derivative and determined by previous transformational rules such as *Pronominalization, Reflexivization,* and *Definitization.* We might call the kinds of rules of which the article insertion rule is an instance *Segmentalizations.* These are rules which insert segmental elements into phrase-markers on the basis of syntactic feature specifications present at earlier, more abstract stages of derivations. It is a difficult and interesting question exactly how such rules should be characterized. I shall not go into this here.[16]

The kind of derivations I am assuming can be illustrated rather schematically and with many oversimplifications. In Figure 1, I sketch the development of the surface form *a boy said he left* on the analysis where *he* refers to *a boy.* As can be seen, the underlying subject noun of the verb *left* of the embedded sentence is identical to the subject noun of the sentence as a whole. This would normally determine an indefinite article for the subject of *left* by virtue of *Segmentalization.* However, the *Pronominalization* and *Definitization* rules turn this noun [+ PRO, + definite, − demonstrative] *before Segmentalization* applies. Therefore, *Segmentalization* determines a definite article. Furthermore, since the noun is at this stage [+ PRO,

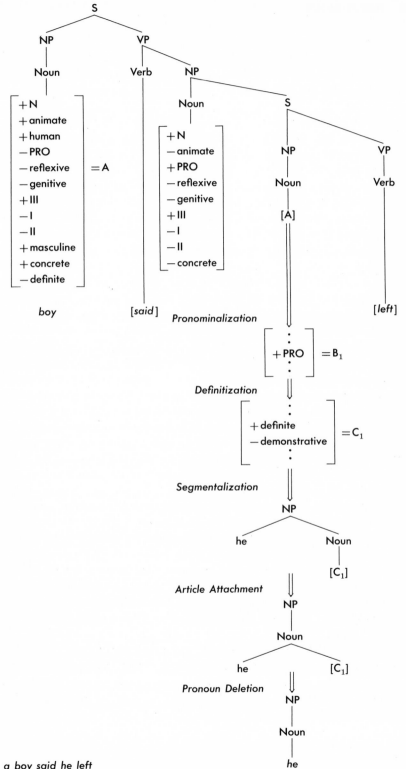

Figure 1

+ human, + masculine, + III, − II, − I, + nominative, − genitive] and since no restrictive relative is present, the relevant article is *he*.[17] I assume here of course that there exist rules which mark nouns with case properties [+ nominative], [+ genitive], etc., before *Segmentalization* applies. These specifications are predictable from context, but we shall not be able to consider their assignment here. *Article Attachment* is the rule designed to account for the fact that *himself, myself*, etc., are single words unlike ordinary article + noun combinations.[18] I assume that this rule works also for nonreflexive pronouns (notice that this is the simplest assumption, since it permits statement of the relevant feature context as [+ PRO] rather than [+ PRO, + reflexive]). It is this rule which then largely accounts for the "deceptive" derived noun status of so-called pronouns. Later we shall give some evidence for assuming that *Article Attachment* works in nonreflexive cases.

In Figure 2, I indicate the derivation of a reflexive form. The derivation is parallel to that of the nonreflexive element in Figure 1 except that the feature [+ reflexive] is specified as well as [+ PRO] because the NP identity is within a simple sentence structure. This determines the operation of *Reflexivization* instead of *Pronominalization*. Furthermore, [+ reflexive] triggers addition of the feature [+ genitive]. There are, of course, many other origins for [+ genitive], all of them transformational. That is, all noun structures start off in the deep structures as [− genitive]. There is, however, an important additional difference, and it is this which has disguised the relationship between ordinary so-called pronouns and reflexive words.

Nothing in our analysis thus far accounts for the difference between the terminal two-morpheme structure of reflexive words and the single formative character of nonreflexive pronominals. That is, what we have said would suggest that the output NP in Figure 1 should be * *heone*. This is not the case here nor is the actual phonological form of the pronoun ever present in analogous forms in the standard language. We can only assume, therefore, the existence of a special rule to drop the nonreflexive pronoun stems in such cases. This is the rule called *Pronoun Deletion* in Figure 1. Although this seems a bit *ad hoc*, it in fact provides the basis for an interesting and important justification for the posited analysis which we shall give in the next section. I am definitely claiming, however, that were it not for this highly restricted and low-level rule, our so-called pronouns would in fact have the terminal forms * *Ione*, * *usones*, * *heone*, * *itone* (or perhaps better * *itthing*, analogous to the indefinite *something*). This should make clear why I said earlier that the contrast pointed out by Allen between pronominals like *he, she, it*, etc., which replace whole NP, and pronouns like *one*, which replace individual nouns, is misleading in part. For in fact I claim that the pronoun which would be pronounced *one, thing*, etc., is also really present in the so-called pronominal cases as well. Further very strong evidence of this will be presented below.

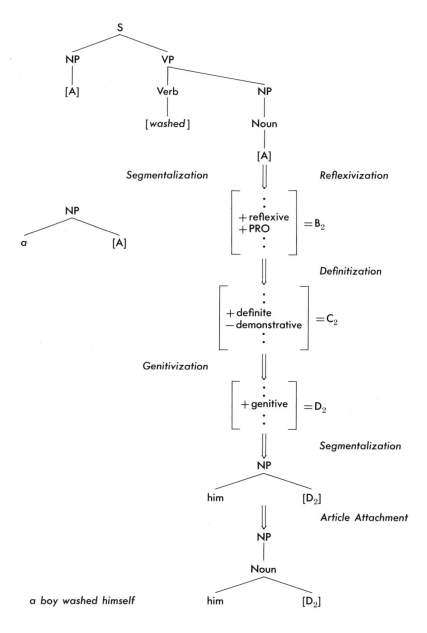

Figure 2

I am assuming, of course, that when transformational rules mark a noun with features like [+PRO], [+reflexive], etc., that this may trigger subsequent effects not only on article form but also in general may determine the phonological form of the noun stem itself. In other words, when a noun is marked [+reflexive] its phonological matrix must be changed from whatever it was originally (for example, that we write *boy, lady, car, goat,* etc.) to *self/selve* depending on [−singular] [+singular].[19] Similarly specification of a noun as [+genitive] in regular cases will have effects on it leading to the suffix written *'s*.[20]

Justification for the Analysis of the So-called Pronouns as Articles

In the previous sections we have outlined an account of forms like *I, us, their,* etc., whereby they are treated as forms of the definite article. In our terms this means that they are segments added to NP whose head nouns are [+definite]. The contrasts among the various definite articles are due to other contrasting features of the head noun. The major motivation of this analysis thus far is the parallelism with respect to properties like animate, masculine, I, II, III, etc., between *he/him* and *himself, it* and *itself, I/me/my* and *myself,* etc. Once it is recognized that the reflexives consist of something plus a noun stem and that this something differs from the forms of pronouns only in case properties ([genitive] and [nominative] values), it is quite natural to assume that pronominalization and reflexivization involve specifying a noun as [+PRO, +definite, −demonstrative], and that these, along with the inherent features of the noun, then determine the form of the article. Hence by parallelism with *himself* we are led to regard *him* as an article whose underlying head noun (which would otherwise show up phonologically as *one*) has been deleted because it was [+PRO] either inherently or derivatively by identity. While perhaps this analysis is not completely implausible, thus far we have certainly given little conclusive ground for accepting it. Basically it has been shown only that it is possible and that it provides a natural way of handling the definiteness of nonderivative pronouns like *I, him, you* and of shaping parallelisms between these and derivative pronoun forms of the reflexive and nonreflexive varieties. Furthermore, the analysis is compatible with the hitherto ignored fact that *self/selve* is a noun stem. However, more serious evidence in favor of the article analysis is available.

It should be emphasized that the analysis accounts for an otherwise unexplained gap in the NP system with respect to the concurrence of third person pronouns, definite articles, and restrictive relative phrases. One finds real pronouns actually occurring with the definite article *the* if there is a restrictive relative phrase or one of its reduced variants present in the NP:

(23)   a. I met the one who Lucille divorced.
       b. I met the man who Lucille divorced.

(24) a. I ate the one Schwartz gave me.
      b. I ate the apple Schwartz gave me.
(25) a. I bred the small one.
      b. I bred the small lion.

but without the restrictives, reduced or not, the pronoun form *one* cannot so occur:

(26) a. * I met the one.
      b.   I met the man.
(27) a. * I ate the one.
      b.   I ate the apple.
(28) a. * I bred the one.
      b.   I bred the lion.

Notice that the analogues with the indefinite article are all right regardless of whether the head noun is [+PRO] or not:

(29) a. I met someone.
      b. I met some man.
(30) a. I ate something.
      b. I ate some apple.
(31) a. I bred something.
      b. I bred some lion.

My suggestion is that the gap left by the definite, nondemonstrative form with [+PRO] head absences in (26) through (28) is actually filled by the so-called pronoun forms, or, more precisely, by that subset which is third person. That is, the so-called third person pronouns, *it, he, her, them,* etc., are exactly the articles assigned to nouns containing the features [+PRO], [+definite], [−demonstrative], [+III],]−II], [−I] *in the absence of restrictive relative phrases in the relevant NP.* This simultaneously explains the failure of the so-called third person pronouns to occur with restrictive relative phrases or their reductions.[21] Schematically what I am claiming is illustrated in Figure 3.

An important issue looms, of course—an issue which relates to a general failure to discuss the way underlying feature specifications are assigned or how the many restrictions among their possible combinations may be stated. In particular, there is only one form of nondemonstrative definite article, namely, *the,* which occurs with a pronoun that has a restrictive relative (with non- first or second persons, see below). But under the present analysis there is a whole contrastive set of nondemonstrative definite articles occurring with the pronouns without restrictives, at least in the singular, namely, *he, she, it,* and their case forms. This means that a set of feature distinctions including those of gender and sex are superficially marked in the definite articles of pronouns without restrictive relatives but not in those of pronouns with restrictives or in those of nouns which are not [+PRO], regardless of restric-

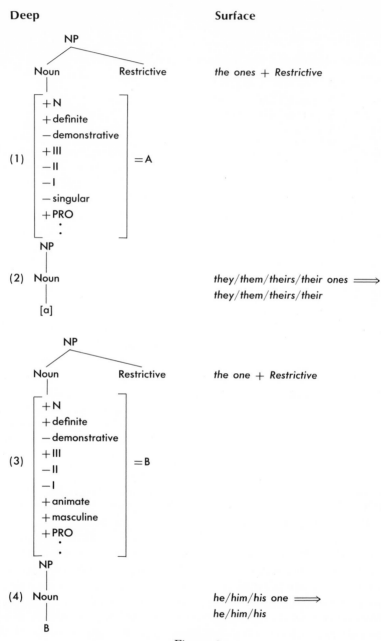

Figure 3

tive occurrence. The first question is whether it is right to assume the underlying distinctions exist even when they yield only the noncontrasting form
the. In fact, there is good reason to assume that these distinctions are present
in the underlying forms in such cases. This follows, for example, from the
fact that all relevant types of reflexives are possible:

(32)   a. The one who I saw behaved himself.
       b. The one who I saw behaved herself.
       c. The one which I saw behaved itself.

In order to maintain the generalization that reflexivization is a function of
NP identity, it is necessary to assume that the underlying pronouns in these
cases contrast in features like animate, masculine, etc. Hence in purely third
person cases it is not necessary to restrict contrasting underlying features
to pronouns without restrictives. Rather it is to be taken as a minor, more
or less morphophonemic fact that we do not say things like * *he boy*, * *she
girl who I like*, etc., instead of the actual forms with the neutralized *the*.

However, in this discussion of underlying features for pronouns we have
ignored the question of features like [I] and [II]. But these involve some
of the most important problems and provide some of the most significant
evidence for our analysis. One's initial impression is that, under the assumptions which have been made here, it will be necessary to restrict underlying
feature specifications [+I] and [+II] in such a way that they occur only
in nouns which are [+PRO] and only in nouns which do not have restrictive
relatives. This will be necessary to prevent such impossible elements as * *I
boy*, * *you person*, * *you girl whom Jack loves*, etc., allowing only abstract
Ione, youone, weones, youones, which become actual surface *I*, *you*, and *me*.
However, although there are real restrictions here, the just given statement
of them is certainly wrong, or rather too general. For it is fundamental to
the present analysis that, in the plural, non-third-person elements can occur
with nonpronouns and/or restrictive relative phrases.

The first forms relevant to this claim are those such as *we men, you guys,*
etc., which we take to be cases of [−PRO], [+II]. Jespersen, who noticed
such forms,[22] of course, implied in effect that they were derivatives from
appositive relative clauses. In transformational terms this would naturally
suggest derivations like, schematically: *we, who are men* ⟹ *we men; you
who are children* ⟹ *you children*. If this solution could be maintained, it
would obviate taking *we* and *you* to be articles in such phrases, as is insisted
here. But in fact this proposal of appositive derivation cannot be right since
forms like *we men*, etc., occur in a variety of contexts where appositive
relatives may not. Thus, for example, Smith (1964) has noted that NP which
are the objects in question may not have appositive relatives:

(33)   a. * Did you see Bill, who is six feet tall?
       b. * Who wrote a novel, which was published by McGraw-Hill?

And, as she also observed, there are negative contexts which exclude appositive clauses:

(34)   a. * He didn't eat the mango, which I bought for him yesterday.
       b. * He didn't write a novel, which was banned as obscene.

Similarly, other negative contexts exclude appositives:

(35)   a. * No American, who was wise, remained in the country.
       b. * None of the cars, which were Chevrolets, was any good.
       c. * They never insulted the men, who were Democrats.

But the forms like *you guys* occur in all such appositive-excluding environments:

(36)   a. Did you see us guys?
       b. Who insulted you men?
       c. He didn't like us Americans.
       d. He did not insult you Communists.
       e. None of you guys is any good.
       f. Neither of us professors is quitting.
       g. They never agreed with us planners.

Furthermore, there are other grounds for doubting the appositive analysis. Notice that the final relative phrase in such prearticle constructions as:

(37)   that one of the men who is sick

is really associated with the first noun *one*, as shown by the agreement with *sick*. Therefore there must be a rule to shift it over the following structure to the end. In nonpronoun NP's this following structure can include article, prenominal modifiers, and postnominal modifiers:

(38)   a. that one of the tall men who is sick
       b. that one of the men here who is sick
       c. that one of the men who I like who is sick.

Observe, however, that the same relative shift rule must operate in pronoun-containing NP:

(39)   a. that one of us who lives here
       b. that one of you guys who betrayed me
       c. that one of you foolish soldiers who deserted his post

Under the analysis suggested here, where *we, us, you,* etc., are articles, the structure over which the relative must shift in (39) is *exactly the same* as that in (38). But under the appositive analysis the structure would necessarily be radically different, complicating the shift rule, since the derived structure of elements like *we men, you foolish soldiers,* etc., would have to be rather like:

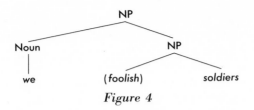

Figure 4

Finally, Jespersen to the contrary notwithstanding, the appositive derivation would assign the wrong interpretation, since in fact such phrases do not have appositive meanings, at least not always. This is shown clearly by such examples as:

(40)   a. You troops will embark but the other troops will remain.
       b. Lets us three men leave first.

which are certainly not paraphrases of:

(41)   a.   You, who are troops, will embark, but the other troops will remain.
       b.   * Lets us, who are three men, leave first; lets us three, who are men, leave first.

The fact that (41b) is, in addition, ungrammatical is further evidence of the inadequacy of an appositive derivation for such forms.

It seems clear then that the only conclusion is that such surface NP's as *we men*, etc., must be derived from underlying nouns which are [−PRO] and yet contain [+I] or [+II] specifications. Hence in such sequences we actually find the so-called pronouns *we/us* and *you* as articles in surface structures. And this is among the strongest evidence for our overall claim that so-called pronouns have essentially the same type of derivation and status as traditionally recognized definite articles.

Having shown that, in the plural, first and second person forms can occur with ordinary nouns, we can turn to the question of their occurrence with restrictive relatives. And here also we find a contrast with the situation in the singular. For in fact such phrases as:

(42)   a. you men who wish to escape
       b. we Americans who have been struggling here

seem perfectly natural. And this is even more true when the restrictives are reduced:

(43)   a. you men here
       b. we honest policemen
       c. you amusing comedians
       d. You diligent Democrats shouldn't put up with lazy ones.
       e. Jonas didn't criticize us intelligent workers, only the dumb ones.

The occurrence of first and second person forms in the plural with restrictive relatives and their reductions leads to a significant justification for the claim that the so-called pronouns are articles and, in particular, for the claim that for standard English a more abstract set of forms *Ione, heone, weones, themones,* etc., underlie the surface elements *I, he, we, them,* etc. In Figure 5 we illustrate a relevant derivation for the *we* case (one/one analysis). (I claim that *we* is in general ambiguous [see below].) Most striking is the fact that the hypothetical pronoun stem *one* actually shows up in surface structures in such forms as:

(44)   a. you great ones
        b. us quieter ones
        c. we religious ones

We take these to have structures exactly analogous to those of *you important men, we diligent Democrats,* etc., except that the head noun is [+PRO], and analogous to the structure in Figure 5 except for the presence of a restrictive relative. It is the reduction of this relative and the preposing of the remaining adjective which then evidentiy prevents the attachment of the articles *you, us, we,* to the following noun and the subsequent deletion of the pronoun stem [+plural] ending. It may be objected that this analysis is dubious because only the forms with reduced relatives are possible. But in fact, for the present writer at least, unreduced relatives in such cases are possible, although with them attachment and deletion occur:

(45)   a. We who are opposing Fascism disagree with those of you who are not.
        b. You who wish to survive had better shape up.

This indicates that the rule of *Article Attachment* takes place only when the article is contiguous to the stem. This conclusion is supported further by forms like:

(46)   a. We here oppose such a move.
        b. You on the East Side have no problems.

where attachment and deletion must be assumed with reduced relative because they are not preposed.

Jespersen (1954),[23] who noticed examples like (44), had the following to say:

> *Ones* may be used after a personal pronoun in the plural. This is not astonishing when an adjective intervenes (as in *you great ones* above ... or ... it is very annoying to *us quieter ones*); but it is more difficult to see why *ones* should have been added to a single *we* or *you*. This is found in Scotch dialect ... , and it is evidently from Scotch that American has taken it. *We'uns* and *you'uns* are especially frequent in the vulgar speech of the Southern states. ...

Jespersen obviously recognizes the problem which such forms as (44) cause

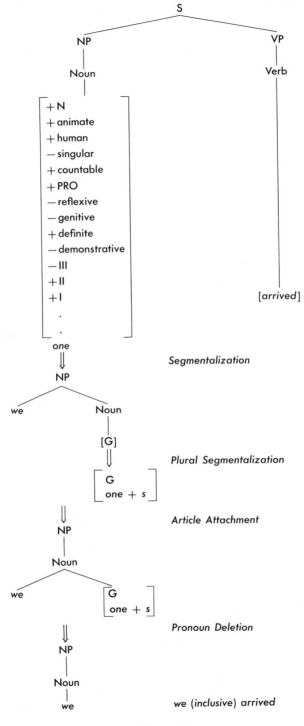

```
                                    S
                          ┌─────────┴─────────┐
                         NP                    VP
                          │                     │
                        Noun                  Verb
              ┌─────────────────────────┐
              │ +N                       │
              │ +animate                 │
              │ +human                   │
              │ −singular                │
              │ +countable               │
              │ +PRO                     │
              │ −reflexive               │
              │ −genitive                │
              │ +definite                │
              │ −demonstrative           │
              │ −III                     │
              │ +II                      │
              │ +I                       │            [arrived]
              │  .                       │
              │  .                       │
              └─────────────────────────┘
                        one
                         ⇓                     Segmentalization
                        NP
                  ┌──────┴──────┐
                 we           Noun
                               │
                              [G]
                               ⇓                   Plural Segmentalization
                          ┌─────────┐
                          │ G       │
                          │ one + s │
                          └─────────┘
                         ⇓                     Article Attachment
                        NP
                         │
                       Noun
                  ┌──────┴──────┐
                 we         ┌─────────┐
                            │ G       │
                            │ one + s │
                            └─────────┘
                         ⇓                     Pronoun Deletion
                        NP
                         │
                       Noun
                         │
                        we              we (inclusive) arrived
```

Figure 5

for a view which treats *we, you,* etc., as pronouns. His remark—that the occurrence of a following noun is not astonishing when an adjective intervenes—is defensive. Why is it not astonishing? But even more, the view falls apart completely when faced with the dialect forms *we'uns, us'uns, you'uns,* etc. These provide one of the most crucial justifications for our analysis. For they illustrate a case where the hypothetical forms *weones, youones,* etc., actually are related to pronunciation without the *ad hoc* rule of nonreflexive pronoun stem deletion which must be posited for the standard language.[24] In comparison to Jespersen's puzzlement, the analysis suggested in this paper provides a natural treatment of such forms. For such dialects as contain *us'uns,* etc., my claim would be that the underlying forms and most of the rules are identical to those suggested here for the standard language. But in these lower-class systems the rule which drops nonreflexive pronoun stems after attached definite articles is, at least in first and second person cases,[25] restricted to the *singular* and does not work for both singular and plural as in the standard language.[26]

In this analysis of first and second person articles, *we, you,* etc., in their occurrences with nonpronouns and restrictives, we have, of course, uncovered differential behavior of the *Article Attachment* rule. If the noun stem is $[+\mathrm{I}]$ or $[+\mathrm{II}]$ the article attaches to a following noun which is $[+\mathrm{PRO}]$ if nothing intervenes, even if there is a following restrictive, reduced or not. But in cases where the noun is both $[-\mathrm{I}]$ and $[-\mathrm{II}]$, attachment occurs only when there is no restrictive. Thus one finds (47a), (47b), and (47c) and not the analogues to (45):

(47) a.   the one who she married
      b.   the one who he married
      c.   the one which I ate
      d. * he who she married
      e. * she who he married
      f. * it which I ate

I have not indicated how the base rules may be formulated to account for the underlying constraints on combinations of feature specifications in nouns or restrictions between these and external elements such as restrictive relatives. Nor shall I do this here. It should be said, however, that variants of the feature apparatus suggested by Chomsky in *Aspects* seem adequate to do the job, i.e., to specify that in the singular $[+\mathrm{I}]$ and $[+\mathrm{II}]$ are incompatible with each other and with $[-\mathrm{PRO}]$ and restrictive relatives, while none of these is true in the plural. Although I cannot go into these matters in detail here, I would like to indicate briefly the kinds of underlying feature bundles which I think must exist and to justify briefly the use of three person features, [I], [II], and [III], which have been implicit in the discussion thus far. In particular, it is important to indicate why we do not simply take first and second persons to be opposite values of one feature.

Given three features of two values, there are eight possible combinations. And in the plural, in fact, six of these occur:

$$
\begin{bmatrix} +\text{III} \\ +\text{II} \\ +\text{I} \end{bmatrix}
\begin{bmatrix} +\text{III} \\ +\text{II} \\ -\text{I} \end{bmatrix}
\begin{bmatrix} +\text{III} \\ -\text{II} \\ -\text{I} \end{bmatrix}
\begin{bmatrix} +\text{III} \\ -\text{II} \\ +\text{I} \end{bmatrix}
\begin{bmatrix} -\text{III} \\ -\text{II} \\ -\text{I} \end{bmatrix}
\begin{bmatrix} -\text{III} \\ -\text{II} \\ +\text{I} \end{bmatrix}
\begin{bmatrix} -\text{III} \\ +\text{II} \\ +\text{I} \end{bmatrix}
\begin{bmatrix} -\text{III} \\ +\text{II} \\ -\text{I} \end{bmatrix}
$$

$$
\qquad\qquad\qquad\qquad\qquad\qquad\qquad * \qquad\quad *
$$

(a)   (b)   (c)   (d)   (e)   (f)   (g)   (h)

Only the combinations (e) and (f) are impossible in the plural. Combination (a), for example, is the analysis of the reflexive form in:

(48) **You and I and John can't perjure ourselves.**

Combination (b) is the analysis of the reflexive in:

(49) **You and John shouldn't bother yourselves about it.**

Of course (c) is the analysis of all so-called third person forms; (g) is the inclusive *we*; and (d) is the exclusive *we*. Notice that only the former occurs in the environment after *let's*.

In the singular, on the other hand, only three of the eight combinations are possible, namely, those in which one of the three features has a plus value and the other two minus values. But since more than four exist in the plural, it is clear that two features will not suffice. It should be emphasized that in these analyses I agree very much with Long (1961, p. 338), who insists that *we* is not the plural of *I* in the same sense in which *boys* is the plural of *boy*. That is, in our terms none of the three possible combinations of features which yields the article *we* differs from the combination which yields the article *I* only in the value of the feature [singular]. Features [II] and [III] necessarily have different values as well, and the feature [PRO] may also differ, since *we* can occur with nonpronouns, while *I* cannot.

An important justification for the three-feature analysis of person properties is that it provides an important part of the basis for giving a general characterization of the first-person–second-person interchange in questions and answers. Given feature analyses like those suggested above, the condition is simply that if the values of the features [I] and [II] do not agree in any noun form of the question, the "corresponding" forms in the answer must have the opposite values for each. Thus, *did you (singular) eat yet,* where the underlying subject noun is $[-\text{I}, +\text{II}]$, must be answered *yes, I ate already,* where the underlying noun is $[+\text{I}, -\text{II}]$. The question *did you (plural) leave* must be answered *yes, we left,* in which the underlying noun is $[+\text{I}, -\text{II}]$, i.e., the *we* is understood as exclusive. But *we* can also answer questions which contain *we: do we have ten dollars; yes we do.* This is possible because the question noun has the specification $[+\text{I}, +\text{II}, \ldots]$, i.e., is inclusive, and does not meet the oppositeness condition requiring a switch in the answer. That *we* questions also may take *you* answers follows from the fact that some *we* are [+I, −II], i.e., exclusive. These facts of question–answer first and second person relations are thus good evidence of the ambiguity of English *we* NP. Obviously these question–answer facts discussed here are not really special to English but again involve universal features of language which ultimately must be built into any correct linguistic theory. That this means features like [I], [II], [III], [PRO], etc., must be universals is simply a further confirmation, since this seems clear on many other grounds.

There is one final minor argument in favor of the claim that the traditional personal pronouns are actually forms of the definite article. Morphophonemically voicing is essentially predictable in dental, nonstrident continuants, i.e., there is no real $[\theta] - [\d]$ contrast in English. In particular, voicing may be predicted in such elements in articles, *the, this, that, these, those,* and in so-called pronouns, *they, them, their, theirs* (not too long ago one could of course have added *thee, thy, thine, thou*). But if we assume that pronouns are articles, these two environments are reduced to one. Analysis of generally so-called adverbial elements also suggests that forms like *then, there, thus* actually have the structure *definite article + certain types of pronoun*[27] so that the same environment covers these as well.

Having mentioned phonology, I can conclude by observing that an analysis like that proposed here for English is to me even more obvious for languages like German and Spanish where, for example, the respective pronoun–definite-article similarities between *er–der, sie–die* and *él–el, ella–la* are evidently no accidents. But I leave it for those who know these languages better than I to consider the possibility of such analyses.

NOTES

1. Cf., for example, Jespersen (1954, pp. 125–126); Curme (1931, p. 557); Long (1961, pp. 338–356).

2. In a paper read to the Linguistic Society of America several years ago.

3. I would argue that there is really no other meaning. The idea that a form like *she* in sentences such as *she dances well* is a "replacement" or "substitute" for some other noun, say in "discourse contexts" or the like, seems to me completely without basis. Such an assumption explains nothing for the quite simple reason that there is nothing really to explain. It is quite sufficient to indicate precisely that such forms refer to object-types whose particular referents are assumed by the speaker to be known to the person spoken to.

4. It is crucial, however, that linguistic theory provide for an indexing of lexical elements. For grammars keep track of whether two or more occurrences of the same lexical item in the deep structure of a single sentence refer to the same entities or not. Thus the underlying structures of *Otis convinced Otis* and *Otis convinced himself*

differ only in that the indices of the two items are identical in the latter case but not in the former. When one speaks of identity in a transformational grammar, as we shall see informally below, it is necessary to include index identity. It seems natural to take the indices to be simply numbers which are assigned to any lexical item when it is taken from the dictionary and inserted in a deep structure. For further discussion of this question of indexing, cf. Chomsky (1965, pp. 145–146); Postal (1966a, pp. 91–92).

5. For latest published discussion of this theory in its most recent formulation, cf. Chomsky (1965).

6. The introduction of syntactic features into linguistic theory is discussed at length in Chomsky (1965).

7. *sm* is the way I shall write here and below the form which occurs in such contexts as *I would like —— applesauce*, a form entirely different from that occurring in contexts like *—— maniac is outside*. The null form of the indefinite article occurs with mass nouns like *blood, soup, rice*, etc., plural nouns like *cars*, and certain unaccountable abstracts like *truth, happiness*, etc.

8. It is easy to show by the criteria to be given below that genitive expressions like *Schwartz's nostril, Sam's horse*, etc., are definite. This follows, however, from the fact that such forms are derived from more abstract structures (but not the most abstract, which involve restrictive relative phases): * *the nostril of Schwartz's*, * *the horse of Sam's*, etc. Evidence for this is given by the article gap with *the* in the otherwise complete paradigm: *a horse of Sam's, some horse of Sam's, this horse of Sam's, that horse of Sam's, these horses of Sam's, those horses of Sam's*, and by the co-occurrence of preposed genitives with superlatives, otherwise restricted to the definite article: *the oldest horse, Sam's oldest horse*, * *an oldest horse*, * *this oldest horse*, etc.

9. It might be objected that indefinites may occur in this context counter to our claim because of such forms as: *expensive as butter is, I still prefer it; strong as gorillas are, they can't outwrestle Superman; cold as a glacier is, it is still not as cold as outer space;* etc. However, it will be observed that in all of these cases the superficially indefinite NP must be interpreted "generically." This very much suggests that one recognizes generic as a syntactic categorization of nouns and insists that [+generic] nouns are [+definite]. Later rules may then switch some generic NP to surface indefinites. As support of this approach, one can note that while definite articles can occur in contexts like (7) with restrictive relatives, this is impossible for these apparent indefinites, a function of the general incompatibility of generic and restrictive: * *expensive as butter which I bought yesterday was . . . ;* * *strong as gorillas who live in Africa are . . . .* The existence of indefinites with adjectives complicates the matter but does not remove the basic point: *rare as good bourbon is . . . ; strong as big men are.* That is, if we treat the apparent counterexamples as generics which later turn indefinite, which is in accord with their semantic interpretation, we account for the failure of indefinite + ordinary restrictive to occur here. On the other hand, if one treats the occurring indefinites in the surface forms as instances of deep indefinites, the nonoccurrence of the restrictives with indefinites is inexplicable and *ad hoc*, since definites do not exclude ordinary restrictives here: *big as the man who I saw yesterday was.* Such facts seem to me to suggest very

strongly that the indefinite examples be taken not as counterexamples to the claim of definiteness in contexts like (7) but only as proof that it is deep structure and not surface structure definiteness which is relevant.

10. In the commentary after the oral presentation it was objected that definite forms can be found in these contexts. The evidence was examples like *there's this guy up here . . .* , etc. But this is a confusion, since although these forms exist they are not instances of the construction I was illustrating. Notice, for example, that they answer different questions. Thus, if asked *what is there on the table,* one can reply *there's some object on the table,* but not *there's this guy on the table.* Moreover, notice that in the so-called counterexamples the *this* is not understood as the definite, demonstrative element, but rather as some kind of "indefinite." While I do not understand this fact, it certainly shows that such forms do not conflict with any claim of indefiniteness.

11. Roberts (1964, pp. 14–17) argues, in effect, that the so-called personal pronouns occur with such indefinite mass and plural NP as *butter, chickens,* etc. However, on page 27 he himself gives part of the evidence showing that this is a mistake. He observes that pronouns occur with prearticle forms *several of, many of,* etc., but takes this only to show the contrast between pronouns and proper nouns. But (obviously) this also shows a contrast between pronouns and those mass and plural NP which do in fact have the null form of the indefinite article: *several of us, many of them,* * *many of chickens.* One can only get *many chickens,* since the *of* is preserved here only with definites: *many of the chickens, many of those artists,* etc. Everything said in the rest of this paper is further argument against the assumption of a "syntactically" indefinite character for pronoun-containing NP. The "semantically" definite character of such NP needs no stress although, under Roberts's analysis, this is an accident, i.e., not a function of the syntactically definite property which yields semantic definiteness in other forms.

12. This is really only a fact about surface forms. Such elements do occur with following indefinite plural nouns in deep structures but deletion and reduction take place. Schematically:

$$\textit{which car of definite cars} \Rightarrow \textit{which one of} \begin{Bmatrix} \textit{the} \\ \textit{these} \\ \textit{those} \end{Bmatrix} \textit{cars}$$

$$\textit{which car of indefinite cars} \Rightarrow \textit{which car}$$

$$\textit{a certain car of definite cars} \Rightarrow \textit{a certain one of} \begin{Bmatrix} \textit{the} \\ \textit{these} \\ \textit{those} \end{Bmatrix} \textit{cars}$$

$$\textit{a certain car of indefinite cars} \Rightarrow \textit{a certain car.}$$

The assumption that the final noun in such constructions must be an underlying plural, although some turn up a surface singulars, explains why nouns which have no plurals do not take such forms: * *a certain blood.* The assumption of indefinite character is supported by such facts as the ungrammaticality of * *there's a certain one of the cars on the rack* and the grammaticality of *there's a certain car on the rack.*

13. Lees and Klima (1963, pp. 17–29).

14. One of these is discussed in Postal (1966a). Another derives from the fact

that underlying NP with head nouns which are identical and have identical reference indices cannot differ in any other element. That is, structures of the form *the big boy helped the small boy* cannot be interpreted as contradictory with the instances of *boy* coreferential. Furthermore, this is apparently not a kind of act particular to English. It seems then that there is a principle of language which requires identical indices to occur only in nouns which have identical "dominating constituents." This latter term is required because such facts are not restricted only to NP and nouns. Facts of this general sort are further evidence to me that much of reflexivization and indeed pronominalization generally is really a universal phenomenon.

15. If, as seems correct, we take reflexive to be a linguistic universal, i.e., a property characterized within linguistic theory, the constraint on [+reflexive] introduction is presumably to be extracted from English grammar as a fact about human language as such. And one ultimate argument for the analysis proposed here, under which *self/selve* is a noun stem with the features [+PRO, +reflexive] rather than an *ad hoc* grammatical formative, will be that this contributes greatly toward permitting a universal statement of the reflexivization operation. That is, properties like [PRO] and [reflexive] are candidates for universal status but a particular formative of English is not.

Reflexivization can be taken as that subtype of pronominalization relevant to identical NP within the same simple sentence structure at the point of pronominalization. This latter constraint is necessary because copresence within the same simple sentence is at times a result of previous transformational operations. Hence it is not copresence within the same deep simple sentence structure which is necessarily relevant. For example, in both English and Mohawk the possessor NP of a genitive construction reflexivizes by identity to the subject NP of a sentence although they start out in different simple sentences. But the processes of genitive formation in both languages insert the possessor NP within the same simple sentence as the subject. Thus *Van Gogh cut off his own ear* is the reflexive of *Van Gogh cut off Van Gogh's ear,* where the two proper nouns have the same reference index. But the latter involves a deep structure object NP containing a relative phrase, i.e., an embedded sentence. Schematically:

   (the ear [Van Gogh has wh some ear])
   N   S   S NP

Here the NP *Van Gogh* which is the subject of *cut off* does not start out as part of the same simple sentence structure as the NP *Van Gogh* which is the subject of *has.* Hence at that stage they are not subject to reflexivization which only comes about because of the results of intervening genitive formation rules. If the relative phrase embedded sentence is not reduced, no reflexivization is possible: * *Schwartz loves the horse which himself has.* Exactly analogous facts can be found in Mohawk. Thus we can possibly assume that some rule(s) to mark the head nouns of repeated identical NP as [+PRO, +reflexive, . . .], if they are within the same simple sentence structure at the point of application, is a universal. An apparent further universal fact is that all "modifiers" within the NP whose head is so marked must be removed, i.e., relative clauses, their reductions, etc. In many languages, of course, and Mohawk is a good example, the reflexive pronouns themselves drop. In Mohawk, at least, this is not *ad hoc* but a predictable result of the fact that all nonemphatic definite pronouns are elided. This is thus some strong evidence for the claim that reflexivization involves assignment of the feature [+PRO], characteristic of nonreflexive pronouns, as well as [+reflexive]. There are many grounds for assuming that both reflexivization and pronominalization involve a further feature, which we might call derivative, which distinguishes inherent pronouns from those derived by identity. For example, in English initial derivative pronoun NP drop in infinitives and gerunds although nonderivative ones do not. Thus *Bill wants to go* must be interpreted to have *Bill* as subject of both *want* and *go* so that the pronominalized form of the repeated *Bill* has dropped. But in *Bill wants him to go,* the subjects of *want* and *go* are not understood as the same. Hence here the pronoun NP is not the result of a pronominalization operation but is instead simply the realization of an inherently [+PRO] noun chosen in the base. A possibility would be to assume that all nouns start out [−derivative] and that pronominalization rules assign [+derivative] thus distinguishing in terms of feature specifications inherent from derivative pronouns.

It should be obvious that all of these suggestions about linguistic universals in regard to pronominalization and reflexivization must be taken as highly tentative and speculative. We are clearly only on the threshold of understanding what is universal in such processes. But it is certainly not too soon to attempt to characterize this, and one must insist that an important constraint on a correct theory of grammar is that it be able to extract what is universal here from particular linguistic descriptions and state it once and for all within the theory of language.

16. It is my feeling, however, that such rules characterize whatever is really common in those features of language which have been referred to as "inflection." That is, inflectional elements are those segments added by *Segmentalization* provided these segments are added in such a way that they become part of the same "word" as does that element whose features they mark.

17. Throughout this discussion we make the simplifying assumption that the segment introduced has only phonological properties. But this is clearly incorrect. It seems clear that these introduced segments must also consist of a set of syntactic features. This will, for example, be the basis for explaining the agreements which show up marginally in English in such cases as *these boys, this boy,* but much more fundamentally in languages like Spanish, etc. Furthermore and even more importantly, it is clear that many transformational rules must refer to the syntactic entity "article." But under our approach there is no constituent or node in trees to formalize this reference. Hence this must be done by assigning common syntactic features to all introduced articles. One of the most difficult questions in considering a theory of *Segmentalization* rules is the relationship between the original set of feature specifications (for example, those of a noun) and those of an introduced segment which superficially mark some features of this element (for example, those of an article). It would seem correct to assume that the introduced segment contains a subset of the features of the original segment as well as certain special features to indicate that it is a grammatical not a lexical element and possibly to indicate what kind of lexical element it "derives from."

18. There is another rule of article attachment which also works for nouns marked [+PRO]. This involves indefinite forms *some, every, any, no,* etc. It is this rule which accounts for the single-word character of *everyone, anywhere, nothing, someone,* etc., in contrast to the two-word character of otherwise parallel [−PRO] forms *every person, any location, no car, some man.* The same rule also explains the one-word

character of the question forms *who, what, where, when, how,* etc., as compared with *what person, what car* (* *what one,* * *what thing*) *what place,* etc., since these single-word forms are derived from *wh* + *some* + [+PRO] and their differences are a function of other features of the noun. In other words, the *who* of the interrogative *who came* is to the *someone* of *someone came* as the *what man* of *what man came* is to the *some man* of *some man came.* Attachment of article to noun takes place only when the noun is [+PRO]. The same rule may just possibly be the explanation of the partially parallel "relative pronouns." That is, *the boy who saw me* derives from a more abstract form *the boy* (*wh some boy saw me*). The identical noun in

$$\text{S} \qquad\qquad\qquad \text{S}$$

the latter may then pronominalize (i.e., turn [+PRO]) which triggers subsequent *wh* + *some* attachment just as if the feature [+PRO] were inherent as in the interrogative forms. This yields the single word form. However, there are problems here having to do with *which/that* and *who/that* alternations which this account does not explain. The type of pronominalization involved in relatives also involves many difficulties. And there are other problems having to do with question-relative parallels and differences.

It would be natural to attempt to combine the article attachment rules for definites with that for indefinites. But there are important differences. Consider: *you big ones;* * *you* (*ones*) *big; someone big;* * *some big one.* This issue must therefore be considered open.

19. Exactly how these shifts of form should be accomplished is not clear. It might be suggested that transformational rules are appropriate here. My own feeling, however, is that this is not correct. Rather I suspect that it should be possible to use the dictionary after the transformational rules have been applied so that the dictionary is used both to fill in the lexical items of deep structures and also to specify those aspects of phonological form which are transformationally determined but *ad hoc,* i.e., not a function of general phonological rules. A similar approach also should be used to describe suppletions. How this proposal to reuse the dictionary should be formalized is, of course, a complicated matter which we cannot go into here. Our assumption, however, is that, for example, *self/selve* is the only noun in the dictionary marked [+reflexive] so that it is the only one which can be correctly selected, on the second pass through the dictionary, for those positions which have been transformationally marked [+reflexive]. The dictionary entry for the noun stem *self/selve* (which has no semantic element) thus represents most of what is *ad hoc* to English in ordinary reflexivization.

20. A difficulty here, of course, is that the phonological suffix is actually added not to the noun but to the final word in the entire NP of which the noun marked [+genitive] is head. Thus: *the boy who is sleeping's dream; the girl I talked to's hairdo,* etc.

21. Notice that, from this point of view, the substandard *them guys,* etc. is a perfectly natural sort of minor morphophonemic difference in article shape which one would expect to differentiate different dialects.

22. Jespersen (1954, Part II, p. 85).

23. Part II, pp. 261–262.

24. Notice how they provide justification for the assumption that *Article Attachment* works also for nonreflexive forms.

25. I do not know whether such dialects have forms like *them'uns* where the

standard language has *them* but this would hardly be surprising. I presume, however, that they do not have singular *I'un, you'un*. A dialect containing the latter is, however, not at all unthinkable. It would simply be one where the deletion rule has been eliminated entirely for non-third-person forms. The simplest dialect of all would, of course, have no deletion of *one/ones* in any of these cases regardless of person or number.

26. The assumption here is that minor syntactic differences between closely related dialects are a function of differences in the transformational rules or in the lexicon, not of differences in the set of base rules which determine the general grammatical properties of deep structures.

27. For some brief discussion, cf. Katz and Postal (1964, pp. 127–138).

Some Remarks on the Action Nominalization in English

BRUCE FRASER

5

In his book, *The Grammar of English Nominalizations,* Lees (1960) takes the position that nearly all (if not all) nominalizations — i.e., noun phrases between whose parts there is a syntactic relationship — should be derived from sentences through the use of syntactic transformations. Thus, a noun phrase such as "his being blind to the realities of war" is derived from an underlying form "the fact that he is blind to the realities of war" and a noun phrase such as "the milking machine" is derived from an underlying form "the machine is for milking." Recently, however, the suggestion has been made both informally and in print (cf. Chomsky, this volume) that, contrary to Lees's claim, certain nominalizations should be lexically, not transformationally, derived. This new position, which I shall refer to as the lexicalist position as opposed to Lees's position, the transformationalist position, maintains that the syntactic relationships in these lexically derived nominalizations are defined by some lexical rules, perhaps not unlike transformations in power. To date, neither of these positions has been presented in sufficient detail to permit a careful evaluation of the structure and claims of each.

In this paper I will attempt to show that action nominalizations such as "John's climbing of the mountain," "the building of the bridge," "the crying of the babies," [the *ing* action nominalizations for Lees (1960)] can be accounted for within the framework of a transformational grammar such as that presented by Chomsky (1965). To do this, I will first characterize this type of nominalization. Next, I will propose an analysis for the derivation of these nominalized forms and show how this particular approach can account naturally for the co-occurrence restrictions on these nominalizations, the limitation on what deep structure sentences can be nominalized, the required derived constituent structure, and, finally, the required semantic interpretation. Finally, I will raise some issues which loom as potential problems to the lexicalist position but which appear either solved or at least easily solvable within the framework of the transformationalist position.

The action nominal exhibits two main forms. The examples in (1) illustrate the first form, followed by the sentence from which it is derived. In all of these examples many irrelevant details have been omitted, and the verbs in the example sentences have been inflected for the sake of readability. In addition, the example nominalizations have been placed in an appropriate environment, enclosed in parentheses, to facilitate the intended interpretation.

(1)   a. John's riding of his bicycle (startled them).
         John rode his bicycle.

      b. His figuring out of the solution (took one hour).
         He figured out the solution.

      c. (I was annoyed by) her yelling.
         She yelled.

The superficial effect of the rule which relates these nominalized forms to the sentence from which they are derived is threefold: (1) the subject noun phrase (e.g., *John*) has the abstract morpheme [poss] (possessive) attached to the end of it; (2) the insertion of the formative *of* after the verb of the sentence (e.g., *ride*) and before the direct object noun phrase [note that in (1c) there is no direct object noun phrase]; and (3) the insertion of an *ing* after the verb.

The interpretation of these action nominalizations is that of an action, an activity, an act, or an event. They must be distinguished from factive nominals such as

(2)   a. John's riding his bicycle (bothered her).
         John rode his bicycle.

      b. His figuring out the problem (astounded us).
         He figured out the problem.

      c. (Were you appalled) at her yelling?
         She yelled.

in which the interpretation is the assertion of a fact, a statement, and not an activity. Furthermore, co-occurrence restrictions are not the same as those of the action nominalization (e.g., one cannot *photograph, participate in,* or *be present at* a fact, only an activity; conversely, one cannot *write down, acknowledge,* or *be struck by* an activity, only a fact). Aside from the different semantic interpretation of these two, the factive nominal permits no insertion of the preposition *of* after the verb. The intransitive cases are superficially identical, however (e.g., *her yelling*), but, as we shall discuss below, have different internal constituent structure.

The action nominals are also similar in form to one type of predicate complement construction. For example:

(3) a. (We watched) John running the race.
     b. (The men worried about) Mary walking through town.
     c. (I saw) the bad guys beating up the heroes.

Aside from the superficial differences between the examples in (3) and those in (1), namely, that the subject noun phrase does not receive an 's and that the verb is not followed by an *of*, we note that the constructions in (3) (e.g., *John running the race*) are not noun phrases at all but consist of a noun phrase (e.g., *John*) followed by a complement (e.g., *running the race*). Moreover, the interpretation of this construction is of the referent designated by the noun phrase engaged in some activity. There is a difference between watching John, the individual, running the race and watching the activity, John's running of the race.

   Another nominal with which the action nominal may be confused is illustrated by the examples in (4).

(4) a. The man's refusal to chair the session (interested us).
     b. Their disgust with the situation (angered him).
     c. The U. S.'s destruction of Vietnam (infuriated us).

These we will call substantive nominalizations. They have the interpretation of a completed activity — thus a fact [cf. Lees (1960)]. We find pairs like *refusing–refusal, destroying–destruction, closing–closure,* etc. The most obvious difference between the substantive and action nominals is that the former almost always have an ending such as *∅, tion, al, ure* attached to the infinitive form of the verb to form the nominal form, while the latter always have the *ing* attached. The semantic interpretation of some nominals which have the substantive nominal form (i.e., the non–*ing* ending) may be that of an action nominal in which case we must extend the definition of the action nominalization to include other endings. Suffice it to say here, however, that the substantive nominal has been but barely investigated and few conclusions can be drawn.

   Finally, for verbs like *eat, cook, drink, drive,* etc., which can occur with or without a direct object noun phrase, a form such as *John's driving* is three ways ambiguous:

1. the fact that John drives;
2. some specific activity: for example, John's driving of the car yesterday;
3. the general name given to the way in which John operates a motor vehicle.

It is this last nominal, the substantive nominal, that Katz and Postal (1964) suggested might be derived from an underlying string "the way in which John drives" and not the action nominalization. We can illustrate the difference between these three homophonous cases by the following examples:

(5)　a. John's driving (was considered a major comeback).
　　　b. John's driving (of the Rolls-Royce) (caused much concern).
　　　c. John's driving (is more proficient than Mary's).

The second form of the action nominalization is shown in (6).

(6)　a. The climbing of Mt. Vesuvius by a lone hiker (is an impossible feat).
　　　b. That breaking of the window by the gangsters (was an act of violence).
　　　c. (I have never seen) a filming of a motion picture.
　　　d. (Did you hear the sound of) that crying by the babies?

The forms in (1) and (6) differ in two ways: 1. the subject noun phrase in (1) has *'s* attached while in (6) it is preceded by the preposition *by* and moved to the position following the verb and its objects take exactly the form and position of the postposed subject of a passivized sentence (e.g., *the giving of money to her by the Red Cross*); 2. a singular article such as *the, this, that, such a,* etc., precedes the deverbalized noun (e.g., *climbing*) in (6).

Looking now at the action nominalization as it has been restricted above, I suggest that it be derived from a noun phrase having a constituent structure such as the one shown in (7a).

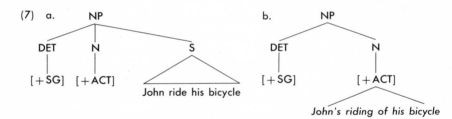

If, for example, the embedded sentence S in (7a) is *John ride his bicycle*, then the transformation relating this underlying form and the corresponding nominal in (1a) moves the subject noun phrase followed by *'s* under the category determiner, DET, and the remaining part of the sentence with the verb followed by an *ing* and *of* under the category noun, N [this is shown in (7b)]. [Cf. Chomsky (1962) for a discussion of the facts motivating this particular constituent structure.] In light of the analysis for the first form of the action nominalization given above, we can account quite naturally for these determiners. In (7a) the DET and N are marked for certain necessary features such as [+SG] and [+ACT], respectively, but no lexical formatives are present. To account for the determiner in these cases, we need only permit a singular determiner such as *the, a,* or *this* to occur and its presence then requires the second form of the action nominalization to be derived. It is necessary to derive these two forms by applying a different rule for each for the following reason: the semantic interpretation of the nominals having any but the article *the* as the determiner differs from that when the possessivized subject noun phrase occurs. The following nominals do not receive an equivalent interpretation:

(8) a. John's chairing of the session
    b. That chairing of the session by John   } (was exciting).
    c. No chairing of the session by John

It remains for us to account for the *by*–NP sequence following the direct object noun phrase in (8). At first glance it appears that we should apply the passive transformation to the sentences underlying these nominals. Certain facts, however, suggest that this approach is incorrect.

First, there are no cases of the action nominalization in which the subject of a passive sentence (the original direct object) can become possessivized. Thus, the strings in (9) are unacceptable action nominals.

(9) a. * His hitting by Mary (startled us).
    b. * Mary's giving of a book by John (was a nice gesture).
    c. * Their attacking by the Indians (sounded the alarm).

Therefore, if the sentences underlying the nominals in (9) were first passivized, the rule deriving them would have to move the passive subject back to its original direct object position.

Second, as we will note below, no model (e.g., *can*, *will*) or part of the aspect (e.g., *have +en*, *be +ing*) of the verb phrase may appear in any form of the action nominalization. The passive rule, however, introduces just such a formative, namely, the verb *be*, followed by the past participle marker EN; thus, the rule deriving the nominalized forms would be slightly more complicated, since it would have to permit the *be*–EN to occur and then delete it.

Third, any sentence with an intransitive verb, which meets the restrictions discussed below, can become an action nominalization. But such a sentence cannot be passivized since it lacks a direct object. To maintain the position that the *by*–NP is the result of the application of the passive rule forces us to redefine this rule to apply to sentences without direct objects, but only in case the sentence is to ultimately become an active nominal. But within the framework of grammar we are assuming — that presented in Chomsky (1965) — this information is not available to the passive transformation at the time it applies to a sentence since it is indicated only by the determiner and noun in (6), constituents which are beyond the scope of a cyclic transformation operating on the embedded sentence S.

In light of these facts, I suggest that the *by*–NP sequence be created as a result of the rule deriving the second form of the nominalization and that it be positioned after the verb and possible direct object, subject to the same restriction as agent placement in the passive transformation. In fact, if we view a transformation as a sequence of operations on a P-marker, we can utilize the agent placement operation of the passive transformation as part of the action nominalization transformation which derives the nominals in (6).

In some dialects the *by* in the second form of the action nominalization can or must be replaced by *of* when the *by* immediately follows the verb, and if the determiner is not demonstrative, the *of* may not occur if a direct object is present.

(10)   a. The loud crying $\begin{Bmatrix} by \\ of \end{Bmatrix}$ the boy (annoyed me).

b. That dancing $\begin{Bmatrix} by \\ of \end{Bmatrix}$ the girls (was energetic).

c. Any shooting $\begin{Bmatrix} by \\ of \end{Bmatrix}$ the hunters (must be stopped).

d. The yelling of insults $\begin{Bmatrix} by \\ * of \end{Bmatrix}$ John $\left.\vphantom{\begin{Bmatrix} by \\ of \end{Bmatrix}}\right\}$

The yelling $\begin{Bmatrix} by \\ of \end{Bmatrix}$ John $\left.\vphantom{\begin{Bmatrix} by \\ of \end{Bmatrix}}\right\}$ (frightened the baby).

Finally, we note that there are action nominalizations like

(11)   a. That playing of the piano of his (is driving me wild).
       b. This blustering of his (must cease).

where it appears that the subject noun phrase, if a pronoun, may become possessivized when the *of* replaces *by*. Why this should be the case is not at all clear.

This particular analysis of the P-marker underlying the various forms of the action nominalization is supported by a number of points. First, as Chomsky (1962) and others have pointed out, the derived constituent structure of these action nominalizations consists of a determiner (e.g., *John's*) followed by a noun (e.g., *riding of his bicycle*). Since transformations as they are characterized in Chomsky (1965) cannot introduce constituents, but can only delete and rearrange the existing constituent structure of a P-marker, it is not possible to derive the nominalization forms from a base P-marker in which the constituent noun phrase dominates only the sentence S which is to be nominalized. If these action nominalizations are to be transformationally derived, the DET and N constituents must be introduced by the rules of the base.

Second, although we do not find the sentences in (12) acceptable

(12)   a. * The activity (that) John climbed the mountain (was fatiguing)
       b. * The act (that) the man destroyed the building (disturbed us)
       c. * The process (that) he melted down the silver (tired him out)

we do find the related sentences in (13) acceptable.

(13) a. The activity of climbing the mountain (was fatiguing).
         The activity, namely, John's climbing of the mountain (was fatigu-
         ing).
         The activity, namely, the climbing of the mountain (by John) (was
         fatiguing).

      b. The act of destroying the building (disturbed us).
         The act, namely, the man's destroying of the building (disturbed
         us).
         The act, namely, the destroying of the building (by the man) (dis-
         turbed us).

      c. The process of melting down the silver (tired him out).
         The process, namely, his melting down of the silver (tired him out).
         The process, namely, the melting down of the silver (by him) (tired
         him out).

Thus, it appears that the P-marker in (7), or one very much like it, is
required to account for the nominalizations in (13) anyway, and, therefore,
our analysis does not require the definition of an empty noun phrase preceding
the sentence being nominalized.

Notice that although the original subject of the nominalizations is deleted
in the first examples in (13a) through (13c) [e.g., *he* in (13c)], we must assume
that one originally existed. In a nominalization such as "the act of giving
the present to himself (pleased John)," the *himself* could only have become
the reflexive because of an identical noun phrase to the left of the reflexive
pronoun. This NP, the subject noun phrase, is later deleted.

Third, action nominalization cannot occur freely, but is restricted to those
environments in which nouns such as *activity, event, act, process,* etc., can
occur. For example, the strings in (14) are unacceptable sentences.

(14) * The breaking of the window by the boys (was written down).
      * The man's writing of poison pen letters (was delicious).
      * Her ripping up of the postcard (owed four dollars).

By positing that the nominalizations originate with a noun phrase whose head
contains the relevant features of nouns such as *activity, action,* etc., these
unacceptable co-occurrences are precluded.

To recapitulate, I have suggested that the various forms of the action
nominalization can be accounted for by positing an underlying noun phrase
consisting of a determiner, noun, and sentence to which two action nominalization transformations may apply to derive the required strings. Moreover,
I have shown this underlying form to be motivated independent of these
nominals.

We turn now to the set of restrictions which must be placed on the embedded sentence being nominalized. For the sake of exposition, we divide

those restrictions up into four types: 1. those on the form of the sentence in general; 2. those on the subject noun phrase; 3. those on the verb; and 4. those on the direct object noun phrase.

The sentence being nominalized must be essentially of the form NP–TNS–V–(NP)–X; that is, the sequence consisting of the subject noun phrase, the tense marker, the verb, possibly a direct object noun phrase, and a (possibly empty) string of adverbials. The tense marker is necessary in order to account for time agreement between the nominalization and its environment — for example, to preclude unacceptable strings like "* John's shooting of a buffalo tomorrow was observed yesterday," where the tense of the nominalization is *present* while that of the matrix verb phrase is *past*. No sentence in which a noun phrase has been questioned and moved forward as in an interrogative question or a relative clause meets this general structure. Modals (e.g., *can, shall, will*) as well as any part of the aspect of the verb phrase (e.g., *have, being*) are also excluded, a fact we mentioned above in the discussion concerning the introduction of *by*. No sentence adverbials (e.g., *certainly, surely*) can occur since their position of occurrence is restricted to sentence initial position and between the subject noun phrase and the verb. No negation of the verb phrase may occur, although direct object negation seems acceptable in some cases (see below). No *-ly* adverbials whether they be analyzed as manner, frequency, or some other kind (e.g., *cleverly, occasionally*) may occur any place in the sentence. However, these same adverbials paraphrased in another form (e.g., *in a clever way, at occasional intervals*) are permitted. Finally, the direct object noun phrase, if one exists, must follow a verb or a verb–particle combination (e.g., *figure out*), but it cannot follow a compound verbal (e.g., *think about, rely on, speak of*) in which the verb plus preposition must be treated as a single lexical unit (i.e., where the interpretation of this V–Prep sequence is not derivable from the meanings of the verb and preposition taken alone, but where, syntactically, the preposition and following noun phrase pattern are like a syntactic constituent — a prepositional phrase). Prepositional phrases in which the preposition is not lexically (i.e., not semantically) tied to the verb (e.g., locative adverbials) seem acceptable. The examples in (15) illustrate the points just discussed.

(15) a. * What's John climbing
       * Who's did the man watching } startled us.
       Whose sounding of the symbols

   b. * The man's will throwing of the ball } concerned no one.
      * Her have swimming

   c. * The king permitted { certainly the giving up of his life.
      your surely sending of the letter.

   d. * The organizing of the party carefully
      * John's writing of poison pen letters occasionally } is a difficult task.
      The conducting of a symphony in a professional way

e. We watched $\begin{cases} \text{* his not looking up of the information.} \\ \text{? no one's swimming of the lake.} \\ \text{? the discovering of nothing by the scientists.} \end{cases}$

f. $\left. \begin{array}{l} \text{* The talking about the problem} \\ \text{* Mary's depending on John} \\ \text{The man's jumping into the pool} \end{array} \right\}$ saved her.

There are only three constraints we must place on the subject noun phrase. The first, which holds for both forms of the action nominalization, requires that the subject not be the expletive *there*, a consequence of the fact that only sentences with nonstative verbs can undergo this nominalization (see below). The second and third apply only to the first form of the nominal and require first that the possessivized noun phrase be marked [+animate] as opposed to [−animate] and, second, that it not be complex. The notion of a complex noun phrase is discussed in Ross (1967); suffice it to say that in rough terms it is a noun phrase which contains either a relative clause, a number of adjectival or adverbial modifiers, some conjoined constituents, or some combination of these. This same notion of complexity arises in attempting to state the condition for moving particles after direct object noun phrases — note the acceptability of "he looked the information up" but the unacceptability of "* he looked all of the relevant information which I needed up" [cf. Fraser (1965)]. The strings in (16) illustrate these points.

(16) a. * There's appearing of an apparition (frightened me).
         * There's occurring of accident (scared the police).

b. $\left. \begin{array}{l} \text{* The machine's crushing of the rock} \\ \text{The crushing of the rock by the machine} \end{array} \right\}$ was noisy.

    $\left. \begin{array}{l} \text{* The wind's snuffing out of the candle} \\ \text{The snuffing out of the candle by the wind} \end{array} \right\}$ caused chaos.

c. $\left. \begin{array}{l} \text{* The man who arrived yesterday's giving} \\ \quad \text{of the lecture} \\ \text{The giving of the lecture by the man who} \\ \quad \text{arrived yesterday} \end{array} \right\}$ assisted us.

The first restriction on the verb requires that it be marked [−stative] [cf. Lakoff (1966b) for a discussion of this concept]. The second requires that if the verb consists of a verb–particle combination, the particle must immediately follow the verb and not the direct object noun phrase. This requirement about particles holds also in some dialects for reduced adverbials (e.g., where we derive the formative *in* from *into* NP, *off* from *off of* NP, *up* from *upwards*) which can normally occur in either post-verb or post-direct object position [cf. Fraser (1965)]. Third, the verb cannot be part of an idiom (e.g., *make love to, take advantage of*). We show these facts using examples in (17).

(17) a. * John's resembling of his mother⎫
           * Her hearing of the music   ⎬ astounded us.

      b. * The looking of the information up   ⎫
           * His figuring of the problem out   ⎪
           * The butler's bringing of the dinner in ⎬ took three hours.
           * His pulling of the lever down   ⎭

      c. * His making of love to her   ⎫
           * The taking of advantage of him   ⎬ caused a commotion.

Finally, the restrictions on the direct object noun phrase must also be stated. First, the noun phrase following the verb must be the direct object, not another noun phrase moved to this position (e.g., the indirect object *Mary* in *give Mary the book*). Second, it must not contain or be a part of a complement construction (e.g., *John* in *persuade John to go* is followed by the complement *to go*). Third, in at least those cases where the verb is *make*, *give*, or *raise*, and where the direct object is a substantive nominal (e.g., *make a reference to, give some advice to, raise two objections to*), the substantive nominal must have a determiner (e.g., *a, some, two*) although the nominal with no determiner is perfectly acceptable in declarative sentences.

(18) a. * Jim's giving of Mary the book   ⎫
           * The renting of the men the house   ⎬ interrupted Harry.

      b. * Our persuading of John to go   ⎫
           * The refusing by her to carry out the plan   ⎬ occurred at noon.

      c. * Your making of reference to the book   ⎫
           Your making of a reference to the book   ⎪ displeased
           * Harry's raising of objection to the book   ⎬ the author.
           Harry's raising of two objections to the book ⎭

Examination of these conditions on a sentence to be nominalized shows that they can be analyzed as falling into two types: (1) those resulting from the application of certain phrase structure rewriting rules, followed by the obligatory application of some transformation(s); and (2) those resulting from the application of optional syntactic transformations. Of the first sort are the following, with the example numbers indicated: the question form of the sentence (15a) — the base complement introduces an interrogative marker Q into a base P-marker, forcing the question transformation to apply; the occurrence of: a modal or aspect (15b); a sentence adverbial (15c); negation (15e); a lexical prepositional phrase (15f); a complex noun phrase (16c); an inanimate subject noun phrase (16b); a stative verb (17a); a verbal idiom (17c); a direct object noun phrase containing or being followed by a predicate complement construction (18b). Of the second type — where it appears that these conditions arise through the optional, not obligatory, application of transformational rules — are the occurrence of: the *-ly* form of the adverbial (15d), derived from a more basic form, for example, *carefully* being derived from *in a careful way; there* as the subject noun phrase (16a), derived, for example, from an underlying form *an apparition appeared to me;* a not too complex subject noun phrase (17c), resulting from the reduction of a complex noun phrase by the application of some transformation, for example, deriving *the innocent child,* a noncomplex noun phrase, from *the child who is innocent,* a complex noun phrase; the particle following the direct object noun phrase, not the verb (17b); the indirect object preceding rather than following the direct object (18a) (e.g., *give Mary the book* rather than *give the book to Mary*). What is especially interesting about these latter conditions is that they cannot be avoided by any judicious ordering of the transformational rules. For notice that all of these transformations operate on the sentence being nominalized before the nominalization rule, operating on the next higher sentence, applies. That is, if we follow Chomsky's (1965) suggestion that the set of transformational rules apply cyclically to a base-generated P-marker beginning at the level of the most deeply embedded sentence, then the particle movement, indirect object movement, and other rules apply at the level below that at which the action nominalization applies. Furthermore, the grammar does not keep a record — what has been referred to as a T-marker — of which transformations have been applied and in which order. Thus, these restricted environments must appear in the structural description of the action nominalization rules. There appears to be no difficulty in defining the rules to account for this.

To examine further these action nominalizations, let us consider the following sentences:

(19)   a. John's occasional writing of poetry (was stopped).
       b. The judicious cutting up of the cake (saved the day).
       c. The loud snoring of her husband (kept Mary awake).

Notice that an adjective (e.g., *judicious*) precedes the deverbalized noun in these examples. The issue here is their source.

Adjectives usually are analyzed as originating in the base P-marker as a predicate adjective of a restrictive relative clause (e.g., we derive *the big bear* from *the bear which is big*). Following this approach would lead us to posit a restrictive relative clause on the host noun phrase (e.g., DET–[+N], [+ACT]) and to claim that subsequent to the derivation of the action nominalization, the relative clause is reduced and the adjective preposed before the noun. Whether these nominals do indeed occur with restrictive relative clauses is not at all clear, as can be seen from the questionable examples in (20).

(20)   a. ? The climbing of the mountain that bothered me (occurred at noon
          yesterday).
       b. ? The man's yelling that we heard (was loud).

My feeling is that these relative clauses (e.g., *that bothered me*) modify not the deverbalized noun (e.g., *climbing*), but rather some noun such as *instance* where the underlying form for this nominalization would consist of *the-instance-of-the-activity*-S. But even conceding that the action nominalizations do have restrictive relative clauses, we find that the adjective (e.g., *judicious*) cannot be the predicate adjective of a sentence whose subject is an action nominal. Thus, note the examples

(21) a.   John hit his sister frequently.
           John's frequent hitting of his sister (enraged her).
         * John's hitting of his sister was frequent.

      b.   She sliced up the cake cleverly.
           Her clever slicing up of the cake (won her a prize).
         * Her slicing up of the cake was clever.

      c.   The crowd yelled at a timely moment.
           The timely yelling of the crowd (woke him up).
         * The yelling of the crowd was timely.

in which the adjectives (e.g., *frequent, clever, timely*) may occur as *–ly* adverbials, may occur as prenominal adjectival modifiers, but not as predicate adjectives for the same action nominals. In light of this, I suggest, as does Lees (1960), that the prenominal adjective be introduced not through relative clause reduction and adjective preposing, but rather by permitting these adjectives, in the most basic adverbial form (e.g., *at frequent intervals, in a clever way, at a timely moment*), to occur in the sentence being nominalized, with the action nominalization moving the adjective forward to the prenoun position.

This approach receives further support from the following facts: in general, only one of these adjectives can occur prenominally although other possible prenominal adjectives can occur in the same sentence, but in adverbial form only. But this correlates exactly with the fact that only one adverbial is introduced by the action nominalization rule. If we were to derive these prenominal adjectives from relative clauses, we would be forced to define some restriction to account for: (1) the fact that only one relative clause per nominalization could occur, with the additional requirement that it reduce and prepose, or (2) in case some of these relative clauses are acceptable, the restriction that only one reduce and prepose. This problem is avoided here. The following examples illustrate the above points.

(22) a. * The occasional careful writing of poetry ⎱
           The occasional writing of poetry in a   ⎰ (has its rewards).
           careful way

      b. * John's clever timely organizing of a party ⎱
           John's timely organizing of a party in a   ⎰ (saved the day).
           clever way

We remark here that there is yet another class of prenominal adjectival modifiers, adjectives like *clever, stupid, ridiculous,* which can be thought of as value judgments rather than as attributes of the nominal. These adjectives have a different source and we discuss them below.

Now, consider the sentences

(23)   a.   The shooting of an elephant by a hunter occurred frequently.
            * The shooting of an elephant by a hunter occurred before it was alive.

       b.   Their murdering of the princess happened at midnight.
            * Their murdering of the princess happened every day.

The second sentence in (23a) is unacceptable because of the semantic contradiction inherent in the sentence *someone shot an elephant before it was alive,* while the second sentence of (23b) is unacceptable because the verb *murder (strangle, die)* cannot co-occur with frequency adverbials (e.g., note the unacceptability of * *they murdered the princess many times*). The point is this: only if the sentence which is nominalized can contain a particular adverbial can this adverbial occur in following verb phrases containing stative verbs (e.g., *occur, happen, be, require*). I do not suggest, however, that the lexical selection rules be made to account explicitly for the co-occurrence restrictions between the verb of the action nominalization and such adverbials. Rather, I propose that the P-marker underlying a sentence such as (23a) contain an actual occurrence of the adverbial in the S being nominalized and that the stative verb be followed by only a set of features characterizing the type of adverbials that can follow it. Thus, the string underlying (23a) will consist of *the-activity-a-hunter*-PAST-*shoot-an-elephant-at-frequent-intervals-occurred*-[+frequency]. Just in case the nominalized S contains an adverbial of the type following the stative verb, this adverbial is moved out of the S and to the position immediately following this verb, before the action nominalization applies.

This accounts first of all for the co-occurrence restriction between the stative verbs and the adverbials (e.g., *took four hours* — * *took frequently*) and, moreover, it precludes the generation of the first strings in (23) in case the second string is unacceptable. That is, only if two adverbials can co-occur in the sentence being nominalized can they co-occur across a stative verb.

I must insert a caveat here, namely, that in presenting these examples, I am suggesting an analysis for each example construction which is in some cases motivated by strong evidence, but in others by only a plausibility argument. Thus, other analyses for these constructions could vitiate the argument. However, I am much more concerned here with showing the kind of argument which can be used to support the transformational as opposed to the lexical approach. To the extent these analyses are substantially confirmed, the main thesis of this paper is further supported.

The first case involves examples such as

(24)   a. John's cutting up of four cords of wood yesterday and his doing
           so again today (was a welcome gesture).
        b. Your organizing of a party for Mary and your doing so for Jane
           as well (took a great deal of time).

which contain instances of the form *do so* replacing the contents of a second,
identical verb phrase of two conjoined sentences. The rule accounting for
the introduction of the *do so* must certainly apply to conjoined sentences
(e.g., to *John ran home and Mary did so too*); it is not clear, however, that
this same phenomenon can be found in substantive (lexically derived) nominals. Thus, the nominals

(25)   a. * John's tendency to sleep along with Mary's tendency not to do
           so (ruined the party).
        b. * Her refusal to go and his doing so also (confused the woman).
        c. * The Russians' oppression of Poland after the war and their doing
           so still (is stupid).

are unacceptable for me. Deriving action nominalization transformationally
permits us to account quite naturally for the acceptable occurrences of *do
so* in (24). However, deriving action nominals lexically requires either
the definition of a rule to account for these in the lexicon, or the extension
of the *do so* transformation to account for just these and no other lexical
nominalizations.

A second case is illustrated in (26):

(26)   a. It was stupid of John to do that.
           Stupidly John did that.
           John stupidly did that.

        b. The man was foolish to throw the fight.
           Foolishly the man threw the fight.
           The man foolishly threw the fight.

The sentences in (26a) and (26b) are semantic paraphrases. Now, suppose
we analyze the third sentence in each group as being derived from the second,
the second from the first. Recall that our analysis of the derivation of the
action nominalization related the following strings, *the man threw the fight
foolishly — the man's foolish throwing of the fight*. But this means that the
sentence being nominalized (e.g., *the man threw the fight foolishly*) is not
a base P-marker, but rather results from the application of (at least) two
transformations to some P-marker, transformations which must apply before
the nominalization is formed.

A third case involves adverbial reduction. Some adverbials in English occur
in alternate form (*downward — down*) while others, initially in the form of
prepositional phrases with an unspecified object, reduce to only the preposition
or the first part of it (*bring the dinner into someplace — bring the dinner*

in). These reduced adverbials can, under certain conditions, be preposed to the post-verb position, thereby preceding the direct object noun phrase. But, for many dialects, only if a reduced adverbial is in this post-verb position can a sentence undergo the action nominalization. The following examples illustrate these facts.

(27) a. The man pulled the lever downward.
          The man pulled the lever down.
          The man pulled down the lever.
          The man's pulling down of the lever (set off the bomb).
       * The man's pulling of the lever down (set off the bomb).
          The man's pulling of the lever downward (set off the bomb).

      b. The butler brought the dinner into the room.
          The butler brought the dinner in.
          The butler brought in the dinner.
          The butler's bringing in of the dinner (caused a fuss).
       * The butler's bringing of the dinner in (caused a fuss).
          The butler's bringing of the dinner into the room (caused a fuss).

Here again it appears that the adverbial reduction rules and the preposing rules ought to precede the derivation of the action nominalization.

Still another case arises in connection with sentences taking conjoined subject noun phrases which are initially introduced by the base component and not as a result of conjunction. Verbs like *commit adultery, coauthor, lose contact* occur in sentences such as

(28) a. John and Mary committed adultery.
         John committed adultery with Mary.
         Mary committed adultery with John.

      b. The man and woman coauthored the book.
         The man coauthored the book with the woman.
         The woman coauthored the book with the man.

where the sentences in each group are semantic paraphrases of each other. Now note that each of these forms has a corresponding action nominal:

(29) a. John and Mary's committing of adultery ⎫
         John's committing of adultery with Mary ⎬ (shocked the city).
         Mary's committing of adultery with John ⎭

      b. The man and woman's coauthoring of the book ⎫ (resulted
         The man's coauthoring of the book with the woman ⎬ in a best
         The woman's coauthoring of the book with the man ⎭ seller).

But if we analyze the sentences containing the *with* as being derived from a more basic sentence containing a conjoined subject noun phrase, the transformation relating these sentences must apply first. Actually, deriving the first sentences of these groups from either of the others still presents the same problem.

Finally, consider the examples in (30)

(30) a. He taught mathematics to John.
He taught John.
His teaching of mathematics to John ⎫
His teaching of John   ⎬ (angered us).
* His teaching of John mathematics ⎭

      b. They called the message to him.
They called him.
Their calling of the message to him ⎫
Their calling of him   ⎬ (occurred at 3 p.m.).
* Their calling of him the message ⎭

which contain verbs occurring with a *to* indirect object (e.g., *John*). However, these verbs occur with the noun phrases formerly occurring as indirect objects now functioning as direct objects. The last examples in each group confirm that more is at stake here than the action nominalization applying to the result of the indirect object movement (recall this was a restriction stated earlier). Rather, at issue is the derivational relationships between the first and second sentences of each group. If we analyze the second as being derived from the first through the deletion of an unspecified direct object noun phrase, then here again the rule accomplishing this must apply before the action nominalization is formed. Otherwise, the rule becomes more complicated.

In conclusion, I have attempted to show that for at least the action nominalization as I have characterized it above, the suggestion that it be lexically and not transformationally derived is not at all convincing. I have proposed an analysis for transformationally deriving the action nominalization which accounts for the limitations on the sentence being nominalized as well as for the privileges of occurrence of this nominal. Finally, a number of issues were raised which pose difficulty to the lexicalist position. To be sure, the level of detail of the analysis of the derivation of the action nominal and the dependence of the arguments against the lexicalist position on the particular (and unjustified) analyses of the relevant construction prohibit any strong claim that the main thesis has been, in some sense, conclusively proven. I think, nevertheless, that the arguments presented are sufficiently strong to throw considerable doubt on the lexicalist position *vis-à-vis* the action nominalization and thus place the burden of proof on that position.

The Accessibility of Deep Structures

D. TERENCE LANGENDOEN

6

Given the conception of language which asserts that for each sentence in a language there is a deep semantic representation and a surface syntactic representation of it, the question is raised: why is there a surface syntactic representation at all; or to put it slightly differently, why are there grammatical rules to convert deep structures into surface structures; or again, why are there transformations?

The fact that transformations exist is a fact that demands explanation, for an "ideal" language would be one which provided direct phonological realizations of its semantic structures. Such an explanation should be based, moreover, on considerations which are independent of such internal linguistic considerations as the fact that a child could not acquire his native language unless he could tacitly assume the existence of transformations. Any such explanation most certainly should not be in terms of simplicity considerations alone; these are appealed to only in the absence of more powerful modes of explanation from outside. In this paper, we shall show that a partial explanation for the existence of transformations in terms of language's function as an instrument of communication — the communication of the information in deep structures — can be given.

In a number of places the relative *unacceptability* of particular sentences is due to the internal complexity of their surface syntactic structures; thus, a sentence such as (1) with three degrees of self-embedding, although completely and fully grammatical, is quite unacceptable:

(1) * The rumor that that the report which the advisory committee submitted was suppressed is true is preposterous.

To distinguish cases of sentence unacceptability arising from internal complexity from other cases, let us say that sentences such as (1) have deep structures which are relatively *inaccessible*. We will also say that their surface syntactic structures *do not provide ready access* to their deep structures. Now consider the sentences:

(2) The rumor that it is true that the report which the advisory committee submitted was suppressed is preposterous.
(3) The rumor is preposterous that it is true that the report which the advisory committee submitted was suppressed.
(4) The rumor that it is true that the report was suppressed which the advisory committee submitted is preposterous.
(5) The rumor is preposterous that it is true that the report was suppressed which the advisory committee submitted.

Sentences (2) through (5) all have the same deep structure as (1), yet their surface structures provide relatively greater access to that deep structure than does (1). The reason for this is that various *extraposition transformations* have been applied to obtain the surface structures of (2) through (5), reducing their degree of self-embedding. In (2), the *that*-clause subject of the adjective *true* has been extraposed to the end of the clause containing it, leaving behind the pronoun *it* as the surface subject of *true*. This rule has been applied in examples (3) through (5) as well. In (3), moreover, the *that*-clause complement of the noun *rumor* has been extraposed to the end of the main clause. This rule has also been applied in (5). In (4), the relative clause modifying the noun *report* has been extraposed to the end of the clause containing it. This rule has also been applied in (5). The results are that the degree of self-embedding has been reduced to two in sentence (2), to one in sentences (3) and (4), and to zero in sentence (5). Thus, sentences (2) through (5) provide more ready access to the deep structure common to (1) through (5) than does (1), (5) more so than (2) through (4), and (3) and (4) more so than (2). Now, if the effect of the various extraposition transformations is to render certain deep structures more accessible than they would be if those transformations were not applied, then we can say that the existence of these transformations is motivated (explained) on the grounds that they facilitate communication of certain deep structures.

Similarly the optional or obligatory character of certain transformations under particular conditions can be explained. For example, it is known that the extraposition of *that*-clause subjects of intransitive verbs such as *seem* is obligatory, while the extraposition of *that*-clause subjects of transitive verbs such as *prove* is optional. The reason for this is that the application of the extraposition transformation to *that*-clause subjects of intransitive verbs never decreases accessibility, while the extraposition of *that*-clause subjects of transitive verbs may. To see this, consider the sentences:

(6) That Tom's told everyone that he's staying proves that it's true that he's thinking that it would be a good idea for him to show that he likes it here.

46068

(7)   It proves that it's true that Tom's thinking that it would be a good idea for him to show that he likes it here that he's told everyone that he's staying.

Sentences (6) and (7) have identical deep structures. However, the surface structure of (7), obtained by application of the extraposition transformation to its subject *that*-clause, provides less ready access to its deep structure than does (6). Therefore, the extraposition transformation must be free not to apply to such *that*-clauses (that is, its application in such circumstances must be optional), so that the most accessible surface structures of particular deep structures will be grammatical.

A similar situation presents itself with regard to the so-called particle-movement transformation in English, whose application can be detected in such sentences as:

(8)   A sudden gust of wind knocked him down.
(9)   A sudden gust of wind knocked the old man down.

In case the object of the verb is a personal pronoun, the particle movement transformation is obligatory, but if it is not, then the transformation is optional. Thus (10) is ungrammatical while (11) is grammatical.

(10)   * A sudden gust of wind knocked down him.
(11)   A sudden gust of wind knocked down the old man.

In Ross (1966b), it was suggested that the transformation be considered inapplicable in case the object noun phrase is complex, that is, contains a subordinate clause. Thus (12) was considered grammatical, but not (13):

(12)   A sudden gust of wind knocked down the man who I saw get out of a car a few minutes ago.
(13)   * A sudden gust of wind knocked the man who I saw get out of a car a few minutes ago down.

However, rather than consider (13), and sentences like it, ungrammatical, it would be more in accordance with fluent English speakers' intuitions of grammaticality to consider them fully grammatical, but relatively less acceptable than their counterparts in which the particle movement transformation has not applied. Such sentences are also less accessible than their counterparts, as the following examples dramatically illustrate:

(14)   * The assailant knocked the man who put the rebellion which caused the banks to close down down down.
(15)   The assailant knocked down the man who put down the rebellion which caused the banks to close down.

Consequently, the particle movement transformation must be optional (at least when the object noun phrase is not a personal pronoun) so that the surface structures which provide greatest access to deep structures such as that which underlies (14) and (15) will be grammatical.

From these examples, it should be clear that a genuinely explanatory theory for the existence of transformations, their effects on the structure of sentences, and the conditions under which they are optional or obligatory can be worked out, at least in part, along the lines suggested here. We do not assert that for every well-formed deep structure there is a surface structure which provides ready access to it — one can imagine, at least, an English sentence so complex that the various extraposition transformations would reduce its deep structure complexity only to reintroduce it elsewhere — but simply that transformations are designed to apply so as to increase accessibility and that their application would in fact decrease accessibility.

In the examples considered so far, degree of inaccessibility had to do with degree of self-embedding in surface structures. There are, however, other reasons why a surface structure will not provide ready access to the deep structures underlying it. Consider the fact that the relative pronoun may be deleted except when it stands for the subject of its relative clause:

(16)   The class which/that I will teach next semester will meet in the evening.
(17)   The class I will teach next semester will meet in the evening.
(18)   The class which/that regularly meets in the seminar room has been moved downstairs.
(19)   * The class regularly meets in the seminar has been moved downstairs.

If (19) is imagined as a possible surface structure for the deep structure expressed by (18), in which the relative pronoun deletion transformation has not been applied, it will be seen that it does not provide access to that deep structure, since indication of the subordinate status of the relative clause has been destroyed. The same is not true of sentence (17), since the subordinate status of the relative clause in it is still indicated by the presence of the subject and verb of that clause. Thus, the inapplicability of the relative pronoun deletion transformation in case the pronoun stands for the subject of its relative clause results in the ungrammaticality of surface structures which fail to provide access to their corresponding deep structures. And, although the accessibility theory cannot provide a direct explanation for the existence of the relative pronoun deletion transformation in the first place, there may be an explanation in terms of the desire for parsimony (this is by no means an entirely unserious proposal).

We can account, on similar grounds, for the fact that when the relative pronoun stands for the subject of a subordinate clause inside the relative clause, the subordinating conjunction *that* introducing that subordinate clause must be deleted. Thus the following sentence is grammatical:

(20)   The committee which I understand investigated the accident has not yet made its report public.

but not:

(21)   * The committee which I understand that investigated the accident has
            not yet made its report public.

The subordinating conjunction may, however, be retained in case the relative
pronoun stands for some other noun phrase in the subordinate clause. Thus
both of the following sentences are grammatical:

(22)   The accident which I understand the committee investigated was the
            worst in the state's history.
(23)   The accident which I understand that the committee investigated was
            the worst in the state's history.

The ungrammaticality of (21) stems presumably from the fact that the reten-
tion of *that* would lead to a false parsing of the sentence, in which *that* is
taken to be the subject of the subordinate clause. This means, of course,
that (21) fails to provide access to the deep structure underlying both it and
sentence (20); the obligatory deletion of the subordinating conjunction may
then be understood as a means of rendering ungrammatical certain surface
structures which do not provide ready access to their deep structures.

From the foregoing considerations, we see accessibility and grammaticality
are partially independent, partially dependent notions. From our consideration of the various extraposition transformations and the particle movement
transformation, we saw that certain surface structures which fail to provide
ready access to their deep structures need not be ungrammatical; there need
only be grammatical surface structures which do provide more ready access
to them. On the other hand, we saw from our consideration of the relative
pronoun and subordinating conjunction deletion transformations, that certain
other surface structures which happen to fail to provide ready access to their
deep structures also turn out to be ungrammatical.

Given the conception of deep structures as semantic structures, it is apparent that for any well-formed deep structure, there must be at least one grammatical surface syntactic realization of it. The conception of the transformational component as a *filter*, to weed out unwanted deep structures, cannot
in the present theory be seriously maintained. This position has some interesting consequences. For example, it is known that there are no grammatical
surface structures in which the semantic content of the following sentences
can be expressed as single noncompound sentences:

(24)   * The landlord is upset about the window which I saw the boy who
            broke it.
(25)   * The committee which I wonder whether it investigated the accident
            has not yet made its report public.

These facts would appear to contradict the thesis just maintained, since
although the semantic content of (24) and (25) is straightforward (hence there
must be deep structures which underlie them), there are apparently no gram-

matical surface structures by which they may be expressed. But in fact there are, namely, the compound sentences:

(26)   I saw the boy who broke the window and the landlord is upset about it.

(27)   I wonder whether the committee investigated the accident; it has not yet made its report public.

The idea that relative clauses arise from deep structure conjunctions has recently been suggested by Annear (1967); these observations suggest that the ungrammaticality of sentences containing relative clauses in which the relative pronoun has been drawn from a relative clause or a subordinate clause introduced by a subordinating conjunction other than *that* is due to the fact that such sentences provide relatively less access than do their coordinate sentence counterparts. Example (24), in turn, is more nearly grammatical, and provides greater access to its deep structure, than the following, in which the final pronoun *it* has been deleted:

(28)   * The landlord is upset about the window which I saw the boy who broke.

Examples like (24), which often turn up in the speech of English speakers, are usually thought of as making the best of a bad job — a speaker having found himself relativizing out of a relative clause retains a pronoun in place of the noun phrase so relativized, thus providing himself and his audience with a trace of the deep structure, and thus rendering that deep structure more accessible than it otherwise might have been.

THE MODEL EXTENDED

part
two

The Two Verbs *Begin*

DAVID M. PERLMUTTER

7

In the current theory of syntax[2] there are two ways available to represent the deep structure of sentences like

(1)   Zeke began to work.

Begin might be an intransitive verb like *seem* and *happen,* which take abstract (sentential) subjects in deep structure, so that the deep structure of (1) would be something like[3]

(2)

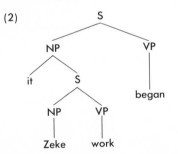

with the subject NP *Zeke* being substituted for *it* by *it*-replacement and the rest of the embedded S being moved to the right and brought under the domination of the matrix VP,[4] yielding the correct derived constituent structure of (1).

On the other hand, *begin* might be a verb like *try,* which takes object complements. Since there are no sentences like

(3)   * Zeke began for Oscar to work.

SOURCE: Revised version of a paper read at the annual meeting of the Linguistic Society of America, December 1967.

Begin, like *try, condescend,* and *refuse,* would manifest the like-subject constraint, requiring that the subject of the embedded S be identical to the subject of the matrix S in deep structure.[5] Under this analysis the deep structure of (1) would look something like

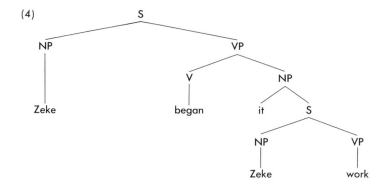

Equi-NP Deletion and other transformations which apply in the derivation of sentences with *try* and like verbs would apply here as well to produce the correct surface structure of sentences like (1).

In this paper evidence is presented to show that *begin* occurs in both types of structures in deep structure.

There is a variety of evidence that *begin* occurs in deep structure as an intransitive verb which takes abstract subjects, as in (2).

First, we note that it takes nominalized sentences as subject in such sentences as

(5)   The doling out of emergency rations began.

Begin must occur in deep structures like (2) if sentences like (5) are to be accounted for.

The second piece of evidence that *begin* is an intransitive verb like *seem* comes from consideration of sentences like

(6)   There began to be a commotion.

Sentences like (6) would be impossible if *begin* occurred only in structures like (4), for to generate them from such structures it would be necessary for *there* to be the subject of *begin* in deep structure, but there is independent evidence that *there* is not present in deep structures at all, but rather is introduced by a transformation.[6] If, on the other hand, *begin* occurs in deep structures like (2), sentences like (6) are easily accounted for. The *there*-insertion rule applies in the embedded sentence, producing a structure like

(7)

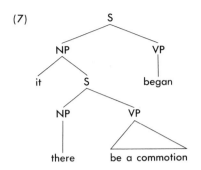

On the second cycle *it*-replacement substitutes *there* for *it* in the matrix sentence, bringing *be a commotion* to the right of *began* and under the domination of that VP.

A third piece of evidence for the existence of deep structures like (2) comes from sentences like

(8)   It began to rain.

in which the dummy subject *it* of weather verbs like *rain* occurs as the surface subject of *begin*. If *begin* occurred only in deep structures like (4), we would have to postulate this dummy *it* as the deep subject of *begin*. If *begin* occurs in deep structures like (2), the embedded subject will be the sentence *it rain* and the correct surface structure will result automatically from rules that are independently motivated.

Fourth, we note the synonymy of the sentences

(9)   a. The noise began to annoy Joe.
      b. Joe began to be annoyed by the noise.

If these sentences were derived from deep structures like (4), we would expect them to exhibit some difference in meaning, since the deep subject of (9a) would be *the noise*, while that of (9b) would be *Joe*. With a deep structure like (2), however, (9a) and (9b) have the same deep structure and differ only in that the passive transformation has applied in the embedded subject of (9b) but not in (9a). Their synonymy is thereby accounted for.

A stronger argument of this type for the existence of deep structures like (2) can be based on the distributional properties of lexical items like *recourse, heed,* and *headway*. These lexical items are not freely occurring nouns; we must exclude such sentences as

(10)   a. * I like heed.
       b. * Heed is nice.

and many others. The restriction on the occurrence of these nouns can be stated as follows: in deep structure they occur *only* in the fixed phrases *have recourse* (*to*), *pay heed* (*to*), and *make headway*.[7] Note that *recourse, heed,* and *headway* must be dominated by an NP node in these fixed phrases, since the passive transformation, which refers to NP, can apply to them to produce such sentences as[8]

(11)   Recourse was had to illegal methods.
(12)   Heed was paid to urban problems.
(13)   Headway was made toward a solution.

Now, since *recourse, heed,* and *headway* occur in deep structure only in the fixed phrases *have recourse, pay heed,* and *make headway,* they cannot be the subject of *begin* (or of any other verb) in deep structure. This being the case, if *begin* occurred exclusively in deep structures like (4), there would be no way to account for the grammaticality of sentences like

(14)   Recourse began to be had to illegal methods.
(15)   Heed began to be paid to urban problems.
(16)   Headway began to be made toward a solution.

If *begin* occurs in deep structures like (2), however, these sentences are automatically accounted for by rules that are independently motivated. The passive transformation, which applies to produce sentences like (11), will apply in the embedded sentence, yielding a derived structure like

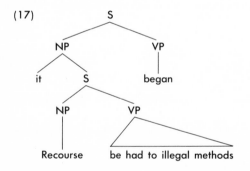

(17)

On the second cycle *it*-replacement substitutes the NP *recourse* for the *it* in the matrix sentence, bringing the rest of the embedded sentence to the right of *began* and under the domination of that VP. If *begin* occurs in deep structures like (2), the grammaticality of sentences like (14) through (16) is automatically accounted for.

There is abundant evidence, then, that *begin* occurs in deep structures like (2), in which it is an intransitive verb with an abstract (sentential) subject. We will now proceed to show that *begin* also occurs in deep structures like (4). The argument will proceed in several steps. First we will show that *begin* takes animate subjects in deep structure; this would be impossible if it occurred exclusively in deep structures like (2). Then we will see that *begin* occurs in sentences in whose deep structure it must have both an animate subject and a complement sentence, as it does in (4). Finally we will indicate the motivation for the NP node which dominates the complement sentence in (4).

That *begin* takes animate subjects in deep structure follows from the fact that it forms agentive nominalizations as in

(18)   Pete is a beginner.

Verbs like *seem* and *happen* which take only abstract subjects in deep structure do not occur in such nominalizations.

(19)   a. * Pete is a seemer.
       b. * Pete is a happener.

There is also evidence that *begin* occurs in deep structures with both an animate subject and a complement sentence, as in (4). As was mentioned above, verbs like *try, condescend,* and *refuse* manifest the like-subject constraint, requiring that the subject of a sentence embedded directly beneath them be identical to their own subject in deep structure. For this reason the deep structure of sentences like

(20)   I tried to begin to work.

must be something like

(21)

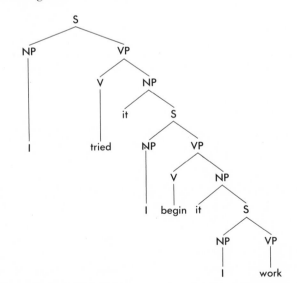

for the subject of the sentence beneath *try* must be identical to the subject of *try* in deep structure. If *begin* occurred exclusively in deep structures like (2), the deep structure of (20) would have to be something like

(22)

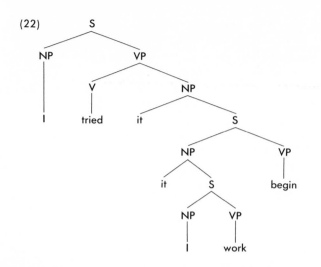

But in (22) the like-subject constraint is not satisfied, for the subject of the sentence beneath *try* is the entire NP containing an embedded sentence, and is therefore not identical to the subject of *try*. Since the like-subject constraint is not satisfied, an ungrammatical sentence must result. For this reason (21) rather than (22) must be the deep structure of (20). The grammaticality of (20) therefore shows that *begin* occurs in deep structures like (4).

A similar argument for deep structures like (4) is provided by the grammaticality of sentences like

(23)   I forced Tom to begin work.

Verbs like *force* require that the subject of a sentence embedded beneath them be identical to their own *object* in deep structure.[9] The deep structure of (23) must therefore be something like

(24)

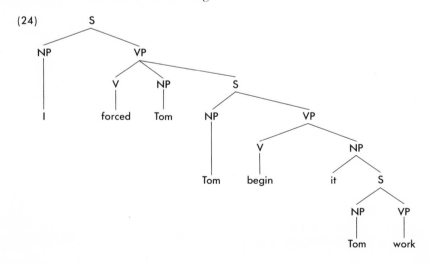

showing that *begin* occurs in deep structures with an animate subject and a complement sentence, as in (4).

Additional evidence for deep structures like (4) comes from imperative sentences like

(25)   Begin to work.

Since imperatives require a second-person subject in deep structure,[10] the grammaticality of sentences like (25) shows that *begin* takes animate subjects and complement sentences in deep structure, as in (4).

Let us now turn to the motivations for another aspect of deep structures like (4) — the NP node which dominates the embedded sentence. In this connection we notice that *begin* takes NP objects, as in

(26)   Sam began the job.

which predictably undergo the passive transformation:

(27)   The job was begun by Sam.

If these sentences are to be accounted for, *begin* must take objects in deep structure.[11]

A slightly more intricate argument for the transitivity of *begin* in deep structure comes from such sentences as

(28)   Mark began enthusiastically, but he got tired by noon.

Here, *begin* occurs without an overt object, and with a meaning like that of such verbs as *eat* and *read* when they have no overt object. If *begin* is a transitive verb, it can be marked for object deletion in the same way that *eat* and *read* are,[12] and this behavior is thereby accounted for in the same way in all such cases. If we are to achieve this parallelism, however, *begin* must take objects in deep structure.

To summarize briefly, we have seen that, on the one hand, *begin* occurs in deep structures like (2) and that, on the other, it takes animate subjects and object complements, as in (4).[13] We will call the former the intransitive *begin*, and the latter the transitive *begin*. No grammar of English can be considered adequate unless it provides for the occurrence of *begin* in both types of deep structures.[14]

This conclusion raises several questions which we will merely mention here without giving a satisfactory answer to them.

The first question concerns what restrictions each *begin* imposes on its subject, the kind of complements it takes, and so on. For example, all verbs which manifest the like-subject constraint require animate subjects. Since sentences like (3) must be ruled out as ungrammatical, the transitive *begin* must also manifest the like-subject constraint. We therefore expect the transitive *begin* to require animate subjects. This would mean that in all sentences in which the subject of *begin* in surface structure is inanimate we are dealing with the intransitive *begin*. That is, sentences like

(29) Oil began to gush from the well.

in which *begin* has an inanimate subject in surface structure must derive from a deep structure like (2) rather than from one like (4). While we will not fully test this hypothesis here, there is some evidence that it is correct. Note that in sentences which we have shown to contain the transitive *begin*, the verb phrase beginning with *begin* can be replaced by *do so*.[15]

(30) Warren tried to begin to work and Jerry tried to do so too.
(31) I forced Warren to begin to work and Paul forced Jerry to do so.
(32) Begin to work and do so at once.

In sentences which contain the intransitive *begin*, however, the verb phrase beginning with *begin* cannot be replaced by *do so:*

(33) * Heed began to be paid to urban problems and attention did so too.
(34) * There began to be a commotion and there did so at four o'clock.

This accords with a valid generalization about English: no verb which occurs in deep structures like (2) in which it takes abstract subjects can be replaced by *do so*. Now, if the transitive *begin* requires animate subjects, and all sentences like (29) in which *begin* has an inanimate subject in surface structure are consequently instances of the intransitive *begin*, it should be the case that in such sentences the verb phrase beginning with *begin* cannot be replaced by *do so*. This seems to be the case, since we do not get sentences like

(35) * Oil began to gush from the well and water did so too.[16]

While this is not conclusive, it can serve to illustrate the kinds of questions that need to be investigated in order to determine when we are dealing with the transitive *begin*, and when with the intransitive one.

The other major question that arises is that of the relation between the transitive and the intransitive *begin*. It has been the purpose of this paper to show that *begin* occurs in two distinct kinds of deep structures. The question will be left open here as to whether we are dealing with two distinct verbs, a single verb with two distinct sets of contextual features, or a single verb whose occurrence in these two kinds of deep structures is predictable in some way.

The properties of *begin* that have been pointed out here are shared by such verbs as *start, continue, keep,* and *stop,* as well as by verbs which appear to be quite different. The verb *threaten,* for example, must be an intransitive verb that occurs in deep structures like (2) because the following sentences are grammatical:

(36)   There threatened to be a riot.
(37)   It threatened to rain.

On the other hand, it must occur in deep structures like (4) because these sentences are grammatical:

(38)   I tried to threaten to resign.
(39)   I forced Tom to threaten to resign.
(40)   Threaten to resign.

The occurrence of *threaten* in both kinds of deep structures produces palpable ambiguities. For example, the sentence

(41)   **The students threatened to take over the administration building.**

has two quite different readings. With the transitive *threaten*, it means that the students made threatening statements to the effect that they would take over the administration building. With the intransitive *threaten* in deep structure, (41) might be used to describe a scene in which a mob of students surged toward the administration building; on this reading it does not entail anyone's making any threats at all.[17]

The question of the range of verbs which are like *begin* in occurring as both a transitive and intransitive verb in deep structure, like the question of how the two verbs are to be related, if at all, will be left open here. It appears, however, that the phenomenon of transitive–intransitive verb doublets is quite widespread, and extends into the modal system. It has been observed by grammarians that modals like *must*, for example, are systematically ambiguous.[18] A sentence like

(42)   Clyde must work hard.

can express some obligation on the part of Clyde to work hard, or it can be paraphrased as: It must be the case that Clyde works hard. This suggests that *must* is a transitive–intransitive verb doublet like *begin* in deep structure, occurring in deep structures like (4) on the former reading and in deep structures like (2) on the latter. Vetter (1967) has shown that this also is the case with *need*. If these analyses are correct, and it turns out that there are syntactic facts in English which can be accounted for only if modals are transitive–intransitive verb doublets in deep structure, this will constitute evidence for the hypothesis argued in Ross (1967) that there is no [auxiliary] constituent in deep structure, and that the so-called "auxiliary verbs" are real verbs in deep structure.

NOTES

1. The subject of this paper is included in my doctoral dissertation *Deep and Surface Structure Constraints in Syntax* (MIT, 1968), where some of the issues raised here are discussed more fully. I am indebted to many friends and colleagues for their helpful

comments and criticism — particularly Stephen Anderson, George Bedell, Noam Chomsky, George Lakoff, and Haj Ross. Errors of course are my own. I am also indebted to the American Council of Learned Societies for support through a graduate fellowship in linguistics and to the National Science Foundation for support through grant GS-2005 to Brandeis University.

2. The theoretical framework presupposed here is basically that of Chomsky (1965) and Rosenbaum (1967). For more recent developments in this theory, see the other papers in this volume and the references cited there.

3. All tree diagrams given here are grossly oversimplified; I have omitted everything that is not relevant to the points under discussion.

4. For a justification of this formulation of *it*-replacement, see Lakoff (1966*a*).

5. For a discussion of the like-subject constraint and the evidence that it is a deep structure constraint, see Perlmutter (1968).

6. *There* behaves like an NP with respect to transformational rules in that it inverts in questions (*Was there a commotion?*), shows up in tag questions (*There was a commotion, wasn't there?*), shows up with *so* (*Joe said there would be a commotion, and so there was*), undergoes *it*-replacement (*We expected there to be a commotion*), and undergoes the passive transformation (*There was expected to be a commotion*). But *there* cannot occur everywhere that NPs occur in deep structure; we must be able to rule out an ungrammatical such sentences as * *I like there*, * *There is nice*, and many others. It is difficult to see how this could be done if *there* occurs in deep structures. If *there* is introduced by a transformation, on the other hand, we can correctly rule out such deviant sentences by stating the constraints on the distribution of *there* in the rule that introduces it. We will now show that these constraints *cannot* be stated in deep structure, and *must* be done by means of a transformational rule. *There* can occur only with a small number of intransitive verbs (such as *be*, in the examples already cited, and a few others, as in *There ensued a controversy*). *There* cannot occur with *kill*, for example, so alongside *A policeman killed a demonstrator* we do not get * *There killed a policeman a demonstrator*. Now, the passive transformation introduces *be*, which can co-occur with *there*. And if the structure underlying *A policeman killed a demonstrator* has been transformed by the passive transformation into the structure underlying *A demonstrator was killed by a policeman*, which contains *be*, then the corresponding sentence with *there* is grammatical: *There was a demonstrator killed by a policeman.* Whether or not *there* can occur in such sentences cannot be determined on the basis of their deep structures alone, for their deep structures do not contain a verb with which *there* can co-occur. It is only if the passive transformation has applied, introducing *be*, that these sentences can contain *there*. In other words, the question of whether or not *there* can appear in certain sentences cannot be decided on the basis of their deep structures, but only after the passive transformation has applied. For this reason the constraints on the distribution of *there* cannot be stated in deep structure. We must conclude that *there* is not present in deep structure, but rather is introduced by a transformation.

7. Some speakers also allow the fixed phrase *take heed* (*of*). Note in passing that these fixed phrases can serve as indicators of environments in which particular verbs can be deleted. For example, Ray Dougherty has noted that although adverbials like *by tomorrow* cannot occur with verbs in the past tense (* *We ordered a bicycle by tomorrow*), sentences like *We needed a bicycle by tomorrow* are perfectly grammatical. This suggests that this sentence is derived from a deep structure with an additional

verb in it: *We needed to V a bicycle by tomorrow*, in which *by tomorrow* is not modifying *needed*, which is in the past tense, but rather the additional verb, which is not. On semantic grounds, the appropriate verb would seem to be *have*, so that the sentences in question would be derived from the structure underlying *We needed to have a bicycle by tomorrow*, by deletion of the verb *have*. Fixed phrases like *have recourse* (*to*) can be used to show that *have* is the correct choice here, since *have* must be able to undergo deletion in this environment anyway in order to account for the grammaticality of sentences like *We needed recourse to some higher authority*. This sentence must be derived from the structure underlying *We needed to have recourse to some higher authority*, since *recourse* can occur only as the object of *have*. The two motivations for an underlying *have* in this environment explain the grammaticality of *We needed recourse to some higher authority by tomorrow*.

8. This was pointed out by Chomsky to show the incorrectness of any analysis under which a passivized sentence like

(i)   **The Mohawks were defeated by the Samoans.**

has a deep structure like

(ii)

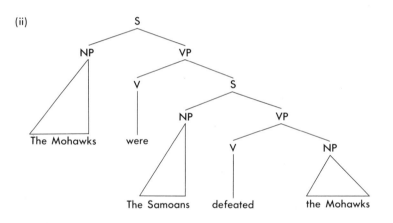

in which the surface subject of the passivized sentence (i) is the subject in deep structure of a higher sentence with the verb *be*. This analysis is incorrect, as (11) through (13) show, because *recourse, heed*, and *headway* occur in deep structure only in certain fixed phrases and therefore cannot be the subject of anything in deep structure. But the analysis of the passive under which (ii) is the deep structure of (i) would require *recourse, heed*, and *headway* to be the subject of *be* in the deep structures of (11) through (13). This analysis is therefore incorrect. Sentences (11) through (13) constitute extremely strong evidence that there is a passive transformation in English which takes deep structure objects and makes them into subjects in surface structure.

9. Evidence for this is to be found in Perlmutter (1968).

10. Evidence for this is to be found in Perlmutter (1968).

11. It might be argued that there are restrictions on the class of NPs that can be the objects of *begin* of a sort that make it necessary to derive these objects from more abstract underlying structures. Regardless of whether or not this is the case,

they must still be dominated by an NP node, as is shown by their ability to undergo the passive transformation in sentences like (27).

12. For some discussion of object deletion of this kind and its relevance to semantic interpretation, see Katz and Postal (1964, pp. 79–84) and Chomsky (1965, p. 87).

13. We have shown that *begin* takes objects in deep structure, but strictly speaking, we have not shown that its complement sentences are object complements. That is, we have not shown that a possible deep structure of (1) is not

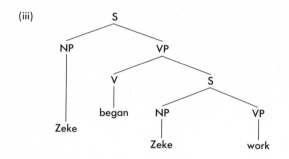

(iii)

rather than (4). Since we *have* shown *begin* to appear in deep structures like

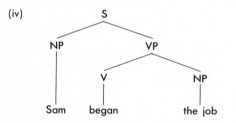

(iv)

however, it is clear that phrase structure rules of the kind justified by Rosenbaum (1967) will produce deep structures like (4) anyway, since these phrase structure rules provide for noun phrase complementation by means of a rule that introduces S under NP. The question therefore is whether *begin* occurs in deep structures like (iii) *in addition to* deep structures like (4) and (2). The answer to this question may well turn out to be negative, even though sentences with *begin* fail to satisfy Rosenbaum's criteria for noun phrase complementation. The fact that we do not get passive sentences like * *To work was begun by Zeke* is irrelevant, as Robin Lakoff has pointed out, since even with verbs which normally passivize we do not get passives when the subject of the embedded sentences is identical to the subject of the matrix sentence. Thus *expect*, for example, takes object complements and normally passivizes, yielding sentences like *For Mike to win was expected by everybody.* But if the matrix and embedded subjects are the same, no passive results: * *To win was expected by Mike.* Since the *begin* that appears in structures like (4) requires that the embedded subject be identical to the matrix subject, we will never get a passive like * *To work was begun by Zeke.* For this reason the lack of a grammatical passive here tells us nothing about whether *begin* takes object complements. George Lakoff has argued that the lack of grammatical pseudo-cleft sentences like * *What Zeke began was to work* is also not a valid argument against noun phrase complementation with such verbs, leading him to call into question the existence of intransitive verb phrase complementation, as in (iii). See Lakoff and Ross (in preparation) for these arguments. However this should turn out, it is only tangentially relevant to the point of this paper, which is to show that *begin* occurs both as a verb with abstract subjects, as in (2), and as a verb with animate subjects and complement sentences, as in (4) or (iii) or both.

14. Garcia (1967) points out that verbs like *begin* lack selectional restrictions on their subjects, and that sentences like (9a) and (9b) are synonymous. She concludes that on formal grounds *begin* should be treated as an intransitive verb that takes abstract (sentential) subjects, analogous to such verbs as *seem* and *happen*. She goes on to say that this solution does not accord with our intuitions about such sentences as *John began to read the book* and offers this as a case where the formally motivated solution and the intuitively correct solution are in conflict. In this paper evidence has been presented to show that no grammar of English is adequate if it does not allow *begin* to occur in two distinct kinds of deep structures. As a result the issue raised by Garcia does not present a problem.

15. For discussion of *do so*, see Lakoff and Ross (1966). This topic is explored in considerably greater depth in Anderson (1968).

16. Sentence (35) may be possible if *did so* is taken as having replaced *gushed from the well*, but *did so* cannot have replaced *began to gush from the well*, which is the reading that is of interest here. For this reason I have starred the sentence.

17. I am indebted to Wayles Browne for pointing out (41) to me. Note in passing that there must be some additional constraints on sentences with *threaten*, for we do not get sentences like * *Recourse threatened to be had to illegal methods.*

18. Within a generative framework, the remarks of Hofmann (1966) are very suggestive.

The Grammar of *Hitting* and *Breaking*

CHARLES J. FILLMORE

8

The contrast between implicit and explicit knowledge is perhaps nowhere greater than in man's use of language. If a person wishes to record and systematize what it is that he "knows" in knowing his language, he cannot simply write it down — he has to discover it first. And in attempting to discover the nature of his linguistic knowledge, he will find that satisfactory statements do not come easily. It is quite certain that the average adult speaker of English, even if given a year's time, simply could not come up with anything like a reliable explanation of how the word *ever* is used and what it means. And yet probably never in his adult life has this same person "made a mistake" in his use of this word, nor has he used it in ways inappropriate to his intentions.

What a speaker of language knows about the individual "words" of his language and the conditions that determine their appropriate use is perhaps the most accessible aspect of linguistic knowledge, but at times it too is extremely subtle and — at least on the face of it — extremely complex. In this paper I hope to explore some of this subtlety and complexity by considering how speakers of English use and understand two very ordinary verbs, *hit* and *break*.

My treatment of these words, and the kinds of evidence I shall appeal to in uncovering their grammatical and semantic properties, will bear some similarity to the style of argument one finds in the writings of the so-called "ordinary language" philosophers, but with two important differences. The

SOURCE: This paper was written while the author was taking part in a research project supported by the National Science Foundation through Grant GN534 from the office of Science Information Service to the Computer and Information Science Research Center, The Ohio State University.

first of these is that, unlike words like *know, good, ought, real,* or *exist,* the words *hit* and *break,* in themselves, have no philosophical interest. The second is that a linguist's analysis of words cannot be accounted satisfactory until his observations can be incorporated into a general empirical theory of linguistic structure. In other words, we cannot be satisfied that our inquiry has been completed until we are convinced that the concepts and principles we have used in organizing our observations are proper to some substantively and formally specific explanatory theory of the nature of human language. What this means in practice is that the linguist keeps the connection with empirical linguistic theory in mind, at least, whereas the philosopher traditionally has not been expected to do so.

A grammatical description of a language is successful if it accounts for precisely the facility that an ideal speaker of a language has in producing and understanding the grammatical sentences in his language. The knowledge that the speaker brings to bear in exercising this ability may be separated into the "general" and the "specific." One's "general" knowledge about a language is organized and displayed in its "grammar"; one's "specific" knowledge about the individual linguistic objects known as words or "lexemes" is collected and itemized in a "dictionary" or "lexicon" of the language. In this paper I shall attempt to determine at least some of the specific things that speakers of English know which account for their ability to use the words *hit* and *break* correctly. Put differently, the goal of this paper is to discover the information that needs to be registered, in one way or another, in the entries for these two words in a scientifically sound dictionary. It is in this sense an exercise in lexicological research.

The reader might at first be inclined to think that the task we have set for ourselves has already been completed — that anyone who wants to learn the lexical facts about *hit* and *break* can do so quite readily by looking the words up in a standard dictionary. It can be shown very easily, however, that there are indeed important facts about words which the makers of dictionaries do not generally bother to tell us. For example, if you look up the words *sick* and *ill* in a standard dictionary, you will be told that they are synonymous in one of their meanings, but what you will not be told is that although both of these adjectives can occur as predicates, only *sick* can occur attributively. Notice examples (1) and (2):

(1)   The children are $\left\{\begin{matrix} \text{sick} \\ \text{ill} \end{matrix}\right\}$.

(2)   the $\left\{\begin{matrix} \text{sick} \\ * \text{ill} \end{matrix}\right\}$ children

Or if you look up the word *good,* you will not find out from the dictionary something that every speaker of English knows, and that every foreign speaker of English needs to know, that (apparently) *good* is the only adjective in

English which can take, in negative and interrogative predicate sentences, the "quantifier" *any.* Notice examples (3) and (4):

(3)   Is it any $\left\{ \begin{array}{l} \text{good} \\ {}_{*}\text{ pink} \end{array} \right\}$?

(4)   They weren't any $\left\{ \begin{array}{l} \text{good} \\ {}_{*}\text{ tall} \end{array} \right\}$.

An ordinary dictionary will not tell us everything there is to know about *hit* and *break;* there is much we shall have to figure out for ourselves. One of the things it will tell us, however, is that each of these words has several senses. We shall concern ourselves here only with what might be called their "basic" or "nontransferred" meanings. We shall consider their use in expressions about *hitting trees* and *breaking sticks,* but we shall ignore their use in expressions about *hitting upon good ideas* or *breaking in a new man,* for example.

The first problem to take note of is that in a grammar which requires "subjects" in the deep structure[2] representation of every sentence, it is necessary to recognize three distinct verbs having the form *break* and two distinct verbs having the form *hit,* and that these distinctions are unaffected by the decision to restrict our attention to the basic meanings of these words.[3]

The three *break* verbs may be referred to as *break-1, break-2,* and *break-3.* The verb *break-1,* which is illustrated in sentence (5),

(5)   **The stick broke.**

is an intransitive verb which asserts of its "subject" the particular deformation or change of state we associate with the meaning of the verb.

The verb *break-2* is seen in sentence (6):

(6)   **John broke the stick (with a rock).**

It is used for asserting of an object the same change of state mentioned in connection with *break-1,* but *break-2* asserts it of its direct object. In general, precisely those noun phrases which can occur as subjects of *break-1* can appear as objects of *break-2; break-2* assigns an "agentive" or "instigative" role to its subject, which is typically animate. As shown in the parenthesized expansion of (6), *break-2* may co-occur with a phrase which identifies the "instrument," i.e., the inanimate object immediately responsible for the action of breaking.

The verb *break-3,* seen in sentence (7),

(7)   **A rock broke the stick.**

differs from *break-2* in accepting inanimate subjects[4] and in not permitting an instrument phrase in the same clause. In other words, a sentence like

(8)   * A rock broke the stick with a hammer.

is unacceptable (where *A rock* is not intended metaphorically), because this verb interprets the role of its "subject" instrumentally, and a simplex clause presumably can identify only one "instrument."[5] Both *break-2* and *break-3* agree in the semantic relation to the direct object.

There are three *break* verbs, but there are only two verbs with the form *hit* (in the meaning we have in mind); and these are *hit-1*, seen in (9),

(9)   John hit the tree (with a rock).

and *hit-2*, seen in sentence (10),

(10)   A rock hit the tree.

Verb *hit-2* parallels *break-3* in assigning an instrumental role to its (inanimate) subject, and in not tolerating an instrumental *with*-phrase. That is, the sentence:

(11)   * A rock hit the tree with a stick.

is unacceptable. And *hit-1* parallels *break-2* in assigning an agentive role to its (animate) subject and in accepting an instrumental phrase [as in the parenthesized expansion of (9)]. The two verbs *hit* agree in their semantic relation to the direct object.

Our two sets of verbs differ in that there is no intransitive verb *hit* corresponding with *break-1*, since there is no sentence of the form (12).

(12)   * The tree hit.

This division of *break* into three verbs and *hit* into two verbs is necessary if we wish to include in our descriptions of what we know about individual verbs constraints on the noun phrases that can occur in construction with them, the sentence types in which they can play a role, and the semantic relations which they express among the constituents of the clauses in which they are used.[6] But clearly there is something wrong with a grammatical model, or with an interpretation of a grammatical model,[7] which requires there to be two *hit*'s and three *break*'s. We shall reject this formulation, then, and propose a different description of the facts we have encountered. We shall assume that in some way certain noun phrases can be designated in the deep structure as having an agentive relation to the verbs they are in construction with, others designated as having an instrumental role. Let us label these noun phrases *agent* and *instrument*, and let us assume that a part of our specific knowledge about each verb in our language is a knowledge of the "kinds" of noun phrases (in the sense we are suggesting) that can occur in construction with it. We are forced to abandon the notions of deep structure subject and deep structure object, if we take this approach, and we must therefore accept a model of grammar in which the subjects and objects that we see in surface structures are introduced by rules.

Temporarily giving the noun phrase *the stick* in examples (5) through (8) the label "X," we may describe *break* as a verb which *requires* an X and which *permits* either an *agent* or an *instrument* or both. Syntactic rules will specify that if there is only an X, the X noun phrase must be the subject. If there is an *agent*, then the X appears as the direct object and the *agent* as subject.[8] If an *instrument* is selected with *break*, it becomes the subject just in case there is no *agent*, but it shows up at the end of the clause, with the preposition *with*, just in case the sentence does contain an *agent*. The selectional possibilities for *break* can be summarized by saying that it can occur in construction with any of the combinations of noun phrases representable by formula (13):

(13)   *(agent) (instrument)* X

The parenthesis notation means that the formula holds whether a parenthesized element is present or not. The left-to-right order of the elements is irrelevant.

By assigning the change of state asserted by *break* to the entity identified by the X noun phrase, by allowing the agentive or instrumental roles of noun phrases to be specified directly by the categories *agent* and *instrument*, by providing for the selection of subjects and objects in the ways mentioned above, and by adopting some formalism which guarantees that noun phrases occurring as *agents* are animate while noun phrases occurring as *instruments* are inanimate, we can account for all of the syntactic and semantic observations that were presented in connection with examples (5) through (8). It is important to realize that this interpretation does not require the separation of *break* into three distinct verbs.

By using the same concepts and rules as those we have just proposed, we can similarly simplify our description of *hit*. We need to say of *hit*, however, that it cannot occur alone with its X element, because sentence (12) is to be excluded. The phenomena we have observed about *hit* can be represented as formula (14)

(14)   *(agent)(instrument)* X

in which the linked parenthesis notation means that at least one of the two elements so linked *must* be present.

Of course, this "simplification" would be no simplification at all if the categories and rules, and the grammatical distinctions we must recognize to make the rules work, were applicable only to the verbs *hit* and *break*. I have developed elsewhere[9] the outlines of a general grammatical theory which incorporates modifications of the type we have been discussing. These matters need not concern us here, but it should at least be pointed out that the observations we have made about *break* and *hit* are true of many other

English verbs as well. Verbs which are semantically similar to *break* and whose occurrence in clause types is accounted for by formula (13) are exemplified in (15); some English verbs sharing with *hit* properties identified by formula (14) are given in (16).

(15)   bend, fold, shatter, crack
(16)   slap, strike, bump, stroke

Since (13) and (14) identify "classes" of verbs, it may be the case that certain properties of *hit* and *break* are associated in general with the verb classes to which they belong, other properties being more uniquely associated with the two words as individual lexical items.

In determining what these shared properties might be, we may first note that all of the verbs we chose to associate with *break* assert that the object identified by the X element is understood as undergoing some kind of change of state. That is, the X element is understood as essentially different after the event symbolized by the verb has "happened" to it. But this does not seem to hold for the verbs classified by formula (14). For the purposes of this essay, we shall refer to verbs like *break* and *bend* as "change-of-state" verbs, and verbs like *hit* and *slap* as "surface-contact" verbs. The surface-contact verbs assert the occurrence of some physical contact between two objects, but from the use of these verbs one cannot necessarily infer that the objects have undergone any essential change.[10] The most direct way of seeing this fact is by comparing our acceptance of sentence pairs like (17) and (18), in which verbs of these two kinds are contrasted.

(17)   I *hit* the window with a hammer; it didn't faze the window, but the hammer shattered.
(18)   * I *broke* the window with a hammer; it didn't faze the window, but the hammer shattered.

There is, then, a semantic as well as a syntactic difference between our two classes of verbs. We can capture some of these facts by replacing our temporary symbol X by *place* in formula (14), which we associated with the surface-contact verbs. For the other X we may use (for want of a better word) the term *object*. Now we can reformulate (13) and (14) as (19) and (20), respectively, and associate part of the meaning of expressions containing our verbs with these newly introduced categories of noun phrases.

(19)   (*agent*) (*instrument*) *object*
(20)   (*agent*)(*instrument*) *place*

The lexical entries for *break* and *hit* are assumed to contain references to formulas (19) and (20) respectively.

Change-of-state verbs, as we have said, are verbs which assert of an object a change in time from one "state" to another. An additional syntactic difference between the two verb classes is that "stative adjectives" can be derived from the change-of-state verbs, but not from the others. These adjectives describe the latter of the two states referred to by their underlying verbs. A consequence of this fact is that sentences like those in (21) are ambiguous in ways in which sentences like (22) are not:

(21)   The window was $\begin{Bmatrix} \text{broken} \\ \text{bent} \\ \text{shattered} \end{Bmatrix}$.

(22)   The window was $\begin{Bmatrix} \text{hit} \\ \text{struck} \\ \text{slapped} \end{Bmatrix}$.

The sentences of (21) may be understood either as passives or as descriptions of states, while those of (22) can be understood only as passives.

One more syntactic difference between change-of-state verbs and surface-contact verbs can be seen when the *object* or *place* noun phrase is a possessed body-part noun. The sentences with surface-contact verbs have paraphrases in which the "possessor" appears as the direct object and the body-part noun appears in a "locative prepositional phrase."[11]

Notice (23) through (26):

(23)   I $\begin{Bmatrix} \text{hit} \\ \text{slapped} \\ \text{struck} \end{Bmatrix}$ his leg.

(24)   I $\begin{Bmatrix} \text{hit} \\ \text{slapped} \\ \text{struck} \end{Bmatrix}$ him on the leg.

(25)   I $\begin{Bmatrix} \text{broke} \\ \text{bent} \\ \text{shattered} \end{Bmatrix}$ his leg.

(26)   * I $\begin{Bmatrix} \text{broke} \\ \text{bent} \\ \text{shattered} \end{Bmatrix}$ him on the leg.

If the sentences paired by (23) and (24) are correctly interpreted as paraphrases of each other, and if that means that they are identical in their deep structure, it follows that our investigation into the classes of verbs associated with *hit* and *break* requires an understanding of the precise ways in which English grammar deals with body-part nouns.[12]

I suggested above that the categories *agent* and *instrument* were to be used somehow to guarantee that the noun phrases that filled these positions in sentences would be animate and inanimate respectively. Perhaps a more satisfactory way of dealing with the same facts is to say that the categories *agent* and *instrument* impose a particular interpretation on the nouns that occur "under" them. The sentences we rejected above were sentences in which interpretations imposed on a noun are contradicted by facts that we know about the objects identified by the noun itself. In sentences (8) and (11), for example, we are forced to interpret *A rock* agentively; but since a rock is not animate, and is therefore known to be incapable of initiating any action, we must either interpret the sentences as meaningless, or as fairy-tale sentences in which *A rock* was "personified" (or perhaps the word we need is "animated"). It must remain an open question just what the best treatment of the distinction between normal and semantically anomalous sentences is, but at least we can be clear about the facts. I shall suggest below that my first formulation is more adequate.[13]

Since we have assigned two different categories to the noun phrases we originally labeled X, we must now ask whether the nouns that occur in the X role with these two verbs must be different (or, alternatively, if nouns are to be interpreted in two different ways depending on whether they are identified as *places* or as *objects*).

Consider, in this regard, sentences (27) and (28):

(27)   I broke the top of the table.
(28)   I hit the top of the table.

In (27), the noun *top* must be referring to the top of a table as a more or less distinct object, while in (28), it can refer either to that or to a portion of the surface area of the table.

This distinction can probably be made clearer with a different kind of example. Suppose you didn't know what *twarge* meant, and you were told two things about some twarge:

(29)   John hit the left side of the twarge.
(30)   John hit the top of the twarge.

You might imagine, on hearing (29) and (30), that a twarge was some kind of solid object, and certainly nothing in the two sentences would contradict that assumption. But suppose you were then told two more things about this twarge:

(31)   John broke the left side of the twarge.
(32)   John broke the top of the twarge.

This time you would be forced to interpret *side* and *top*, not as words designating portions of the surface area of the twarge, but as more or less separable parts of it. The ideas you could have about what a twarge looked like would be much more constrained after you heard (31) and (32) than before. It is clear, in other words, that the X nouns that can occur with *hit* must be partly different (or differently interpretable) from those which occur with *break.*

The fact that in sentences (28) and (30) the noun *top* may be understood as referring *either* to an object *or* to a location suggests to me that one of the roles of the symbols *agent, place*, etc., is in the "selection" of nouns, and that they are not restricted in their effect to the "imposition of an interpretation" on nouns. To appear as an *object*, a noun must identify something that can be a physical object. To appear as a *place*, a noun must identify something that can either be an object or a location.[14]

The ways in which we can understand the nouns that occur with *hit* are almost entirely accounted for by referring to the category *place*, but those connected with the change-of-state verbs appear to involve idiosyncratic properties of individual verbs. In other words, the kinds of objects that *twarge* might refer to are quite different for the various verbs in (34), but not so for these in (33):

$$(33) \quad I \begin{Bmatrix} \text{hit} \\ \text{slapped} \\ \text{struck} \\ \text{smote} \end{Bmatrix} \text{ the twarge.}$$

$$(34) \quad I \begin{Bmatrix} \text{bent} \\ \text{folded} \\ \text{shattered} \\ \text{broke} \end{Bmatrix} \text{ the twarge.}$$

Here for the first time our observations become "lexically" specific. We must now consider what there is to say about objects concerning which it is appropriate to use the word *break.* We have seen already that the object must be in some sense "separable" or discontinuous with other things, but that aspect of the meaning is perhaps best associated with the category *object.*

A sentence like (35)

(35)   I broke the dog.

can be interpreted as referring to something which happened to a figurine in the shape of a dog, or perhaps to a frozen dog, but not to an ordinary dog. That is because *break* requires of the entity named by its *object* noun that it be "rigid" in some of its dimensions. One can *break* a dog's bone, but not, ordinarily, a dog.

To show that we are here dealing with a property of the word *break*, rather than with change-of-state verbs in general, we may compare *break* with *bend.* An object that can be *bent* must be "rigid" to the extent that it offers resistance (one doesn't *bend* a handkerchief, normally), but it must also be flexible. Then too, there are more constraints on the permitted "shapes" of objects that can be *bent* than for objects that can be *broken*; but here the best I can do is expect the reader to know what I mean.[15]

There are, then, these more or less specific, and at least intuitively grasp-able, properties of objects named by nouns capable of appearing nonanoma-lously with the verb *break*. One could make these observations *seem* more formal, of course, by writing "rigidity" with an initial capital letter and postulating it as a semantic feature of certain nouns, but I believe it would be quite misleading to do so. It seems very unlikely to me that anything is gained by treating these particular "selectional" properties of *break* (and *bend, fold,* etc.) in terms of semantic features that are assignable in any natural way to "other words." It is rather that the verb "presupposes" that the "real world objects" named by the nouns that occur with it have certain "physical properties."

But we have still said nothing about what *break* "means." By comparing *break* with *bend* we can see that the former implies, while the latter does not, the appearance of some discontinuity in an external or internal surface of the object; but if there is more to say than that, it is something that can be said as well by dictionary makers as by linguists.

I am inclined to think that the systematic study of the semantic structure of these words ends pretty much with what we have already noted. To seek critical differences between *break, smash, shatter,* to say nothing of the attempt to discover what distinguishes *hit, strike, slam, smite, bump,* etc., from each other, is to involve oneself in judgments that may vary widely from person to person and that may individually have nothing to do with *other* facts about the English language.

Our findings can be summarized by noting that some of the syntactic and semantic properties of our two words can be blamed on the fact that they are words of a particular type; that is, many of the facts we have encountered are instances of general facts about whole classes of words or about uses and interpretations of grammatical categories the existence of which is determina-ble independently of questions of lexicography.

Both of these verbs can be used transitively, with subjects that are under-stood agentively as well as with subjects that are understood instrumentally. But *break*, unlike *hit*, can also be used intransitively. *Break* is one of a class of verbs used to express a change of state in some object, and as such it provides, in the form of its past participle, a stative adjective which is capable of describing the object in its latter state. One of the properties of *hit*, namely the existence of certain kinds of paraphrases when it is used with body-part nouns, is apparently accounted for by referring to the ways in which body-part nouns are used as indicators of places rather than as indicators of objects. And constraints on the specific nouns that can occur in constructions with these verbs are partly determined by the categories *agent, instrument, place,* and *object.*

All of these phenomena are either ascribable to larger grammatical facts or to whole classes of verbs. They fall under what really amounts to our "general" knowledge of English, and are therefore to be treated only in the grammar. The only word-specific information that is related to the preceding observations is: (a) that given in formulas (19) and (20), the information that indicates, for each of these verbs, the syntactic environments in which it is appropriate to use it; and (b) the information that *break* semantically expresses a change of state.

Apart from the information about their general semantic character (as change-of-state verbs or not) and the needed indication of the environments into which they can be inserted, the only really specific lexical information that we have encountered are: (a) the special ways in which speakers of English accept the *object* nouns that occur with *break* and interpret them; and (b) the specific meaning of the two words. The word *break* can be appropriately used only with an object that is "rigid" in some of its dimensions, and it expresses the appearance of some discontinuity therein. (But why one can *break* a thread but not a cloth is not easily covered by this statement.) The nouns that can occur with *hit* apparently do not need to satisfy any requirements not associated with their categorization as *places,* and what exactly is meant by *hit,* in the sense of the kind of surface contact asserted by *hit* in particular (as opposed to *strike,* etc.), is extremely difficult to pin down.

Not every change-of-state verb can be used intransitively: consider *smash* and *cut* in this respect. Not every verb having syntactic properties of the kind represented by formula (19) is a change-of-state verb: there is a large class of motion verbs syntactically like *break,* including *move, turn, rotate, spin,* etc. Not every verb that is semantically a change-of-state verb and is syntactically transitive or intransitive in a way analogous to that represented by formula (19) takes an *object:* some take animate nouns, such as *wake* (*up*). Some change-of-state verbs are understood as affecting a place on an object rather than an object as a whole. The verbs *cut* and *bite,* for example, are of this type, and show paraphrase relations of the type seen in (25) and (26) with body-part nouns. And some change-of-state verbs have associated adjectives that are not identical in form with their past participles. The word *awake* is the stative adjective for *wake* (*up*), and that must have something to do with the fact that nobody knows what the past participle of *wake* is!

What these observations show is that many of the apparent regularities suggested by this study are slightly spurious, and what that means is that the lexical description of some of the other verbs we have mentioned will be somewhat more detailed than that of *break* or *hit.*

One of the conclusions that can be drawn from this study is that the data we have examined fail to support the distinction between syntax (as providing a "level" of representation) and semantics. Modifications that are being devised in the theory of deep structure are tending more and more to provide concepts of the kind that can be used quite directly for expressing semantic assertions about linguistic expressions. The designation of noun phrases as *agents, places,* etc., that has been used in my approach, has a role in semantic interpretation, and such properties of verbs as the change-of-state feature we have associated with *break* are semantic in a more obvious way.

The assignment of such semantic features has, however, clear "syntactic consequences." Current developments within the theory of generative trans-formational grammar suggest that all "purely syntactic" concepts in grammar relate to the application of syntactic rules, not to the underlying representation of sentences.[16]

Certain other matters that have been considered proper to semantics but distinct from syntax include formalizations of the notion of semantic anomaly through semantic projection rules of the type proposed by Katz and Fodor (1963). These authors distinguish between "markers" and "distinguishers" among the features that compose semantic characterizations of lexical items. The distinguishers are those features of the semantic description of a word which are idiosyncratic to that word. The markers are those features which enter into semantic generalizations, features in terms of which various semantic judgments on sentences — including judgments on semantic anomaly — can be formalized and made explicit.

Since a part of the description of certain words is a statement of their selectional restrictions — that is, a statement of the conditions that determine their meaningful use — it should be the case that all semantic anomalies should be describable by a single device. Our consideration of the conditions of appropriateness for the use of words like *break, bend,* and *fold,* however, suggests that selectional information can be as idiosyncratic as the kinds of properties that have been referred to as semantic distinguishers. The treatment of the selectional properties of verbs cannot be carried out in a non-*ad hoc* way, it seems to me, by seeking features on nouns which do or do not violate restrictions associated with particular change-of-state verbs. In fact, it looks very much as if for a considerable portion of the vocabulary of a language, the conditions determining the appropriate use of a word involve statements about properties of real world objects rather than statements about the se-mantic features of words.

Some facts about language that have been hitherto treated in terms of a semantic interpretive component viewed as distinct from the syntactic com-ponent have been absorbed into the latter — that is, they have been shown to be explainable within a combined syntactic–semantic component. Other facts that have been treated by some as belonging to semantic theory proper are believed to be more correctly assigned to the study of the speakers' "practical" knowledge of their language. It seems to me that the explanatory scope of semantics as such, to the extent that semantic knowledge can be separated from knowledge of syntax (or syntax–semantics) and knowledge of the world, should be limited to a clarification of the conceptual inter-relatedness of lexical items and the semantic judgments on sentences that can be directly accounted for in terms of this interrelatedness.

NOTES

1. The author wishes to express his gratitude to Gaberell Drachman and David L. Stampe for many helpful suggestions.

2. For a statement of the distinction between "deep" and "surface" representations of the structure of sentences, see Chomsky (1966, pp. 31–51) and Chomsky (1965).

3. Although it is certainly possible to rephrase the facts under examination in such a way that there is *one* verb *break* with several distinct "uses," it is important to realize that the formal complexity that concerns us here is in no way affected by this reformulation.

4. There are good reasons for saying that an instrumental noun phrase (in the intended sense) is always underlyingly inanimate. A sentence like *The dog broke the stick*, when it is used to refer to what happened to the stick when we threw the dog at it, must then be interpreted as containing in its deep structure the noun phrase *the dog's body*. The word *body*, then, being inanimate, is capable of fulfilling an instrumental function in the clause. There are languages in which the distinction betwen *the dog* as agent and experiencer and *the dog* (= *the dog's body*) as physical object must be made overt. Mohawk, Paul Postal has informed me, is one such language.

5. At most, a simplex clause identifies one "noun phrase" as having an instrumental role. This is not to deny that the noun phrase can be compound.

6. The nature of these differences between our two verbs and the necessary complexity of their description in grammars which require underlying subjects for all sentences are discussed in detail in Hall (1965).

7. In this essay I have considered only interpretations of (5) through (10) that regard them as simplex sentences. A competing view very convincingly presented in Lakoff (1967) would have them *all* be complex (involving successive embeddings) and would assign to them deep structures of an extremely abstract character. I know at the moment no empirical data that would be relevant to a choice between these two views, and it seems to me that neither the facts about *hit* and *break* nor the concluding message about the role of a semantic theory would be affected by a choice between them.

8. We ignore here the rules that result in "passive" sentences. A more detailed description of the operation of syntactic rules in a grammar of the type suggested here may be seen in Fillmore (1968).

9. Fillmore (1968).

10. Of course, the surface-contact verbs can also be said to identify a "change of state" of some kind. In a purely abstract sense, a cheek which has once been

slapped is different from the same cheek before the slapping event took place. The semantic structures of *some* words recognize properties of objects discoverable not in the objects themselves but in their "histories" (words like *bastard* or *widow*), but such matters have no relevance to the distinction between the two kinds of verbs we are discussing here.

11. This fact, incidentally, tends to lend support to our choice of the category *place* for the "direct objects" of surface-contact verbs. Some surface-contact verbs, further-more, permit either the *place* or the *instrument* to become the direct object (where there is an *agent* to serve as subject), allowing such paraphrases as

  (i) I hit the roof with the stick.
  (ii) I hit the stick on the roof.

It should be noticed that when the *instrument* noun phrase is made the direct object, the *place* preposition shows up, and that when the *place* noun phrase is made the direct object, the *instrument* preposition shows up. This is because the rule for forming direct objects, like the rule for forming subjects, has the effect of *deleting the preposition* that would otherwise be associated with the category *agent, place, instrument*, etc.

12. One suggestion on the way in which body-part nouns are to be treated in a grammar is found in the section entitled, "The Grammar of Inalienable Possession," in Fillmore (1968).

13. For a careful discussion of this difference (or rather, a similar difference), see D. T. Langendoen (1967*b*).

14. The distinction could be made more forcefully if we would find nouns which can occur as *places* but never as *objects*. The word *lap* might possibly be such a noun, but I am not sure. At least I am surer about the unacceptability of * *I broke his lap* than I am about that of *I hit his lap*.

15. Notice, too, that *bend* differs from *fold* in respect to both kinds of properties, resistance and shape. The resistance required when one is correctly using the word *bend* is not required for *fold*, and there are further constraints still on the shape of objects that can be *folded*. One cannot, for instance, *fold* a string.

16. I have in mind unpublished manuscripts by J. D. McCawley, J. R. Ross, G. Lakoff, and D. T. Langendoen.

On Very Deep Grammatical Structure

R. B. LEES

9

We can be thankful, I believe, for at least the following major contributions of contemporary linguistic research:

1. It has made available to this field the methods and results of the mathematical study of formal systems, so that now theories of grammatical description can be considered on the basis of their internal logical structure.

2. As a result we have been led to formulate the description of a language in the form of a set of abstract generative rules which specify the grammatical structure of all well-formed utterances in a language.

3. To achieve greater generality in these rules and to explain a speaker's knowledge of innumerable cases of paraphrase or difference of meaning we have been forced to return within technical linguistic analysis to the traditional separation of "logical" and "grammatical" structure, or as they are now often called, "deep structure" and "surface structure" of sentences.

4. As our formulation of the relation between abstract grammatical structure and the way the speaker–hearer understands his sentences has become more sophisticated, our attention has centered more and more upon the most time-honored concern of linguistics, the study of meaning.

During this gradual return to the traditional question of language study we have not had to surrender any real gains afforded by modern linguistics. I shall mention only two. Older semantic studies were weakened by quixotic efforts to derive syntactic structure from intuitive characterizations of meaning

SOURCE: This paper was read at the symposium at the University of Illinois, May 1967. A more technical version of this paper was read at the Tenth International Congress of Linguistics, Bucharest, September 1967.

and by the assumption that an adequate semantic description must specify directly the relation between each expression and the general setting within which it is used on each occasion. We now can make use of an independently motivated syntactic description of sentences, and we now see clearly that there is a semantic aspect of sentences which can be studied and formulated independently of settings.

Much recent grammatical research has been directed toward an explanation of the fact that the native user of a language understands as similar many expressions with quite divergent sequences of word classes and inflections. The method has been to reconstruct for each set of similarly understood expressions an abstract underlying grammatical form which is automatically converted to each of these divergent surface forms by means of certain grammatical transformations each of which is itself of some greater or lesser generality by virtue of independent motivations.[1]

For example, ignoring many minor details, we might construe as variants of the same general process of "extraposition" the three transformational rules central to the analysis of the following English expressions:

1. To explain the relation between

How big is he?

and

He is bigger than I am.

we represent the latter sentence in the abstract form:

He is er than I am big big.

and assume that a transformational rule extraposes the embedded sentence *I am big* together with the prefixed particle *than;* the expression *er + than + sentence* is, accordingly, construed as a preadjectival modifier whose interrogative form is *how.*[2]

2. To explain the relation between

We sent him away to school.

and

He was sent away to school.

and still preserve the generality of a passive rule we represent each sentence in the abstract form:

We sent away to school him.

and assume that in the active a transformational rule extraposes the verb complement *away to school.*[3]

3. To explain the relation between

For you to wear a Beatle haircut disturbs the class.

and

It disturbs the class for you to wear a Beatle haircut.

we represent each sentence in the abstract form:

It for + to you wear a Beatle haircut disturbs the class.

and assume that a transformational rule optionally extraposes the *for + to* nominalization of the sentence embedded within the subject noun phrase (in which case the noun *it* of that noun phrase is not deleted).[4]

Now in the most recent studies of syntactic structure using such methods, an interesting, though not very surprising, fact has gradually emerged: as underlying grammatical representations are made more and more abstract, and as they are required to relate more and more diverse expressions, the deep structures come to resemble more and more a direct picture of the meaning of those expressions!

I shall first review very succinctly for you two efforts in this direction which have recently come to my attention, and then I shall draw our attention to an older study of my own on nominal compounds in English which may motivate such a deep analysis. Although I have only what Fillmore calls a "preliminary version" of his recent monograph (1968), I take the liberty of discussing it in public. Fillmore reviews a wide variety of expressions which fall into sets of related types of which the following are typical:

I broke the window.
The window was broken by me.
The window broke.

I struck the window.
* The window struck.

John bought a car from Bill.
Bill sold a car to John.

Flies swarm in the room.
The room swarms with flies.

Acetone dissolves nail polish.
Nail polish dissolves in acetone.

A fan is in the room.
There is a fan in the room.
The room has a fan in it.

I see it.
He shows it to me.

I like it.
It pleases me.

I own it.
I acquire it.

I hear it.
I listen to it.

I know it.
I learn it.

I see it.
I watch it.

He also considers the difference between languages which contrast nominative and accusative suffixes, such as Latin, and those which contrast ergative and nominative affixes. On the basis of many different considerations Fillmore concludes that the syntactic relations of *subject* and *object* belong to a relatively superficial level of syntactic representation of expressions but that underlying these there is a deeper one in which sentences are represented in another way. There are two major constituents, a *modality* component containing elements for tense, mode, negativity, etc., and a *proposition* component containing elements for nouns, verbs, adjectives, etc. The latter contentful constituent itself consists of a verb and one or more nominals, each of the latter said to be in a certain "case." A sentence may contain only one of each case type, and each verb is marked for which cases it may "take." Rules of topicalization select one of these nominals under certain conditions to be the *subject,* another to be the *object,* and other rules may, in some languages, choose certain prepositions to prefix to some of the nouns in certain cases, while in other languages certain affixes may be chosen instead. There are among the cases one for *agent,* one for *instrument,* one for *place,* one for *beneficiary,* etc.

In other words, in Fillmore's view, the deep structure of a sentence represents directly who does what to whom for whose benefit, with what, where, when, how, and why; and what the subject or object of a verb is is a question of more superficial formal syntactic requirements.

The other work which I shall mention here is as yet only alluded to in various unpublished communications from John Ross of MIT and George Lakoff of Harvard. Ross and Lakoff note that during the last few years the notion of "deep structure" has developed under the somewhat tacit assumption that one and the same level of linguistic structure is defined by the following four different and independent motivations:

1. the simplest base over which plausible transformational rules can be defined;

2. the representations over which reasonable co-occurrence and selectional restrictions can be defined;

3. the structures in terms of which significant syntactic relations, such as *subject*, can be defined;

4. the trees into which lexical items can be inserted correctly.

Now, McCawley (1967) had already argued cogently that all selectional restrictions are actually semantic, not syntactic. But co-occurrence restrictions must also be semantic; for example, it is inconceivable that a verb might permit as subject the word *cathode* but yet reject on grammatical grounds the synonymous expression *negative electrode.* Also, although some verbs may require female subjects, none ever require feminine subjects; no verb which requires a plural subject can take a grammatically plural but semantically singular subject, such as *scissors.* Ross and Lakoff also note with Fillmore that *subject* and *object,* although they are distinguished to be sure, do not seem to be required for correct semantic interpretations. Finally they remark that whatever level of grammatical structure is defined by considerations of simplicity of transformational rules does not seem to be clearly related to any other facts of linguistic knowledge.

Lakoff (1967) has also studied the relation between instrumental sentences and corresponding ones in *use:*

Galileo observed Jupiter with a telescope.
Galileo used a telescope to observe Jupiter.

He enumerated a surprising number of plausible formal syntactic motivations for deriving both from the same deep structure. But that just means that the ordinary conception of deep structure falls under some suspicion, for the first sentence type appears to be a simplex sentence with an instrumental adverbial phrase, while the second appears to contain an embedded sentence; moreover, the main verb of the former is the embedded verb of the latter, which itself contains another independent main verb. It seems at best unlikely that the ordinary notion of deep structure is capable of accommodating such a case.

The implications of these researches is that what we have been calling "deep structure" may well actually be some intermediate level of representation, in fact perhaps not even a definable level of linguistic structure at all — something like what is represented in a traditional phonemic transcription as compared with a systematic morphophonemic representation or a frankly phonetic transcription.

Secondly, there is a strong implication that the deepest syntactic level of representation which functions in a linguistic description is so close to what we might call the meaning of a sentence that there may be no validity to maintaining a distinction between these. I shall return later to some suggestions about what such a result, if true, would entail for our conception of the internal organization of a descriptive grammar of a natural language.

I turn now to the analysis which I gave to nominal compounds in 1957.

The fourth chapter of Lees (1960), an antediluvian monograph on English syntax, was designed to explain in some measure the knowledge an English speaker has of indefinitely many expressions, each consisting of two nouns, characteristically the first with primary, the second with tertiary stress, the whole functioning itself as a noun within noun phrases. A part of that knowledge which is to be accounted for is the intuition that for each of the ways a given compound can be understood, the two members are related as are certain constituents of some sentence of English; among these constituents are the subject noun, the verb, the object noun, and an oblique object (i.e., the object of a preposition in an adverbial phrase). There are also some compound types related to the two parts of a copula sentence.

The treatment I gave consisted in the formulation of a small set of transformational rules to derive the various compound types from their underlying-sentence representations. For example, omitting certain unessential details, from the abstract tree representing the deep structure of a noun phrase containing a head noun *bridge* and an embedded sentence-tree which underlies the sentence *Someone draws the bridge,* successive trees (represented below by a version of their last lines only) could be derived, each by means of a certain formal and general rule:

a bridge which is for someone to draw the bridge
a bridge for someone to draw the bridge
a bridge for someone to draw
a bridge to draw
a dráwbrìdge

Thus, the two parts of the nominal compound *drawbridge* were described as related to one another as are the verb and its object in a sentence, since the internal organization of both the compound and the sentence in question is specified in terms of the same underlying deep structure (in part). It was shown that the overwhelming majority of compound types can be derived from an immediately underlying expression by a very general inversion rule, roughly:

$$N_1 + P + N_2 \rightarrow N_2 + N_1$$

Although this general rule was formulated, and it was indicated which compound types can be construed as requiring the application of this rule in their derivational history, all the compounds which fell into the scope of the study were classified not according to this fact but by a different set of criteria, namely, according to the underlying syntactic relations reflected in the two members. But these two different points of view were never clearly distinguished in the study.

This ambivalence was not the only disturbing feature of my analysis of nominal compounds. I ignore here such trivial complaints as that my assignment of a particular compound to a type could be questioned by someone who understands it in some other, alternative way, for as I have repeatedly emphasized, nominal compound expressions are massively and multiply ambiguous. But closer inspection of many of the classes which I isolated reveals that they often contain subsets of compounds which are understood differently though consistently.

For example, the compounds in a class represented by *gunpowder* were grouped together as derived by an NPN rule from a copula-sentence expression $N_1 +$ for $+ N_2$, as in:

The powder is for guns. →
... powder for guns ... →
... gúnpòwder ...

and among them were included:

bríefcàse, cóffee crèam, dóg fòod, évening weàr.

Consider just the first two; notice that while we do indeed have both *case for briefs* and *cream for coffee*, we understand the spatial relations oppositely: the briefs go into the case, but the cream into the coffee. Moreover, these are not isolated fortuitous facts about the world we live in; each is matched by a set of compounds of the same type:

bríefcàse, áshtràly, ícebòx, pígpèn, bírdcàge,
cóffee crèam, pócket bòok, fiéld artìllery.

As another example, a large and varied class of compounds was isolated in which the first noun was related to the second as are the object and subject of a verb, respectively:

... mason who lays bricks ... → ... bríck màson ...

and among them were included:

cár thìef, wáter pìstol, oíl wèll, and fiéld mòuse.

But these each fall easily into classes of their own:

1. blóod dònor, bríck màson, cár thìef, físhwìfe, lócksmìth
2. búg spràly, fíre èngine, hóur glàss, lífe boàt, wáter pìstol
3. fúr sèal, grável pìt, hóney bèe, límestòne, oíl wèll
4. cáve màn, fiéld mòuse, séa-hòrse, wáter snàke.

Now, in case 1, N_2 of the compound $N_1 + N_2$ represents someone who actually does something to or with what is represented by N_1: gives, lays, steals, sells, treats, etc. But in the *wáter pìstol* case the head nouns are all inanimates representing objects which do nothing but instead can be *used* by someone to do something. In case 3, someone may obtain N_1 *from* N_2, but otherwise the object represented by N_2 does nothing itself (as portrayed in the compound). Finally, in case 4, these creatures again do nothing — they are simply characterized by their natural *location*. Notice that, just as Fillmore conjectured, an *agent* noun, the one which, if present, appears as subject of a transitive verb, appears always to be animate, even characteristically human; and the nouns in case 4 are not restricted to animates:

gróund wàter, spáce chàrge, bódy flùids, kídney stòne.

There are many other similar examples I might cite of the insight offered by this deeper analysis. It seems at this point to support Fillmore's contention that *subject* and *object* are superficial, or at least more superficial than the features we have been isolating (we already know, of course, that these features cannot be characterized in terms of surface structures, but they now appear not to be part even of the so-called deep level). Also our reanalysis seems to support Fillmore's proposal that the underlying categories of the deepest level are generalized *cases*, that is, nominals with such functions as *agent*, *place*, *instrument*, etc., plus the *verb*.

Returning now briefly to Fillmore's contention that the *agentive* and the *dative* nouns are obligatorily animates, let me conclude by saying that it is devilishly hard to find convincing counterexamples from nominal compounds. For example, one might suppose that compounds like *wínd eròsion* or *smóke dàmage*, *wíndmìll* or *wáter whèel*, and *cóver cròp* or *púnchlìne* all reflect the syntactic relations in a sentence type with transitive verb and inanimate subject:

The wind erodes something.
The wind powers the mill.
The crop covers the ground.

Modern chemistry is based on the insight that matter is atomic in nature. But we do not suppose that it can simply repeat what was already known to Leucippus and Democritus. Chemistry has done much more than fill in a few details; it is important to see that the assumption of atoms is not merely a solution to the philosophical inconceivability of unbounded subdivision, but it is also a good theory to account for constant combining proportions in compounds, for the malleability of metals, for the gas laws, and for innumerable other facts. The major function of a successful explanatory theory is just to establish understandable relations among a wide variety of otherwise arbitrary and fortuitous observations.

Contemporary transformational studies attempt to do that for the ancient intuitions about language. The great grammarians of the past felt in their bones, and quite correctly, that what we wish to say determines in part what we utter; only now can we begin to say in any detail and with any assurance just what that connection consists in.

NOTES

1. Since the technical literature developing linguistic traditions in these directions into our times has by now become so copious, it is confusing and repetitious to acknowledge in detail the sources of the insights to which I have referred. We owe our current deep concern for them above all to the Chomskyan Revolution in our field, though, as Chomsky himself has been at pains to argue, many of the ideas are ancient. Perhaps *every* linguist has contributed something to our limited knowledge of man's most striking talent, his ability to learn and use languages.

2. This simple and obvious, though perhaps too primitive, proposal was advanced in Lees (1961).

3. Such an analysis would require, of course, that we confirm the implied description of *be at school* and *send to school* as containing the same underlying place adverb; the details may never have been worked out, even if correct.

4. The proposal is due to Rosenbaum (1967).

REVISING THE MODEL

part
three

Pronominalization, Negation, and the Analysis of Adverbs[1]

GEORGE LAKOFF

10

Introduction

Studies in transformational grammar have made it clear that the grammatical analysis of sentences must be carried on at two levels, deep structure and surface structure. The surface structure of a sentence is roughly equivalent to its parsing, in traditional terms. The deep structure is more abstract. It reflects the logic of the sentence, exhibiting only elementary grammatical relations. And in all cases, the deep structure contains more elements than does the relatively abbreviated surface form of the sentence. In most cases, deep structure will even contain full sentences that do not appear as sentences in surface structure. For example, Chomsky (1957 and 1965) has argued that attributive adjectives are derived from full sentences in deep structure. "The tall man left" would have the sentence "the man is tall" in its deep structure, even though this sentence does not appear as a clause in surface structure. If Chomsky's arguments are correct, and I believe they are, then there is an extra deep structure sentence for every attributive adjective that appears in surface structure. In what follows I will argue that the same is true of either (a) certain adverbial modifiers, in particular, time and place adverbials, or (b) negatives, or (c) both.

1. Pronominalization

Since the inception of transformational studies of pronominalization,[2] it has been assumed that anaphoric pronouns do not occur in underlying structures; rather, they are derived by transformation from the full noun phrases to which they refer. For example, it has been assumed that (1) is derived from (2):

(1)   *The man who John knows* shaved *himself.*
(2)   *The man who John knows* shaved *the man who John knows.*

The two occurrences of "the man who John knows" in (2) are assumed to refer to the same individual.[3] We will refer to the view that pronominalization is a syntactic process as Assumption 1.

ASSUMPTION 1: Anaphoric pronouns are derived by a transformational rule from the full noun phrases to which they refer.

A priori, there is no reason to believe Assumption 1. One might just as easily suppose that anaphoric pronouns occur in underlying structure and that there is a rule of semantic interpretation that indicates what the antecedent is for each pronoun. In the absence of any compelling evidence, one could just as well make Assumption 2:

ASSUMPTION 2: Anaphoric pronouns occur in underlying structures and their antecedents are given by semantic rules.

I should like to raise the question as to whether there is any good reason to believe that Assumption 1 is true and Assumption 2 false.

2. Anaphoric "It"

There are a wide variety of cases in English where the anaphoric pronoun "it" stands in place of a noun phrase complement sentence. Consider (3), for example:

(3) **John said that Bill finked on Max, but I didn't believe it.**

The *it* in (3) is understood as referring to the noun phrase complement of (4).

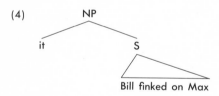

(4)

If we were to make Assumption 1, we would guess that (5) would be the structure underlying (3).

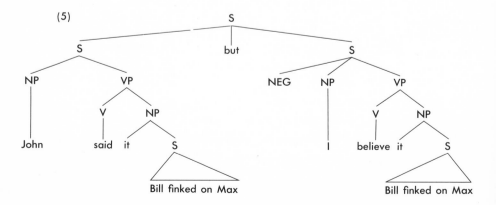

(5)

If this deep structure is correct, (3) would be derived from (5) by a rule having the effect of deleting the rightmost S "Bill finked on Max" and leaving behind "it" as an anaphoric pronoun. It is an open question as to whether the process of S-deletion in this case is just a subcase of the ordinary pronominalization rule. At present, there is no reason to believe that it is not, while there is one very strong reason to believe that it is a subcase of ordinary pronominalization.

Anaphoric "it" of the type found in (3) patterns just like other anaphoric pronouns with respect to the constraints of right-to-left pronominalization. Langacker (1966) and Ross (1968) have shown that right-to-left pronominalization is impossible in certain situations.

(6) a. Although *Irv* was sick, *he* went to the party.
     b. Although *he* was sick, *Irv* went to the party.
     c. *Irv* went to the party, although *he* was sick.
     d. * *He* went to the party, although *Irv* was sick.

(The italicized noun phrases are assumed to refer to the same individual.) Pronominalization is impossible in (6d), where the antecedent is inside an independent subordinate clause and the anaphoric pronoun is in the main clause. The same constraint holds in the case of anaphoric "it," as in (3).

     e. Although Sid asserted *that Max left*, I didn't believe *it*.
     f. Although Sid asserted *it*, I didn't believe *that Max left*.
     g. I didn't believe *that Max left*, although Sid asserted *it*.
     h. * I didn't believe *it*, although Sid asserted *that Max left*.

Since the anaphoric "it" referring to noun phrase complements has the same privileges of occurrence as ordinary anaphoric pronouns, there is good reason to believe that S-deletion is a subcase of ordinary pronominalization.

Suppose this is true. What follows? If I can show that Assumption 1 is true of the above cases of anaphoric "it," then it follows that Assumption 1 is true of ordinary pronouns. In the following section, I will try to show that Assumption 1 is true of a certain class of cases involving anaphoric "it." Given this, I will make the claim that the formation of anaphoric pronouns should be a single unified process: if Assumption 1 is true for some anaphoric pronouns, then it is true for all of them. The basis for this claim is Occam's razor: why should there be two processes of rather different sorts to do the same job? I will discuss this in somewhat more detail below.

3. Negatives

Before going on to our discussion of anaphoric pronouns, let us consider a rule of English called "*not*-transportation," which will provide indirect, but crucial, evidence concerning the nature of pronominalization. "*Not*-transportation" is the rule that relates (7) and (8):

(7)   I believe that John isn't coming.
(8)   I don't believe that John is coming.

Sentence (8) is ambiguous. It can be merely an ordinary negative, meaning "it is not so that I believe that John is coming." This is simply a denial of the sentence "I believe that John is coming" and does not commit the speaker to any belief at all. But (8) has another meaning — that of (7). It is the latter sense of (8) that we are concerned with. Here the negative appears overtly in the main clause, though logically it is the embedded clause that is negated.

It was proposed by Fillmore (1963) that the latter sense of (8) is derived from the same structure as that which underlies (7), and that the rule of *not*-transportation moves the negative from the embedded clause into the main clause. There is rather strong evidence, as Klima (1964) has pointed out, to indicate that Fillmore's analysis is correct. The evidence involves the possibility of using *until*-adverbials with punctual verbs such as "leave." These adverbials can occur with "leave" only if a negative is present.

(9)   * John will leave until tomorrow.
(10)   John won't leave until tomorrow.

This fact allows us to make two predictions. The first concerns verbs that do not undergo *not*-transportation, that is, those that do not occur in synonymous sentence pairs like (7) and (8). This includes most verbs that take object complements, for example, *state, claim, hope, know,* etc. Sentences (11) and (12) are not synonymous:

(11)   I claimed that John wasn't coming.
(12)   I didn't claim that John was coming.

Under Fillmore's analysis, we would maintain that the *not* of (11) cannot move up from the embedded sentence to the main sentence, and that the *not* of (12) has only one deep structure source, in the main sentence rather than in the embedded sentence. Now consider (13):

(13)   I claimed that John wouldn't leave until tomorrow.

We would predict that the *not* in (13) cannot move to the main sentence, and that (14) would therefore be ungrammatical:

(14)   * I didn't claim that John would leave until tomorrow.

Sentence (14) is ungrammatical: it contains the ungrammatical sentence (9) embedded as the object of "claim." The negative element required to make "leave" modified by "until tomorrow" grammatical must be in the same sentence, and not in a higher sentence, as it is in (14).[4]

Our second prediction concerns the small class of verbs like *believe, expect, think, want,* etc., that do undergo *not*-transportation, that is, those that do occur in synonymous sentence pairs like (7) and (8). Consider (15):

(15) I believed that John wouldn't leave until tomorrow.

If Fillmore's analysis of (7) and (8) is correct, then we would expect that "not" in (15) would be able to undergo *not*-transportation and move from the embedded clause to the main clause. That is, (16) should be grammatical, which it is.

(16) I didn't believe that John would leave until tomorrow.

Note also that (16), unlike (8), is unambiguous. Sentence (16) cannot be understood as an ordinary negation, " * it is not so that I believed John would leave until tomorrow." This is impossible because the positive sentence " * I believed that John would leave until tomorrow" is ungrammatical. Thus, (16) can have only the meaning of (15), and the *not* of (16) must have originated in the embedded clause, not in the main clause.

Let us now return to anaphoric pronouns. Consider (17):

(17) Bill believed that John wouldn't leave until tomorrow, and I believed that John wouldn't leave until tomorrow too.

Sentence (17) is grammatical, though its style is rather infelicitous, because of the repeated noun phrase complement "that John wouldn't leave until tomorrow." Sentence (17) can be paraphrased without repetition if one substitutes the anaphoric pronoun "it" for the second occurrence of the noun phrase complement.

(18) Bill believed that John wouldn't leave until tomorrow, and I believed it too.

As before, we will ask whether the "it" in (18) occurs as such in deep structure, as would follow from Assumption 2, or whether the "it" is derived from a full underlying noun phrase complement, according to Assumption 1. That is, the deep structure of (17) is essentially that of (19).

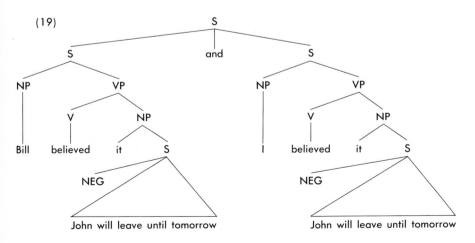

(19)

Under Assumption 1, (19) would also be the deep structure of (18). Under Assumption 2, however, the deep structure of (18) would be (20).

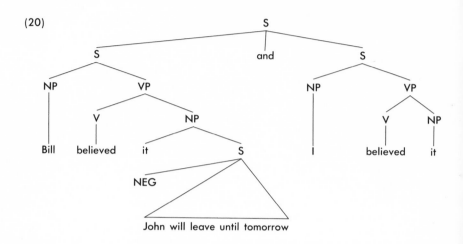

(20)

So far we have presented no evidence to decide between Assumption 1 and Assumption 2. Consider (21):

(21)   Bill didn't believe that John would leave until tomorrow, and I didn't believe that John would leave until tomorrow either.

Sentence (21) must have the same deep structure as (19). As we saw above, the occurrences of *not* in (21) cannot originate in the main clauses, but must originate in the embedded complement clauses, as shown in (19). Neither occurrence of *not* can originate in the main clause for the same reason that the occurrence of *not* in (16) could not originate in the main clause, but had to be moved out of the embedded clause. Now consider (22):

(22)   Bill did*n't* believe that John would leave until tomorrow, and I did*n't* believe it either.[5]

As in the case of (21), the *not* in the first half of the sentence cannot originate in the main clause, but must be moved there from the embedded clause. But what about the second occurrence of *not* in (22)? It is understood in the same way as the corresponding *not* in (21) and the *not* in the first half of (22). Since it cannot have originated in the main clause either, it must have been moved there by *not*-transportation from the embedded clause. But that means that there must have been an embedded clause in the second half of (22) at some point in its derivation. First the *not* moved into the main clause, and the remainder of the clause was deleted.

This explanation is possible under Assumption 1, which states that the embedded clause is there in deep structure. But such an explanation is not possible under Assumption 2 — if we continue to assume that a negative is to be analyzed as part of the sentence that it negates, that is, if we assume the analysis of (23).

(23)

Under Assumption 2, the rightmost S of (19) would not be present in deep structure, as in (20), and hence there would exist no S for the NEG to hop out of. Given our assumptions about the source of NEG, Assumption 2 could not explain the *not* in the second half of (22). Thus, (22) would appear to indicate that Assumption 1 was correct and Assumption 2 incorrect.

However, such a conclusion would depend crucially on the assumption that an analysis of negatives like that in (23) was correct. There are, of course, other possibilities that ought to be considered. For example, in symbolic logic, the negative is treated as a special sort of operator or predicate, external to the proposition it negates. One possible way of translating such a notion into syntactic analysis would be to have deep structures like (24).

(24)

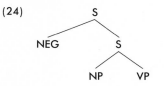

Another possibility would be to consider NEG not a special sort of element but an ordinary predicate, as in (25).

(25)

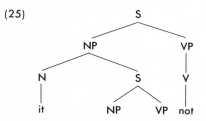

Such an analysis of negation would raise a considerable number of serious questions involving the details of working out such a proposal and the justification of such an analysis which are beyond the scope of this paper. For

our present discussion it will suffice to say that an analysis of negation something like (25) will allow us to save Assumption 2 in the face of the above
argument. Under such an analysis, the deep structure of (22) would be (26).

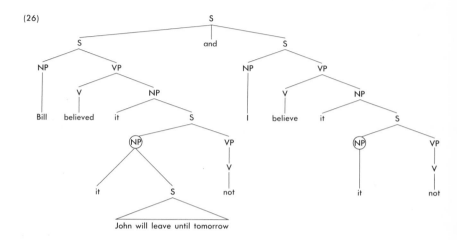

It is assumed that the two encircled noun phrases in (26) are coreferential;
that is, the encircled NP *it* on the right is the anaphoric pronoun that refers
back to the encircled NP on the left. Diagram (26) might then be a possible
deep structure for (22), with the two occurrences of *not* undergoing *not*-
transportation. If such an analysis can be worked out in detail, then Assumption 2 could be saved. But, as should be obvious, this would be a tricky
business. First, there are two occurrences of *it* on the right, and it is not
at all clear which one should be deleted, what the details of the rule should
be, and how such a rule might receive independent justification. Second,
suppose that *not*-transportation does not apply to (26). How could the resulting bad sentence be blocked? These are but some of the problems that arise
from the claim that (26) underlies (22). They are hard, but not necessarily
unsolvable. Our ability to maintain Assumption 2 depends on their being
solvable.

It ought to be mentioned that analyses like (24) and (25) have some
independent support. Consider (27) (pointed out by N. Chomsky) and (28)
(pointed out by W. Browne):

(27)   John didn't marry Mary, although the fortune teller had predicted *it*
       (that John *would* marry Mary).
(28)   It is believed that Sally is not cruel to animals, but I wouldn't put
       it past her (that Sally *is* cruel to animals).

In both cases there is a negative sentence on the left side and an anaphoric *it* on the right side which refers back not to the negative sentence, but to the *positive* sentence corresponding to the negative sentence. In proposals like (24) and (25), the positive proposition is separated from the element which negates it, and so it becomes possible for anaphoric pronouns to refer back to the proposition without the negative. In analyses like (23), where the negative is part of the sentence that it negates, this is not possible. For example, under Assumption 1, (27) would have the deep structure of (29).

(29)

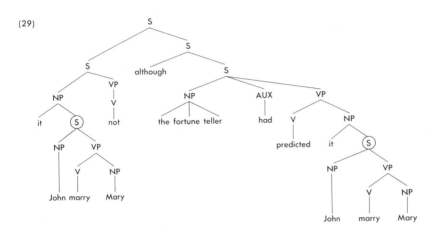

The encircled S on the right is identical to the encircled S on the left. The S on the right will delete by S-deletion. If one makes Assumption 2, then the tree above, minus the encircled S on the right, will be the deep structure of (27), and the *it* following *predicted* will be coreferential with the noun phrase [$_{NP}$ it [$_{S}$ John marry Mary $_{S}$] $_{NP}$].

It should be noted in passing that in accepting (25) as a deep structure for negative sentences, one would be making the claim that an anaphoric *it* may refer to the positive version of a negative sentence [as in (27) and (28)], but not to the negative version of a positive sentence. So far as I know this is correct.

Thus far, we have shown that if the *not*-transportation arguments are correct, then either

(30)   a. Assumption 1 is correct for anaphoric "it."

or

b. Negatives appear in deep structure as in (25).

4. Locative and Time Adverbs

From (30a) it follows that whenever one finds an anaphoric "it" of the sort discussed above, the deep structure source of that "it" is a noun phrase of the form

(31)

In the process of pronominalization, the S is deleted under identity with another S elsewhere in the sentence.

Given this assumption, we can derive some rather startling consequences. Consider (32):

(32)   Goldwater won in the West.

In traditional grammar as well as in most transformational studies, (32) would be analyzed essentially as in (33):

(33)

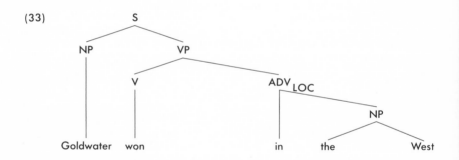

That is, it is generally assumed that "in the West" is a locative adverb modifying "won" and that "won in the West" forms a single deep structure constituent. Now consider (34):

(34)   Goldwater won in the West, but *it* didn't happen in the East.

The "it" in (34) must come from an underlying NP of the form

(35)

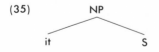

What is the S in (35)? Note that it cannot be "Goldwater won in the West," since the meaning would be wrong — something like that of "Goldwater's

victory in the West didn't happen in the East." (34) does not contain any such strange meaning. The "it" in (34) simply refers to "Goldwater's winning," which means that the S in (35) can only be "Goldwater won." Thus the underlying structure of (34) must be something like (36).

(36)

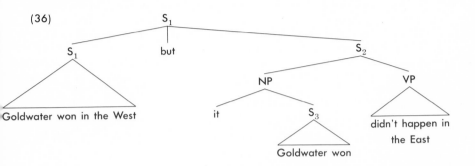

We know that S_3 is deleted in the process of pronominalization and we also know that it can be deleted only if it is identical with some other S elsewhere in (36). The only other occurrence of "Goldwater won" in (36) is in S_1. This means that "Goldwater won" in S_1 *must itself be an S* — in order for S_3 to delete under identity with it. Thus, (36), filled in somewhat more precisely, must have at least the structure of (37).

(37)

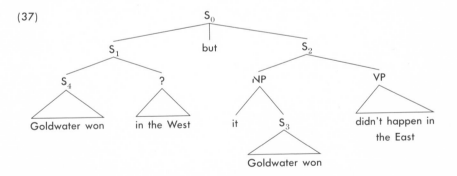

But if "Goldwater won" is an S in S_1, then the analysis in (33) must be grossly wrong. In (33), "Goldwater won" is not even a constituent, much less an S. Thus, if our line of reasoning is correct, locative adverbs like "in the West" do not occur in the same VP constituents as the verbs that they modify in underlying structure. Perhaps it is inappropriate to speak of a locative adverbial modifying a verb; logically, it "modifies" an event, which is specified by a full sentence (in this case, "Goldwater won"). If something like (37) is correct, then locative adverbs are not part of the sentences they modify in deep structure.

Note that our result holds not only for the particular locative adverbial in (37), but for the full range of such adverbials. For example,

(38) a. A Brink's truck was robbed outside of town, but it could never have happened within the city limits.
  b. John proposed to Mary by the river, although everyone had guessed that it would happen indoors.
  c. The train exploded near Mexico City, although the assassins had planned for it to happen at the border.

Moreover, similar results can be obtained for time adverbials.

(39) a. Goldwater won in 1964, but it won't happen in 1968.
  b. A Brink's truck was robbed in the evening, but it couldn't have happened during the daytime.
  c. John proposed to Mary in May, although everyone had guessed it wouldn't happen until August.
  d. The train exploded before noon, although the assassins had planned for it to happen at 3 o'clock.

By the same arguments that were used in the case of (34), we can show that the time adverbials in (39) are, like locative adverbials, outside of the sentence they modify in deep structure.

Let us now ask what it means to say that such adverbials are outside the sentences they modify. I would certainly not be willing to claim that the underlying structure of (32) is (40)

(40)

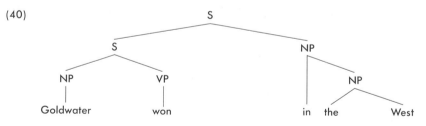

although that is all the structure that we have evidence for. My best guess is that the structure underlying (32) is something like (41):

(41)

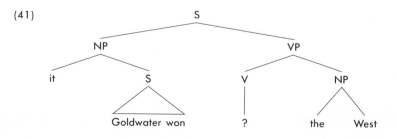

The verb in (41) indicated by "?" would have a meaning something like "took place in" or "was located in" and would be deleted by some as yet unknown rule. This rule would be specific to English and other similar languages, but would not apply in languages like Chinese, Javanese, and several West African languages, where the verb "to be" precedes locative adverbs. In those languages, a deep structure analysis like (41), with "be" replacing "?," seems to be well motivated on the basis of fairly obvious surface structure facts.

It ought to be noted that the fact that I do not know exactly what the structure of (41) looks like and the fact that I do not know what would be the rules involved in the deriving (32) from such a structure do not at all invalidate the line of reasoning that I have pursued. All that I have argued is that some such structure and some such rules must exist. Given (30a) and the principle of recoverability of deletion, the above results follow.[6]

5. *Conclusion*

If the line of reasoning we have pursued is correct, then we must conclude that either

(42)   a. Time and locative adverbs do not occur in deep structure as parts of the sentences that they modify. Rather they appear to be derived from predicates of other, "higher" sentences, as in (41).
       b. Negatives occur in deep structure outside of the sentences that they negate, perhaps as in (33).
       c. Both (42a) and (42b) are true.

Condition (42a) follows from Assumption 1 (for anaphoric "it"), and (42b) follows from Assumption 2.

Suppose Assumption 2 is correct and anaphoric pronouns occur in deep structures. Then there must be some semantic apparatus to indicate what these pronouns may refer to. A reasonable constraint on such would be (43):

(43)   Anaphoric pronouns may refer only to single constituents. (Perhaps only to NP constituents.)

Suppose we were to adopt Assumption 2 with condition (43). Consider (34):

(34)   Goldwater won in the West, but *it* didn't happen in the East.

Since "it" refers to "Goldwater won," condition (43) says that "Goldwater won" must be a single constituent (presumably an S) in (34). If locative adverbs are inside the sentences they modify, this is not possible. Thus it follows from Assumption 2 and condition (43) that locative adverbs are external to the sentences they modify. (The same case can be made for time adverbs.) Thus in order to disprove (42a) one must show *both* that Assumption 2 is right and that (43) is wrong.

If (42a) is correct, then the deep structures of English sentences will look more like those of the corresponding sentences in languages like Chinese, Javanese, etc., thus increasing the likelihood that a common set of deep structures for these languages can be found. At the same time, it would indicate that the supposed grammatical category *locative adverb* does not appear as such in the deep structures of English sentences and open to serious inquiry the question of whether such a category exists in the deep structure of any natural language. But no matter which of (42a), (42b), or (42c) is true, our results indicate that deep structures are somewhat more abstract, further removed from surface structures, than had previously been thought. Considering other recent results in transformational studies, this should hardly be surprising.[7]

NOTES

1. This work was supported in part by grant GN-1934 from the National Science Foundation to Harvard University.

2. See Lees and Klima (1963).

3. For discussions of identity of reference, see Katz and Postal (1964); Chomsky (1965); and Postal (1966*a*).

4. Dwight Bolinger has pointed out (personal communication) that *not*-transportation, if formulated as an optional transformation (as I have suggested), would not be meaning-preserving. Consider the following:

(a)   I don't think Bill left.
(b)   I think Bill didn't leave.

If one asks whether the speaker is more certain of his assertion in (a) or in (b), one must conclude that he is more certain in (b) and that, in (a), where *not*-transportation has taken place, he is somewhat uncertain. Thus the occurrence of *not*-transportation is correlated with some uncertainty on the part of the subject of *think*, or whichever verb happens to be present. This explains the observation by Paul and Carol Kiparsky in their paper *Fact* that *not*-transportation never occurs with factive verbs. Since it is presupposed that the subject of a factive verb knows that the complement of the verb is true, he cannot be uncertain about it. Consider

(c)   John regrets that Bill didn't leave.

It is presupposed in (c) that John knows that Bill didn't leave. Therefore, John can't be uncertain about it. If *not*-transportation indicates uncertainty, then, for strictly semantic reasons, the rule cannot apply with factive verbs.   .

It ought to be noted that Bolinger's observation does not affect our argument at all, since in sentences like (a) the negative still belongs logically to the embedded sentence, and, as (13) through (16) show, the negative is in the embedded sentence grammatically as well. Further grammatical evidence that there is a rule of *not*-transportation is provided by expressions like *lift a finger*, which require a negative in the same sentence in deep structure.

(d)   * John lifted a finger to help Bill.
(e)   John didn't lift a finger to help Bill.

With *lift a finger*, we get the same pattern as with *until tomorrow* in (13) through (16).

(f)   I claimed that John didn't lift a finger to help Bill.
(g)   * I didn't claim that John lifted a finger to help Bill.
(h)   I thought that John didn't lift a finger to help Bill.
(i)   I didn't think that John lifted a finger to help Bill.

And sentences like (22) show up as well:

(j)   Max did*n't* believe that John would lift a finger to help Bill, and I did*n't* believe
         it either.

It has been claimed by Jackendoff (1967) that there is no rule of *not*-transportation. Rather, the negative is introduced in deep structure just where it occurs in surface structure, and a rule of semantic interpretation associates the negative with the sentence that it logically negates. I would like to consider just what innovations in linguistic theory would be required to make such a proposal work.

Jackendoff claimed that one could predict from the meaning of a verb whether or not it participated in *not*-transportation. In other words, Jackendoff claimed that the *not*-transportation verbs formed a natural semantic class (or a disjunction of such classes), and that it would never be the case that there would exist two synonyms such that one participated in *not*-transportation and the other did not. Since Jackendoff's claim involves meaning, it would necessarily be a cross-linguistic claim, involving synonyms in different languages.

These claims are simply false. There are only a handful of verbs in English that undergo *not*-transportation: *think, want, believe, likely, seem, reckon, guess, expect, suppose, anticipate*, and perhaps a few others. The class differs from person to person. A number of people I've spoken to do not have *reckon, guess*, or *anticipate* as *not*-transportation verbs. This fact alone is sufficient to show that one cannot predict the ability to take *not*-transportation just from the meaning of the verb. Now consider individuals (and there are quite a number) for whom *expect* takes *not*-transportation but *anticipate* does not. If the rule refers to natural semantic classes, then there will have to be a natural semantic class that includes *expect* but excludes *anticipate*. The same is true of *expect* and *guess*, of *guess* and *suppose*, and of *guess* and *anticipate*. To show that this is possible, one would have to take sentences like

(k)   I expect that Bill will leave.
(l)   I guess that Bill will leave.
(m)   I anticipate that Bill will leave.
(n)   I suppose that Bill will leave.

and show that any one of them can be true while the others are false. I doubt that this is possible.

Similarly, *want* is a *not*-transportation verb, while *desire* is not.

(n)   I don't want you to lift a finger to help Bill.
(o)   * I don't desire that you lift a finger to help Bill.

Jackendoff's proposal would require that *want* be included in a natural semantic class, from which *desire* is excluded. To show this, one would have to consider sentences like

(p)   I want Bill to leave
(q)   I desire that Bill leave.

and show that one can be true while the other is false. This seems unlikely.

There are cross-linguistic counterexamples to Jackendoff's hypothesis as well. In German, *hoffen* is a *not*-transportation verb, while *hope* in English is not one.

What these examples show is that one cannot predict from the meaning of a verb whether or not it will take *not*-transportation. This means that if the phenomenon is to be handled by a rule of semantic interpretation, the rule will have to have exceptions; hence a theory of exceptions for semantic rules must be added to the theory of grammar. Moreover, since *not*-transportation applies only to a handful of irregular verbs and adjectives, and not to the mass of regular cases, the theory of semantic exceptions would have to permit minor semantic rules. Thus, the exception apparatus for syntax would have to be duplicated for semantic rules. I know of no independent motivation for this apparatus in semantics.

Even if we were to accept such a revision of semantic theory, Jackendoff's proposal would require even further drastic revisions in the theory of grammar. This follows from the fact that the *not* can occur indefinitely far away from the verb it negates, so long as each of the intervening verbs may take *not*-transportation (i.e., *believe*, *want*, *think*, etc.). Consider the following:

(a) I believe that John wants Bill *not* to lift a finger to help Irv.
(b) I believe that John doesn*'t* want Bill to lift a finger to help Irv.
(c) I do*n't* believe that John wants Bill to lift a finger to help Irv.

If *not*-transportation is a syntactic rule, then it can apply cyclically, moving the *not* step by step up the tree. However, if *not*-transportation is to be handled by a rule of semantic interpretation, then the rule must apply anticyclically, working its way down the tree and checking at each step for the presence of the appropriate type of lexical exception. Thus, the concept of an anticyclical semantic rule would have to be introduced into semantic theory. There is no independent motivation that I know of for such an addition to semantic theory.

Still, the facts require an even more drastic revision of the theory of grammar. All known selectional restrictions on the occurrence of lexical items are finite in scope. Usually they apply in the same sentence (subject–verb and verb–object selections) and sometimes one sentence away (verb–verb selections; i.e., *force* requires an activity verb in its complement). If *not*-transportation is a syntactic rule, then this can be maintained for cases like X, where *lift a finger* would require that a negative be present in the same sentence in deep structure. The negative could then be moved away by successive application of *not*-transportation. However, Jackendoff's proposal requires that a negative be present somewhere, perhaps indefinitely far away, for *lift a finger* to be selected. Thus Jackendoff's proposal requires that selectional restrictions extend over an indefinitely large stretch of tree. But that is the least of the difficulties, since *lift a finger* requires not only that there exist a negative commanding it somewhere up the tree, but also that there exist, between the negative and *lift a finger*, a continuous sequence of *not*-transportation verbs, each commanding *lift a finger*. Since *not*-transportation verbs must be represented as lexical exceptions to a minor semantic rule, the selectional apparatus must refer to indefinitely long sequences of lexical exceptions of a particular sort. Again there is no independent reason for supposing that such a selectional apparatus exists.

To make Jackendoff's proposal work, the following apparatus must be introduced into the theory of grammar:

1. A theory of exceptions and minor rules for rules of semantic interpretation.

2. Anticyclical semantic rules.

3. Selectional restrictions of indefinite scope.

4. The use of indefinitely long chains of lexical exceptions in the statement of selectional restrictions.

Since none of these has any independent motivation, there is no good reason to believe that they exist. However, there are some very good reasons to believe that they do not exist.

(1)   The theory of exceptions necessary for just this one semantic rule would be duplicating the exception apparatus in syntax, which is justified on independent grounds.

(2)   Anticyclic semantic rules have the same effect as cyclic syntactic rules. The cycle is independently motivated for syntax, so inventing anticyclic semantic rules for this one case is again unnecessary duplication of theoretical apparatus.

(3)   Allowing selectional restrictions to range indefinitely vastly increases the power of the theory of grammar and predicts that there should be other such selections of indefinite scope. Until there is independent evidence for this, there is every reason to try to maintain that selectional restrictions are finite in scope.

(4)   This shows that there would be a generalization missed in Jackendoff's proposal. According to this proposal, it is an accidental fact that *lift a finger* would require the presence of *not* **and** the presence of lexical exceptions to the semantic equivalent of *not*-transportation. Why this rule and not some other? Surely this is no accident. Moreover, Jackendoff's proposal would require that the same lexical exceptions be mentioned twice in accounting for sentences with *lift a finger*, once to permit the selectional restrictions and once to permit the operation of the semantic rule. Again, something is being missed. Lexical exceptions should be employed only in permitting the operation of the appropriate rule. They shouldn't have to be duplicated in selectional restrictions.

From this, I conclude that *not*-transportation is a syntactic phenomenon, and that it is handled by a syntactic rule, as was claimed by Fillmore.

So it is apparent that *not*-transportation is a syntactic rule, which is all that our argument requires. However, Bolinger's observation does have other important consequences for syntactic theory. *Not*-transportation is a syntactic rule that is correlated with a fixed meaning. In the Katz–Postal and *Aspects* theories, the deep structure would have contained a syntactic representation of this meaning — perhaps an arbitrary marker, U, bearing the appropriate meaning and restricted in occurrence to *not*-transportation verbs. The rule could then be made obligatory, triggered by the presence of U. This solution is obviously a fudge; there is no independent motivation for hypothesizing U in just such cases. If we reject such an *ad hoc* solution, there are just two alternatives that I can think of:

(a)   **The rule is obligatory and sensitive to semantic information.**

or

(b)   **The rule is optional and changes meaning if it applies.**

My guess is that (a) is correct, since there is other evidence that syntactic rules must take semantic information into account.

The phenomenon of *not*-transportation is relevant to a number of issues in syntactic theory, and certainly deserves further study. Any such investigation should, however, take into account a further observation of Bolinger's. In the case of English *not*-transportation, we find the following situation:

(I)	Certainty	Negative appears with the verb it negates.
	Uncertainty	Negative is moved away from the verb it negates.

However, there is another logical possibility that might occur in some natural language:

(II)	Uncertainty	Negative appears with the verb it negates.
	Certainty	Negative is moved away from the verb it negates.

Any of the theories that we have mentioned that can describe the situation in (I) can also describe the situation in (II). According to these theories, it is an *accidental* fact of English that (I) occurs and that (II) does not. All of these theories would predict that if *not*-transportation occurred in some other language, one would have just as much reason to expect it to be correlated with certainty (II) as with uncertainty (I). Bolinger suggests that this is wrong, that it is not at all an accident that the movement of the negative away from the verb it negates represents uncertainty. Rather, he says, the movement of the negative away from its normal position is a natural way of softening a negative statement. In accordance with this view, (I) would be a very natural phenomenon and (II) would be impossible (or at least highly un-natural). I do not know if there are any languages where (II) occurs, but my intuition (for what it is worth) tells me Bolinger is right. If he is, then none of the theories of grammar that I know of, or can even imagine, can describe his observation — and to that extent all present theories of syntax are inadequate.

5. In the examples that we have given so far, *not*-transportation has applied either in both of the conjoined sentences, or in neither. However, there is no mechanism in our present version of the rule to keep it from applying to one sentence but not the other. Thus *not*-transportation could apply in the first conjunct, but not the second, and vice versa. However, if this happens, then pronominalization with "it" becomes impossible.

(a) * Bill believed that John wouldn't come until tomorrow and I didn't believe it either
(b) * Bill didn't believe that John would come until tomorrow and I believed it too.

How can we account for this? Note that in order to account for (22) we must assume that *not*-transportation must apply before the formation of the anaphoric pronoun. The latter rule can apply only if the two noun phrases in question (the objects of "believe") are identical. They will be identical only if *not*-transportation has applied in both or in neither. Otherwise, there will be a *not* present in one that is absent in the other; the two noun phrases will not be identical, and the formation of the anaphoric pronoun will be blocked. The resulting sentences, without pronominalization, would be:

(c) ? Bill believed that John wouldn't come until tomorrow, and I didn't believe he would come until then either.
(d) ? Bill didn't believe that John would come until tomorrow, and I also believed that he wouldn't come until then.

These are stylistically awkward because of the repetition involved and the lack of parallelism, but they are considerably better than (a) and (b).

6. For further results along a similar line of reasoning, see Lakoff and Ross, in preparation.

7. Between the time this paper was submitted to the publisher (September 1967) and the time of editing (June 1969), there have been a number of discoveries which have a bearing on the topic discussed in this paper. First, Robin Lakoff (1969) has found an even stronger argument for the existence of a syntactic rule of *not*-transportation. The argument is based on tag-questions. With a positive declarative sentence one gets a negative tag and vice versa.

(a) The Knicks won, didn't they?
(b) The Knicks didn't win, did they?

With most verbs that take complements, the tag goes on the main verb, not the verb inside the complement.

(c) John knows that the Knicks didn't win, $\left\{ \begin{array}{l} \text{doesn't he?} \\ \text{* did they?} \end{array} \right\}$

(d) John doesn't know that the Knicks won, $\left\{ \begin{array}{l} \text{does he?} \\ \text{* didn't they?} \end{array} \right\}$

When the main verb, however, has the meaning of "suppose" and is used performatively, that is, with a first person subject, present tense, nonrepetitively, then the tag goes with the verb in the complement, not the main verb.

(e) I suppose the Knicks didn't win, $\left\{ \begin{array}{l} \text{* don't I?} \\ \text{did they?} \end{array} \right\}$

(f) I suppose the Knicks won, $\left\{ \begin{array}{l} \text{* don't I?} \\ \text{didn't they?} \end{array} \right\}$

Mrs. Lakoff now considers sentences like (g):

(g) I don't suppose the Knicks won, did they?

She observes that the tag goes with the verb of the complement, as in (e); note the plural *they*. However, the tag is positive even though *won* has no overt negative. Thus, at the time that the rule of tag-formation applied, the negative must have been on *win*, not on *suppose*; the negative must have been moved up to *suppose* by a subsequent application of the rule of *not*-transportation. This is corroborated by the fact that *suppose* occurs in (g) in a performative usage, but since performative utterances are not subject to logical negation, the *not* associated with *suppose* in (g) could not have been there in underlying structure.

Since this paper was submitted, a tremendous amount of work has been done in the area of pronominalization, some of which vitiates some of the minor arguments in this paper. For example, it was assumed, since anaphoric pronouns in general obey the same constraints on occurrence, that they were therefore to be accounted for by a single unified process. This assumption was made because it was also assumed that such constraints were to be stated as part of some sort of transformational rule. However, it is demonstrated in Lakoff (1968) that the pronominalization constraints discussed by Langacker and Ross are not part of a rule, but are rather output conditions. Thus, it would no longer follow that Assumptions 1 and 2 would have to be mutually exclusive, and it might be possible that some pronouns are derived by deletion rules, while others are present in underlying structure. In fact, strong evidence is presented in Lakoff (1969) that pronouns indicating identity of sense must be derived by deletion rules, while those indicating identity of reference must not. Since the anaphoric *it* discussed in the bulk of this paper is of the identity of sense sort and must be derived by a deletion rule, the main argument of this paper is not vitiated by this result.

Chomsky (1969) has attempted to provide a *reductio* argument against the main conclusions of this paper by arguing that if (38) and (39) show that locative and time adverbs are from "higher" sentences, then (h) must show that direct objects are from "higher" sentences.

(h)   Irving refused the peanut butter sandwich, but *it* wouldn't have happened with a bagel.

This is a fallacious argument. Recall that Ross (1967) points out that in rules deleting constituents under identity, pronouns commanded by their antecedents are ignored in the definition of "identical constituents." Ross discusses sentences like (i).

(i)   Having the police after him bothered John, but *it* would never bother Mary.

As Ross points out, the *it* in (i) must be derived from "having the police after *her*." Since *Mary* commands *her* prior to the deletion, the difference between *him* and *her* is ignored by the general principle cited above. For a detailed discussion of such cases, see Lakoff (1969). Given Ross's observation, it is clear what is going on in (h). Prior to the deletion rule, the sentence on the right of (h) would be of the form: [$_{NP}$ *it* [$_S$ *Irving refuse it*$_i$]] *would never happen with a bagel*$_i$. Since *bagel*$_i$ commands *it*$_i$, *it*$_i$ is ignored in checking for identity of constituents.

One might then ask the following question: Why not say that in sentences like (j)

(j)   Nixon won in 1968, but *it* won't happen in 1972.

the sentence on the right is derived from an underlying: [$_{NP}$ *it* [$_S$ *Nixon win then*$_i$]]*won't happen in 1972*$_i$? The answer, I think, lies in a very interesting construction pointed out to me by Ross (personal communication).

(k)   Noon found Harry making love to Zelda.
(l)   1969 found Richard Nixon in the White House.
(m)   Opening day found Amos Otis the third baseman of the Mets.

Found functions here as a two-place predicate relating a time expression (its subject) to a complement sentence (its object). Thus, (k) would be derived from a structure of the form (n).

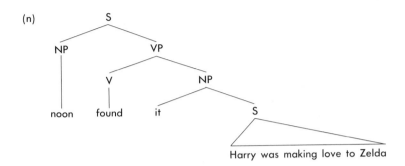

(n)

Found requires that subject-raising apply and that its complement contain the copula. Thus, *found* seems to be an overt occurrence of the predicate hypothesized above for ordinary occurrences of time adverbs, namely, one relating a time expression to a complement sentence. The only difference would be one of order, which could be accounted for if the rule of subject–object inversion had applied to *found*.

Now note that the complement sentence in the object of *found* cannot contain time adverbs, either in full or anaphoric form.

(o) * Noon found Harry making love to Zelda at 12 o'clock.
(p) * Noon found Harry making love to Zelda then.

This is natural, since the function of *found* is to specify the time reference for its complement sentence. If *found* is an overt manifestation of the abstract predicate hypothesized above, then sentences like (o) and (p) would rule out the possibility of an embedded time adverb in such cases.

It should be noted in addition that (k) is synonymous to (q).

(q) Harry was making love to Zelda at noon.

Thus, we have the situation where a time expression which shows up on the surface as an adverb in (q) appears in a synonymous sentence as a superficial subject. Under any analysis, *noon* in (k) will have to be either an underlying subject or underlying object of *found*, depending on whether or not one assumes subject–object inversion. Thus, if semantic representations preserve the grammatical relations found in deep structure, *noon* in (q) will have to enter into the same grammatical relations as it does in (k) — namely, subject or object.

Where Do Noun Phrases Come From?[1]

11

JAMES D. McCAWLEY

1. Background

The contents of this paper are clearly transformational grammar although not so clearly generative grammar. In discussing English I will be treating the English language not as a class of sentences but as a code which relates messages (semantic representations) to their encoded forms (the surface form of sentences). The possibility or impossibility of a given (surface form of a) sentence depends on two quite separate factors, namely, the details of the code and the restrictions on the possible messages: a surface structure is possible only if there is a message which the code pairs with it. This paper is transformational grammar in that I maintain that the code has roughly the form of the "transformational component" of a grammar as discussed in Chomsky (1965), i.e., that the "encoding" of a message can be regarded as involving a series of intermediate stages, each obtained by applying some transformation to the preceding stage. It is not obviously generative grammar, in that to a certain extent I leave open the question of what a "possible message" is.

There are several conceivable kinds of constraints on "possible message." One kind of constraint relates to what might be called the "logical well-formedness" of the message. For example, *or* is a predicate which may be combined with two or more propositions. However, *or* by itself is not a well-formed message, nor is *or* combined with a single proposition, nor is *or* combined with things which are not all propositions; the following loosely represented structures are thus not "possible messages":

> or
> or (John is a fool)
> or (China is industrializing rapidly; the Pope)

These constraints on "possible message" correspond roughly to what is called "strict subcategorization" in Chomsky (1965).

SOURCE: Part of this paper was originally published in McCawley (1967).

In Chomsky (1965), another kind of constraint, called "selectional restrictions," which are supposed to exclude sentences such as

(1)   * That idea is green with orange stripes.

is discussed. While Chomsky treats "selectional restrictions" as constraints on his level of "deep structure" (which I reject in this study), they can equally well be considered as constraints on the set of possible messages, a point of view which is implicit [though not unambiguously; cf. McCawley (1968)] in Katz and Fodor (1963). Both Chomsky (1965) and Katz and Fodor (1963) treat these constraints as requirements imposed by a verb or adjective whereby a noun phrase[2] is required to possess some property such as "animate" or "physical object."

I see no reason for believing that selectional restrictions have any independent status in linguistics. All of the selectional restrictions which I have seen cited either are completely predictable from the meaning of the lexical item in question or are not in fact real restrictions. Moreover, selectional restrictions appear to divide into two types, of which only one can really be said to constitute a restriction on "possible messages."

As regards the status of selectional restrictions as an independent factor in language, if selectional restrictions were not predictable from the meanings of the lexical items in question, then it would be possible to have different lexical items which had the same meaning but differed in selectional restrictions. While a number of examples of such lexical items have been proposed, in each case the difference between the lexical items has turned out actually to be one of meaning rather than one of selectional restriction. For example, one might gloss the Japanese verb *kaburu* as *put on, said of a hat; hameru* as *put on, said of gloves; haku* as *put on, said of footwear;* etc., and assert that these verbs have the same meaning but differ in selectional restrictions. However, such a description is incorrect, since the verbs in fact refer to the quite different actions involved in putting on the articles of clothing involved, as is demonstrated by the fact that if one puts on an article of clothing in an unnatural manner (e.g., puts a pair of socks on his hands, uses a necktie to hold up his trousers, etc.), the choice of a verb is determined not by the article of clothing involved but by the manner in which it is put on, e.g., covering one's head with a pair of gloves would be described by *kaburu*, not by *hameru*. Similarly, the English verbs *kick, slap,* and *punch* have been defined by some as *strike with the foot, strike with the open hand,* and *strike with the fist,* suggesting that they have the same meaning but different selectional restrictions. However, John Robert Ross (personal communication) has observed that in the bizarre situation in which a person had been subjected to surgery in which his hands and feet were cut off and then grafted on to his ankles and wrists respectively, it would be perfectly correct to speak of that person as kicking someone with his fist or slapping someone with his foot, which implies that the verbs refer to the specific motion which the organ in question performs rather than being simply contextual variants of strike.[3] Moreover, it appears incorrect to regard many so-called "selectional violations" as not corresponding to possible messages, since many of them can turn up in reports of dreams:

(2)   I dreamed that my toothbrush was pregnant.
(3)   I dreamed that I poured my mother into an inkwell.
(4)   I dreamed that I was a proton and fell in love with a shapely green-and-orange-striped electron.

or in reports of the beliefs of other persons:[4]

(5)   John thinks that electrons are green with orange stripes.
(6)   John thinks that his toothbrush is trying to kill him.
(7)   John thinks that ideas are physical objects and are green with orange stripes.

or in the speech of psychotics. While one might suggest that a paranoid who says things like

(8)   My toothbrush is alive and is trying to kill me.

has different selectional restrictions from a normal person, it is pointless to do so, since the difference in "selectional restriction" will correspond exactly to a difference in beliefs as to one's relationship with inanimate objects; a person who utters sentences such as (8) should be referred to a psychiatric clinic, not to a remedial English course.

I thus conclude that in many sentences which various authors have wanted to exclude as "selectional violations," the peculiarity of the sentence is completely a consequence of extra-linguistic factors and that the sentence indeed corresponds to a "message" which a person will have occasion to express under appropriate circumstances. On the other hand, there are many selectional restrictions which must be considered as constraints on "possible messages." For example, the constraint that the complement of the progressive *be* must be headed by a nonstative verb may not be violated even in sentences such as

(9)   * I dreamed that John was knowing the answer.
(10)   * Arthur believes that John is knowing the answer.

I am at present unprepared to state what range of selectional restrictions constitute legitimate restrictions on "possible message."

2. Semantic Representation

In referring above to the "logical well-formedness" of a semantic representation, I used the terms "proposition" and "predicate" in the sense in which they are used in symbolic logic. I will in fact argue that symbolic logic, subject to certain modifications, provides an appropriate system for semantic representation within the framework of transformational grammar. I thus hold that the much-criticized title, *The Laws of Thought,* which George Boole (1840) gave to the first work on symbolic logic, is actually much more appropriate than has generally been thought the case.

Since the representations of symbolic logic appear at first glance to be of a quite different formal nature from the labeled trees which constitute syntactic representation, it might appear that the processes which link semantic and surface syntactic representation would divide into two separate systems, a system of "semantic rules" which operate on representations of the one kind and a system of "syntactic rules" which operate on representations of the other kind, with the two kinds of representation meeting at a "level" corresponding to what Chomsky calls "deep structure." However, Lakoff[5] has pointed out that the difference in formal nature between syntactic and semantic representation is only apparent. Lakoff observes that some of the traditional categories of symbolic logic are reducible to others, e.g., quantifiers can be considered as two-place predicates, one place corresponding to a set and the other to a propositional function, and that [as shown by recent work of Lakoff (1965), Bach (1968), and others] only a small inventory of syntactic categories functions in the "deeper" stages of the "derivational history" of sentences. Many syntactic categories are "derived" rather than basic; for example, most prepositions originate as parts of verbs; prior to a transformation which adjoins the "prepositional" part of a verb to a noun phrase, a verb-plus-PrepP combination has the form verb-plus-NP. Likewise, many category differences which had figured in previous analyses have turned out to hinge merely on whether certain lexical items do or do not "trigger" certain transformations. For example, there is no need to set up the categories PredP, Aux, and Modal, which appear in Chomsky (1965): one can treat the various auxiliary elements as simply verbs[6] which [like the verbs *seem, appear,* etc.; cf. Rosenbaum (1967)] trigger a transformation of "VP-promotion," which detaches the VP from the embedded sentence and puts it after the verb in question (see Figure 1), and which have the additional peculiarity of being combined with the tense element by a very early transformation[7] and which are thus affected by various transformations which operate on the "topmost verb" of a sentence. Lakoff and Ross have argued in lectures at Harvard and MIT in Autumn 1966 that the only "deep" syntactic categories are *sentence, noun phrase, verb phrase, conjunction, noun,* and *verb,* and that all other traditionally recognized categories are special cases of these categories corresponding to the "triggering" of transformations by certain lexical terms. Bach (1968) then discovered some quite convincing arguments that the *noun–verb* distinction need not be part of this inventory of categories. He argues that all nouns originate in the predicate position of a relative clause construction (e.g., *the anthropologist* arises from a structure roughly paraphrasable as *the x who is an anthropologist*) and that the difference between nouns and verbs is that nouns but not verbs are subject to a transformation which

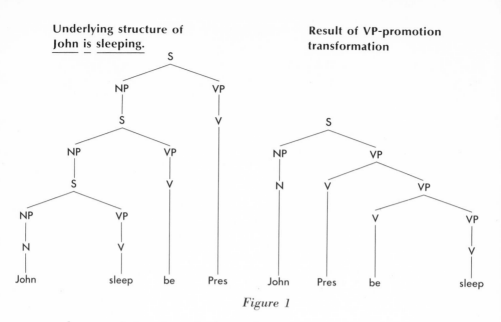

Figure 1

replaces a relative clause by its predicate element. At the conference mentioned in Note 5, Lakoff observed that the resulting inventory of categories (*sentence,* NP, VP *conjunction,* and *"contentive"* — the term introduced by Bach for the category containing nouns and verbs) matches in almost one-to-one fashion the categories of symbolic logic, as reinterpreted above, the only discrepancy being that the category VP has no corresponding category of symbolic logic, and that if one accepts Fillmore's proposal[8] that VP is not a "basic" category but a "derived" category which arises through a transformation in roughly the following manner:

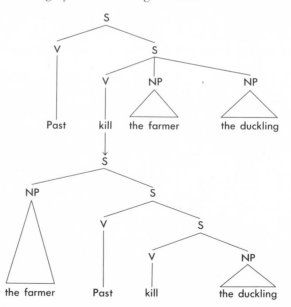

then not only is the correspondence between "deep" syntactic categories and the categories of symbolic logic exact, but the "phrase structure rules" governing the way in which the "deep" syntactic categories may be combined correspond exactly to the "formation rules" of symbolic logic, which define recursively the concept "well-formed formula," e.g., the phrase structure rule that a sentence consists of a contentive plus a sequence of noun phrases corresponds to the formation rule that a proposition consists of an n-place predicate plus an "argument" for each of the n places in the predicate.

Since I believe that the correspondence between syntactic categories and the categories of symbolic logic is slightly different from that proposed by Lakoff (in that I believe that a slightly different kind of symbolic logic is required for semantic representation), I will not go into the details of the correspondence which Lakoff set up. However, I observe that if such a correspondence is valid, then semantic representations can be considered to be objects of exactly the same formal nature as syntactic representations, i.e., trees whose nonterminal nodes are labeled by symbols interpretable as syntactic categories. One might object that the trees of syntax are different in formal nature from those which symbolic logic formulas may be interpreted as, in that the nodes of syntactic trees have a left-to-right ordering relation, whereas it is not clear that there is any ordering relation on the nodes of the trees which I am proposing as semantic representations. Whether this objection is correct depends on whether one holds that things which mean the same must have the same semantic representation or merely that there is an equivalence relation on semantic representations such that things which mean the same have equivalent semantic representations. The former position would, of course, imply that semantic representations cannot have ordered nodes, since

(11)   John and Harry are similar.
(12)   Harry and John are similar.

would have to have the same semantic representation, and that representation thus could not have the node corresponding to *John* preceding the node corresponding to *Harry* or vice versa. However, no evidence has as yet been adduced for accepting this position rather than the other one. Until such evidence is found, the question of the ordering of nodes gives no reason for believing semantic representation to be different in formal nature from syntactic representation. I will thus treat the elements of symbolic logic representations as having a linear order and assume that there are rules such as

(13) $p \text{ or } q \equiv q \text{ or } p$

which define an equivalence relation on these representations.

These considerations suggest that there is no natural breaking point between a "syntactic component" and a "semantic component" of a grammar such as the level of "deep structure" was envisioned to be in Chomsky (1965)[9] and imply that the burden of proof should be on those who assert that such a breaking point exists. In McCawley (in press), I present an argument that setting up a level of "deep structure" makes it impossible to treat as unitary processes certain phenomena which in fact are unitary processes, in particular, that the use of *respective* and *respectively* in English involves a phenomenon which can be stated as a single rule if there is no level of "deep structure," but must be divided into special cases, some of which correspond to "semantic projection rules" and others to "transformations," if a level of deep structure is accepted. Since the argument is rather involved, I will not reproduce it here but refer the reader to McCawley (1968) for details. The general outline of this argument for rejecting a level of "deep structure" is, of course, identical to that of Halle's (1959) celebrated argument for rejecting a "phonemic level."

3. Noun Phrases and Semantic Representation

The principal respect in which I maintain that symbolic logic as it has been represented hitherto is insufficient for the representation of meaning has to do with noun phrases. Consider the sentence

(14)   The man killed the woman.

If, following Chomsky (1965), one assumes each noun phrase occurrence in a syntactic representation to have attached to it an "index," which corresponds to the "intended referent" of that noun phrase occurrence, then the structures underlying (14) will have some index x_1 attached to *the man* and some index x_2 attached to *the woman*. The meaning of (14) will then involve the proposition that there exists some event of killing which took place prior to the speech act and involved x_1 as agent and x_2 as patient. In addition, it will involve the proposition that x_1 is a man and the proposition that x_2 is a woman. One might propose tying all of this information together into a formula such as[10]

(15) $\exists_y [\text{kill}_y (x_1, x_2) \wedge \text{past} (y)] \wedge \text{man} (x_1) \wedge \text{woman} (x_2)$

with perhaps some further modification to incorporate the meaning of *the*, which I have ignored. However, a representation such as (15), in which the meanings of the noun phrases appear as terms of a conjunction, does not correctly represent the meaning of the sentence. Note that if one says

(16)   I deny that the man killed the woman.

he is not denying (15). To deny a conjunction is to assert that at least one of the terms is false. However, in (16) the speaker is not merely asserting that one of the three terms of (15) is false but is asserting that the first term is false: it would not be correct to say (16) when one means that x_1 did in fact kill x_2 but that x_1 is not a man. Similarly, when one asks

(17)   Did the man kill the woman?

he is not asking whether the conjunction (15) is true (i.e., whether all three terms are true) but is assuming the truth of the second and third terms and asking whether the first term is true. It thus appears that in some sense the meanings of the expressions *the man* and *the woman* play a subordinate role in the meaning of (14).

To represent meaning correctly, symbolic logic will have to be supplemented by a way of representing this type of "subordination." The fact that no such device has been used in symbolic logic until now is a result of the fact that symbolic logic has largely been used as a device for representing the content of propositions of mathematics. This "subordination" relates to an important way in which the sentences of natural languages differ from the propositions involved in mathematics. In mathematics one enumerates certain objects which he will talk about, defines other objects in terms of these objects, and confines himself to a discussion of objects which have been either explicitly postulated or explicitly defined and have thus been assigned explicit names; these names are in effect proper nouns. However, one does not begin a conversation by giving a list of postulates and definitions. One simply starts talking about whatever topic he feels like talking about, and the bulk of the things which he talks about will be things for which either there is no proper noun (e.g., there is no proper noun *Glarf* meaning *the nail on the third toe of Lyndon Johnson's left foot*) or the speaker does not know any proper noun (e.g., one can use an expression such as *the pretty redhead who you were talking to in the coffeeshop yesterday* even if he does not know that girl's name). Moreover, people often talk about things which either do not exist or which they have identified incorrectly. Indices exist in the mind of the speaker rather than in the real world: they are conceptual entities which the individual speaker creates in interpreting his experience. Communication between different persons is possible because: 1. different individuals often correctly identify things in the world or make similar identifications, so that what one speaker says about an item in his mental picture of the universe will jibe with something in his hearer's mental picture of the universe; and 2. the noun phrases which speakers use fulfill a function roughly comparable to that of postulates and definitions in mathematics: they state properties which the speaker assumes to be possessed by the conceptual entities involved in what he is saying and are used chiefly to give the listener sufficient information to identify the things that the speaker is talking about. I conclude that it is necessary for the semantic representation of an utterance to separate the utterance into a "proposition" and a set of noun phrases, which provide the material used in identifying the indices of the "proposition," e.g.,

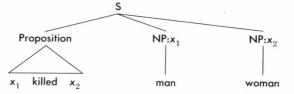

That representations such as the above play a role in syntax is shown by an interesting class of ambiguities, which appear to have escaped notice until recently. The sentence

(18)   John said that he had seen the woman who lives at 219 Main Street.

is appropriate either when John has said something such as *I saw the woman who lives at 219 Main Street* or when John has said something such as *I saw Mary Wilson* and the speaker is describing Mary Wilson as *the woman who lives at 219 Main Street*. This ambiguity is brought out by the fact that the sentence can be continued in two ways, each of which allows only one of the two interpretations:

(19)   . . . but the woman he saw really lives on Pine Street.
(20)   . . . but he doesn't know that she lives there.

similarly, while it is in principle possible that the sentence

(21)   John says that he didn't kiss the girl who he kissed.

is a report of John's having uttered the contradictory sentence *I didn't kiss the girl who I kissed*, it is more likely to involve a statement such as *I didn't kiss Nancy*, reported by a person who is convinced that John really did kiss Nancy; similarly with

(22)   John admits that he kissed the girl who he kissed.
(23)   John doesn't know that your sister is your sister.

These facts indicate that in certain kinds of embedded sentences the lexical material relating to noun phrases in the embedded sentence may be either part of the embedded sentence or part of the main sentence. But the proposal of the last paragraph makes such representations possible; for example, the two meanings of (18) can be represented as

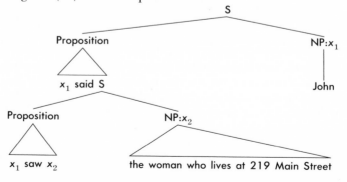

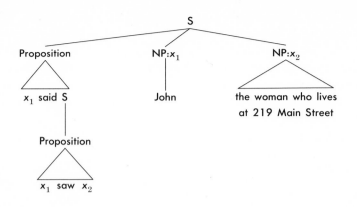

In the one case *the woman who lives at 219 Main Street* is part of what John is supposed to have said; in the other case it is not. Distinctions relating to what sentence a noun phrase is a constituent of are also involved in sentences such as

(24)   **Nancy wants to marry a Norwegian.**

which may mean either that there is a Norwegian who Nancy wants to marry or that Nancy wants her future husband to be Norwegian, even though she may not have yet found a Norwegian to marry. In the first case *a Norwegian* is a constituent of the main sentence, and in the second case it is a constituent of the sentence which is the underlying object of *want*. There is a similar ambiguity in

(25)   **John wants to find the man who killed Harry.**

In cases of multiple embeddings, it is possible to get multiple ambiguities; for example,

(26)   **John says that Nancy wants to marry a Norwegian.**

can be interpreted in these three ways: 1. there is a person who John says Nancy wants to marry and who the speaker describes as a Norwegian; 2. John says that Nancy wants to marry a certain person and John describes that person as a Norwegian; and 3. John says that Nancy wants her future husband to be Norwegian. It is difficult to see how these three senses could be assigned different deep structures unless those deep structures allowed noun phrases to occur separate from the propositions in which they are involved and to be constituents of sentences in which those propositions are embedded.[11]

The hypothesis that English sentences are derived from semantic representations of the form just discussed implies that English must have a transformation which substitutes each noun phrase for an occurrence of the corresponding index. In the case of the pair of diagrams given above, since there is only one occurrence of x_1 and only one occurrence of x_2, there is only one way in which this substitution could be performed, and in both cases (18) will result. However, if an index occurs several times in a semantic representation, it is sometimes possible to substitute the noun phrase in question for any of several occurrences of the index, thus giving rise to alternate superficial terms such as

(27)   After John left his apartment, he went to the bank.
(28)   After he left his apartment, John went to the bank.

If underlying structures such as the above are postulated, then pronominalization must be regarded in a quite different light than hitherto has been the case: pronominalization consists not of replacing repetitions of a noun phrase by pronouns but rather of determining which occurrence of an index will have the corresponding noun phrase substituted for it. Those occurrences of indices for which the substitution is not made are then filled by pronouns. Note, incidentally, that not all occurrences of an index are possible places to substitute the noun phrase: the sentence

(29)   After he left John's apartment, he went to the bank.

is not a variant of (27) (here the first *he* could refer only to someone other than John). Also, changes in word order affect the possibilities for substituting noun phrases: while

(30)   John went to the bank after he left his apartment.

is synonymous with (27),

(31)   He went to the bank after John left his apartment.

is not (here *he* cannot refer to John). Ross (in press) and Langacker (in press) have independently arrived at a characterization of the cases in which a pronoun may have a given noun phrase as its antecedent. Working from the assumption that pronouns are derived by a transformation which replaces a noun phrase by a pronoun if it is identical to some other noun phrase, they conclude that a noun phrase may trigger the pronominalization of an identical noun phrase either if it precedes it or if it follows it and is a constituent of a clause which the other noun phrase is in a clause subordinate to; for example, in (28) the pronoun *he* is in a clause subordinate to that of which the antecedent is a constituent. The effect of this constraint can be imposed on the rule proposed in this paper by saying that a noun phrase may be substituted for any occurrence of the corresponding index which either precedes or is in a "higher" sentence than all other occurrences of that index.

The conception of pronominalization which I propose here is supported by the following sentence, to which my attention was called by Susumu Kuno:

(32)   A boy who saw her kissed a girl who knew him.

Here *her* is to be interpreted as referring to the girl mentioned in the sentence and *him* to the boy mentioned in the sentence. Under the conception of pronominalization which derives a pronoun from a copy of the antecedent noun phrase, this sentence would have to have infinitely many sentences embedded in it: *her* would have to come from a copy of *a girl who knew him,* which would in turn have to come from a copy of *a girl who knew a boy who saw her,* etc., and both noun phrases would thus have to be derived from infinitely deep piles of relative clauses. However, with the conception of pronominalization which I propose here, this problem would vanish: the sentence would be derived from a structure roughly representable as

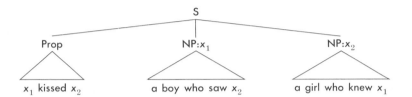

The substitution of noun phrases for the corresponding indices takes place sequentially. The process may begin either with the substitution for x_1 or the substitution for x_2; what results under the prop node will be respectively

(33)   A boy who saw x_2 kissed x_2.
(34) x_1 kissed a girl who knew x_1.

In (33), both occurrences of x_2 are possible places for the insertion of the remaining noun phrases; inserting it in place of the first occurrence of x_2 yields

(35)   A boy who saw a girl who knew x_1 (= him) kissed x_2 (= her).

and inserting it in place of the second occurrence of x_2 yields (32). In (34), only the first occurrence of x_1 meets the constraint given above, and substituting the noun phrase there yields (32). I call the reader's attention to the fact that there are thus two derivations which lead from the tree given above to the surface structure of (32), which may or may not be a defect of this account of pronominalization.

4. *Implications*

The above treatment of noun phrases necessitates some changes in the "base component" of a grammar: a distinction between "sentence" and "proposition" must now be drawn, a proposition is now a "contentive" plus a sequence of indices rather than a "contentive" plus a sequence of noun phrases, and an overall constraint on semantic representations must be imposed to insure that each representation contains neither too many nor too few noun phrases. An obvious way to formulate this constraint is to say that for each index in a semantic representation of a sentence there must be at most one corresponding noun phrase, and that that noun phrase must be directly dominated by an S node which dominates all occurrences of that index. Such a constraint is needed anyway to exclude the possibility of saying

(36)   Napoleon loves Bonaparte.

to mean that Napoleon loves himself [cf. Gruber (1965)]. The constraint can be sharpened somewhat. If a personal pronoun occurs in a sentence which does not contain an antecedent for that pronoun, then either the pronoun has an antecedent in some preceding sentence in the discourse (possibly a sentence uttered by someone other than the speaker) or the pronoun is used deictically (i.e., is a direct reference to someone or something physically present as the sentence is uttered) and is stressed and accompanied by a gesture. Since the semantic function of the gesture which accompanies a deictic pronoun is the same as that of the lexical material of an ordinary noun phrase, it is tempting to suggest that in these sentences the gesture *is* a noun phrase, that the substitution transformation of the last section attaches that noun phrase to one of the occurrences of the index in question, and that the phonetic reflex of a gesture is stress. As evidence in support of this treatment, I point out that a deictic pronoun may serve as the antecedent of a pronoun under exactly the same conditions under which an ordinary noun phrase may; for example, in

(37)   After he left the office, *he* (gesture) went to the bank.

the first *he* may have the second as its antecedent, but in

(38)   He went to the bank after *he* (gesture) left his apartment.

it may not. This suggests tightening the constraint to make it say that for every index in the semantic representation of a sentence there is exactly one corresponding noun phrase, except that a noun phrase may be omitted if there is a corresponding noun phrase in an earlier sentence of the discourse.

Regarding the distinction between "sentence" and "proposition," I observe that verbs differ as to whether they take a "sentence" or a "proposition" as complement, i.e., whether the complement may contain noun phrases as well as a proposition. The discussion in Section 3 implies that *say, deny,* and *want* take sentences rather than propositions as their complements. On the other hand, *seem* and *begin* take propositions as complements; note that the sentences

(39)   John began beating the man who lives at 219 Main Street.
(40)   John seems to know the man who lives at 219 Main Street.

do not admit the ambiguity which was noted in (18). However, if these sentences are embedded as the complements of verbs such as *say* and *want,* the result has the ambiguity in question:

(41) John wants to begin beating the man who lives at 219 Main Street.
(42) Harry says that John seems to know the man who lives at 219 Main Street.

Another interesting example is provided by the phenomenon of "extraposition" which is manifested in sentences such as

(43) It surprises me that John beats his wife.

as opposed to

(44) That John beats his wife surprises me.

Rosenbaum (1967) analyzes (43) and (44) as arising from the same deep structure.

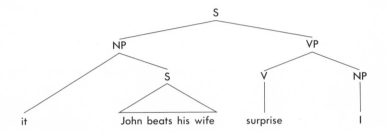

Rosenbaum sets up an optional transformation of extraposition, which moves certain embedded sentences to the end of the clause [thus giving rise to (43)], followed by a transformation which deletes *it* in a noun phrase of the form *it* + S, which will give rise to (44) if extraposition has not applied. While this approach generated the correct sentences and assigned them the correct structural descriptions, there remained a couple of respects in which it was unsatisfactory, namely: 1. it posited deep structures containing an element (the *it*) which contributed nothing to semantic interpretation; and 2. it failed to provide explanation of why *it* and not something else (perhaps *that* or *something*) should appear in extraposed sentences. Since *it* is what results from the pronominalization of a sentence:

(45) That John killed his wife bothers Frank, but it doesn't bother me.

the obvious place to look for an explanation of the *it* is pronominalization. Thus one might propose that extraposition simply reduplicates the embedded clause and that one copy of it is pronominalized.

That proposal is untenable due to the fact that if extraposition reduplicated a sentence, the resulting structure would not meet Ross and Langacker's condition for "backwards" pronominalization, so that only the copy and not the original could be pronominalized, which is the reverse of the actual state of affairs. However, within the framework proposed above, one can make a closely related proposal which will in fact explain the *it*. Specifically, note that the embedded sentences, being noun phrases, would have to originate in the same positions as items such as *John, your sister,* etc., and then substituted for the corresponding index. I know of no reason why extraposition would have to follow the noun phrase substitution transformation. If it in fact precedes it, then extraposition can be formulated as a transformation which optionally puts a "propositional" noun phrase at the end of a clause containing the corresponding index. If this option is not carried out, the proposition will be substituted for the index, thus yielding sentences such as (44), whereas if the option is carried out, that index will remain by itself and will thus be realized as a pronoun, giving sentences such as (43). The sentence

(46)   It surprises John that it bothers Frank that Harry killed his wife.

thus arises from the structure

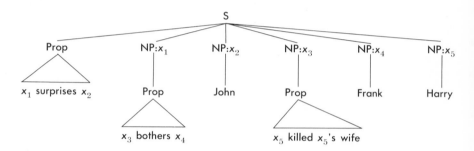

Note that "propositional" NPs can participate in the same ambiguities as can ordinary NPs.

(47)   John admits that Arthur was right.

may be a report of John's having said *I admit that Arthur was right* or his having said *I admit that Muhammed Ali is the greatest living American,* which the speaker describes as an admission that Arthur was right. Exactly how to represent these two structures is not completely clear to me at the moment; the following represents my current best guess:

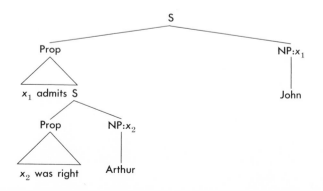

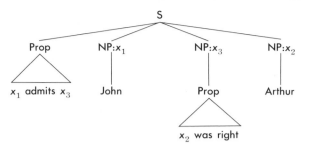

The proposal that sentences are derived from structures in which the adjuncts to "contentives" are indices rather than full noun phrases renders fairly trivial certain problems which would otherwise present considerable difficulty. For example, it is hard to see how the sentences

(48)   Everyone loves himself.
(49)   Everyone loves everyone.

could be assigned different "deep structures" and how the reflexivization transformation could be formulated without *ad hoc* restrictions if syntax were to start with "deep structures" in which full noun phrases like *everyone* rather than indices were to be the subjects, objects, etc., of verbs and reflexivization were contingent on noun phrases being identical. However, if sentences are derived from structures in which the adjuncts of "contentives" are simply indices, as is the case in semantic representation, (48) and (49) can be derived from the structures

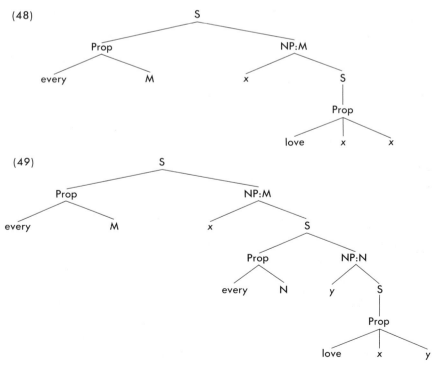

of which only the second is subject to reflexivization.[12] Moreover, this proposal explains why the sequence of words (49), when appropriately stressed, may mean either that everyone has the characteristic of loving everyone or that everyone has the characteristic that everyone loves him.[13] The former of these meanings corresponds to tree (49), and the latter to tree (50):

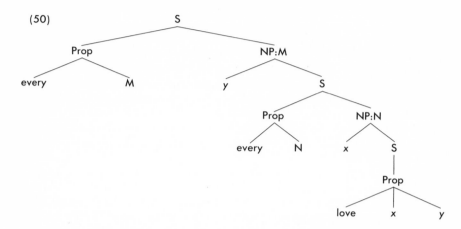

(50)

Both structures will yield the same sequence of words, since in either case the two indices occurring next to *love* are the only places where the two occurrences of *everyone* may be substituted.

Finally, I observe that the data which I have discussed here show to be completely untenable the familiar proposal [Chomsky (1957)] that each language has a limited repertoire of "kernel sentences" and that the full range of sentences in the language is obtained by combining and deforming these kernel sentences in various ways. Note that the sentences discussed require analyses in which structures containing less material than would make up a sentence (i.e., they have "slots" for noun phrases but no corresponding lexical material) are embedded in structures which contain more lexical material than there are slots to put it into.

NOTES

1. It has come to my attention that Paul Postal independently arrived at ideas similar to many of those contained in this paper a short while before I thought of them.

2. Actually, Chomsky regards the condition as imposed not on the entire noun phrase but on its head noun. The untenability of that view is demonstrated in McCawley (1968), where it is also observed that selectional restrictions cannot be regarded as requiring a noun phrase to possess a property such as "animate" but only as excluding those having contradictory properties; note that as selectional restrictions are formulated in Katz and Fodor (1963), etc., a noun phrase which is unspecified

for the property in question ought to violate the selectional restriction, whereas in fact a noun phrase such as *my neighbor*, which is unspecified as to maleness or femaleness, may perfectly well be used with a verb which Katz and Fodor would describe as "requiring a male subject" or "requiring a female object."

3. It is occasionally suggested [e.g., Bierwisch (1967)] that there is a linguistically significant distinction between interpretations which are possible only by imagining some bizarre situation and interpretations which require no such effort of the imagination. However, it is not clear that this criterion really defines a classification of sentences. How easy it will be to imagine a situation in which a given sentence would be appropriate depends on such extra-linguistic factors as a person's factual knowledge, the strength of his imagination, and the possible presence of LSD in his bloodstream. I suspect that sentences which one interprets without thinking up some story to embed them in are simply those which it is so easy to imagine someone's using that it would require no effort to think of such a story.

4. Jakobson (1941, Sections 25–27) points out that many persons, especially children, associate colors with sounds and, for example, will not hesitate to say that the vowel [a] is red.

5. Remarks delivered at the Texas Conference on Language Universals, April 15, 1967.

6. This proposal was first made in Ross (1967b). A slight change which I have made in Ross's analysis forces me to use the name "VP-promotion" for the analogue of the transformation which he and Lakoff call "*it*-replacement" after Rosenbaum's "pronoun replacement."

7. This transformation is discussed in Hoffman (1966).

8. Fillmore (1968). In order to avoid questions extraneous to this paper, I have changed Fillmore's labeling drastically.

9. Since the publication of Chomsky (1965), Chomsky has modified his conception of deep structure considerably. Rather than regarding "deep structure" as a "level" intermediate between semantic representation and surface structure, he now holds [Chomsky (1967a, p. 407)] that "deep structure completely determines certain highly significant aspects of semantic interpretation . . . [but] surface structure also contributes in a restricted but important way to semantic interpretation."

10. The symbols in this representation are to be interpreted as follows: If p and q are propositions, then $p \wedge q$ is the proposition that p and q are both true. $\exists_x f(x)$ means that there exists a value of x for which $f(x)$ is a true proposition.

11. A valiant attempt at a description of these sentences is given in Bach (1968).

12. A similar account of the structure of such sentences is given in Lakoff and Ross (1967).

13. These two meanings are "logically equivalent"; if either is true, then so is the other. It is of course reasonable to say that logically equivalent things need not have the same meaning, since any two contradictory propositions are logically equivalent, but one would hardly want to say that the sentences

(i)   That horse is not a horse.
(ii) My father had no children.

have the same meaning. The meanings of (49) give a much less trivial example of things which are logically equivalent but different in meaning.

Remarks on Nominalization[1]

NOAM CHOMSKY

12

For the purposes of this paper, I will assume without question a certain framework of principles and will explore some of the problems that arise when they are applied in the study of a central area of the syntax of English, and, presumably, any human language.[2]

A person who has learned a language has acquired a system of rules that relate sound and meaning in a certain specific way. He has, in other words, acquired a certain competence that he puts to use in producing and understanding speech. The central task of descriptive linguistics is to construct grammars of specific languages, each of which seeks to characterize in a precise way the competence that has been acquired by a speaker of this language. The theory of grammar attempts to discover the formal conditions that must be satisfied by a system of rules that qualifies as the grammar of a human language, the principles that govern the empirical interpretation of such a system, and the factors that determine the selection of a system of the appropriate form on the basis of the data available to the language learner. Such a "universal grammar" (to modify slightly a traditional usage) prescribes a schema that defines implicitly the infinite class of "attainable grammars"; it formulates principles that determine how each such system relates sound and meaning; it provides a procedure of evaluation for grammars of the appropriate form. Abstractly, and under a radical but quite useful idealization, we may then think of language-learning as the process of selecting a grammar of the appropriate form that relates sound and meaning in a way consistent with the available data and that is valued as highly, in terms of the evaluation measure, as any grammar meeting these empirical conditions.

I will assume that a grammar contains a base consisting of a categorial component (which I will assume to be a context-free grammar) and a lexicon. The lexicon consists of lexical entries, each of which is a system of specified features. The nonterminal vocabulary of the context-free grammar is drawn from a universal and rather limited vocabulary, some aspects of which will be considered below. The context-free grammar generates phrase-markers, with a dummy symbol as one of the terminal elements. A general principle of lexical insertion permits lexical entries to replace the dummy symbol in ways determined by their feature content. The formal object constructed in this way is a *deep structure*. The grammar contains a system of transformations, each of which maps phrase-markers into phrase-markers. Application of a sequence of transformations to a deep structure, in accordance with certain universal conditions and certain particular constraints of the grammar in question, determines ultimately a phrase-marker which we call a *surface structure*. The base and the transformational rules constitute the syntax. The grammar contains phonological rules that assign to each surface structure a phonetic representation in a universal phonetic alphabet. Furthermore, it contains semantic rules that assign to each paired deep and surface structure generated by the syntax a semantic interpretation, presumably, in a universal semantics, concerning which little is known in any detail. I will assume, furthermore, that grammatical relations are defined in a general way in terms of configurations within phrase-markers and that semantic interpretation involves only those grammatical relations specified in deep structures (although it may also involve certain properties of surface structures). I will be concerned here with problems of syntax exclusively; it is clear, however, that phonetic and semantic considerations provide empirical conditions of adequacy that must be met by the syntactic rules.

As anyone who has studied grammatical structures in detail is well aware, a grammar is a tightly organized system; a modification of one part generally involves widespread modifications of other facets. I will make various tacit assumptions about the grammar of English, holding certain parts constant and dealing with questions that arise with regard to properties of other parts of the grammar.

In general, it is to be expected that enrichment of one component of the grammar will permit simplification in other parts. Thus certain descriptive problems can be handled by enriching the lexicon and simplifying the categorial component of the base, or conversely; or by simplifying the base at the cost of greater complexity of transformations, or conversely. The proper balance between various components of the grammar is entirely an empirical issue. We have no a priori insight into the "trading relation" between the various parts. There are no general considerations that settle this matter. In particular, it is senseless to look to the evaluation procedure for the correct answer. Rather, the evaluation procedure must itself be selected on empirical grounds so as to provide whatever answer it is that is correct. It would be pure dogmatism to maintain, without empirical evidence, that the categorial component, or the lexicon, or the transformational component must be narrowly constrained by universal conditions, the variety and complexity of language being attributed to the other components.

Crucial evidence is not easy to obtain, but there can be no doubt as to the empirical nature of the issue. Furthermore, it is often possible to obtain evidence that is relevant to the correct choice of an evaluation measure and hence, indirectly, to the correct decision as to the variety and complexity that universal grammar permits in the several components of the grammar.[3]

To illustrate the problem in an artificially isolated case, consider such words as *feel*, which, in surface structure, take predicate phrases as complements. Thus we have such sentences as:

(1) John felt angry (sad, weak, courageous, above such things, inclined to agree to their request, sorry for what he did, etc.).

We might introduce such expressions into English grammar in various ways. We might extend the categorial component of the base, permitting structures of the form noun phrase–verb–predicate, and specifying *feel* in the lexicon as an item that can appear in prepredicate position in deep structures. Alternatively, we might exclude such structures from the base, and take the deep structures to be of the form noun phrase–verb–sentence, where the underlying structure *John felt* $[_S John \ be \ sad]_S$[4] is converted to *John felt sad* by a series of transformations. Restricting ourselves to these alternatives for the sake of the illustrative example, we see that one approach extends the base, treating *John felt angry* as a NP–V–Pred expression roughly analogous to *his hair turned gray* or *John felt anger* (NP–V–NP), while the second approach extends the transformational component, treating *John felt angry* as a NP–V–S expression roughly analogous to *John believed that he would win* or *John felt that he was angry*. A priori considerations give us no insight into which of these approaches is correct. There is, in particular, no a priori concept of "evaluation" that informs us whether it is "simpler," in an absolute sense, to complicate the base or the transformation.

There is, however, relevant empirical evidence, namely, regarding the semantic interpretation of these sentences.[5] To feel angry is not necessarily to feel that one is angry or to feel oneself to be angry; the same is true of most of the other predicate expressions that appear in such sentences as (1). If we are correct in assuming that it is the grammatical relations of the deep structure that determine the semantic interpretation, it follows that the deep structure of (1) must not be of the NP–V–S form, and that, in fact, the correct solution is to extend the base. Some supporting evidence from syntax is that many sentences of the form (1) appear with the progressive aspect (*John is feeling angry*, like *John is feeling anger*, etc.), but the corresponding sentences of the form NP–V–S do not (* *John is feeling that he is angry*). This small amount of syntactic and semantic evidence therefore suggests that the evaluation procedure must be selected in such a way as to prefer an elaboration of the base to an elaboration of the transformational component in such a case as this. Of course this empirical hypothesis is extremely strong; the evaluation procedure is a part of universal grammar, and when made precise, the proposal of the preceding sentence will have large-scale effects in the grammars of all languages, effects which must be tested against the empirical evidence exactly as in the single case just cited.

This paper will be devoted to another example of the same general sort, one that is much more crucial for the study of English structure and of linguistic theory as a whole.

Among the various types of nominal expressions in English there are two of particular importance, each roughly of propositional form. Thus corresponding to the sentences of (2) we have the gerundive nominals of (3) and the derived nominals of (4):[6]

(2) a. John is eager to please.
     b. John has refused the offer.
     c. John criticized the book.

(3) a. John's being eager to please
     b. John's refusing the offer
     c. John's criticizing the book

(4) a. John's eagerness to please
     b. John's refusal of the offer
     c. John's criticism of the book

Many differences have been noted between these two types of nominalization. The most striking differences have to do with the productivity of the process in question, the generality of the relation between the nominal and the associated proposition, and the internal structure of the nominal phrase.

Gerundive nominals can be formed fairly freely from propositions of subject–predicate form, and the relation of meaning between the nominal and the proposition is quite regular. Furthermore, the nominal does not have the internal structure of a noun phrase; thus we cannot replace *John's* by any determiner (e.g., *that, the*) in (3), nor can we insert adjectives into the gerundive nominal. These are precisely the consequences that follow, without elaboration or qualifications, from the assumption that gerundive nominalization involves a grammatical transformation from an underlying sentencelike structure. We might assume that one of the forms of NP introduced by rules of the categorial component of the base is (5), and that general rules of affix placement give the freely generated surface forms of the gerundive nominal:[7]

(5) [$_S$NP *nom* (Aspect) VP]$_S$

The semantic interpretation of a gerundive nominalization is straightforward in terms of the grammatical relations of the underlying proposition in the deep structure.

Derived nominals such as (4) are very different in all of these respects. Productivity is much more restricted, the semantic relations between the associated proposition and the derived nominal are quite varied and idiosyncratic, and the nominal has the internal structure of a noun phrase. I will comment on these matters directly. They raise the question of whether the derived nominals are, in fact, transformationally related to the associated propositions. The question, then, is analogous to that raised earlier concerning the status of verbs such as *feel*. We might extend the base rules to accommodate the derived nominal directly (I will refer to this as the "lexicalist position"), thus simplifying the transformational component; or, alternatively, we might simplify the base structures, exluding these forms, and derive them by some extension of the transformational apparatus (the "transformationalist position"). As in the illustrative example discussed earlier, there is no a priori insight into universal grammar — specifically, into the nature of an evaluation measure — that bears on this question, which is a purely empirical one. The problem is to find empirical evidence that supports one or the other of the alternatives. It is, furthermore, quite possible to imagine a compromise solution that adopts the lexicalist position for certain items and the transformationalist position for others. Again, this is entirely an empirical issue. We must fix the principles of universal grammar — in particular, the character of the evaluation measure — so that it provides the description that is factually correct, noting as before that any such hypothesis about universal grammar must also be tested against the evidence from other parts of English grammar and the grammars of other languages.

In the earliest work on transformational grammar [cf. Lees (1960)], the correctness of the transformationalist position was taken for granted; and, in fact, there was really no alternative as the theory of grammar was formulated at that time. However, the extension of grammatical theory to incorporate syntactic features [as in Chomsky (1965, Chapter 2)] permits a formulation of the lexicalist position, and therefore raises the issue of choice between the alternatives.[8] My purpose here is to investigate the lexicalist position and to explore some of the consequences that it suggests for the theory of syntax more generally.

Consider first the matter of productivity. As noted above, the transformation that gives gerundive nominals applies quite freely.[9] There are, however, many restrictions on the formation of derived nominals. The structures underlying (6), for example, are transformed to the gerundive nominals of (7) but not to the derived nominals of (8):

(6)   a.   John is easy (difficult) to please.
       b.   John is certain (likely) to win the prize.
       c.   John amused (interested) the children with his stories.

(7)   a.   John's being easy (difficult) to please
       b.   John's being certain (likely) to win the prize
       c.   John's amusing (interesting) the children with his stories

(8)   a. * John's easiness (difficulty) to please
      b. * John's certainty (likelihood) to win the prize
      c. * John's amusement (interest) of the children with his stories

There are, of course, derived nominals that superficially resemble those of (8), for example, those of (9), which pair with the gerundive nominals of (10):

(9)   a. John's eagerness to please [(2a), (4a)]
      b. John's certainty that Bill will win the prize
      c. John's amusement at (interest in) the children's antics

(10) a. John's being eager to please [(2a), (3a)]
      b. John's being certain that Bill will win the prize
      c. John's being amused at (interested in) the children's antics

These discrepancies between gerundive and derived nominals call for explanation. Specifically, we must determine why the examples of (8) are ruled out although those of (9) are permitted.[10]

The idiosyncratic character of the relation between the derived nominal and the associated verb has been so often remarked that discussion is superfluous. Consider, for example, such nominals as *laughter, marriage, construction, actions, activities, revolution, belief, doubt, conversion, permutation, trial, residence, qualifications, specifications,* and so on, with their individual ranges of meaning and varied semantic relations to the base forms. There are a few subregularities that have frequently been noted, but the range of variation and its rather accidental character are typical of lexical structure. To accommodate these facts within the transformational approach (assuming, as above, that it is the grammatical relations in the deep structure that determine meaning) it is necessary to resort to the artifice of assigning a range of meanings to the base form, stipulating that with certain semantic features the form must nominalize and with others it cannot. Furthermore, the appeal to this highly unsatisfactory device, which reduces the hypothesis that transformations do not have semantic content to near vacuity, would have to be quite extensive.[11]

The third major difference noted above between gerundive and derived nominals is that only the latter have the internal structure of noun phrases. Thus we can have such expressions as *the proof of the theorem* (* *the proving the theorem,* with a gerundive nominal), *John's unmotivated criticism of the book* (* *John's unmotivated criticizing the book*), and so on. Correspondingly, the derived nominals cannot contain aspect; there is no derived nominal analogous to *John's having criticized the book.* Furthermore, many derived nominals pluralize and occur with the full range of determiners (*John's three proofs of the theorem, several of John's proofs of the theorem,* etc.). And derived nominals, in fact, can appear freely in the full range of noun phrase structures. For example, the sentence *John gave Bill advice* is just like any other indirect object structure in that it has the double passive[*advice was*

given (to) Bill, Bill was given advice]. It is difficult to see how a transformational approach to derived nominals can account for the fact that the
structures in which they appear as well as their internal structure and, often,
morphological properties, are those of ordinary noun phrases. None of these
problems arises, as noted earlier, in the case of gerundive nominals.

These properties of derived nominals are quite consistent with a lexicalist
approach and, in part, can even be explained from this point of view. Before
going into this matter, let us elaborate the lexicalist position in slightly greater
detail.

I noted earlier that the lexicalist position was not formulable within the
framework of syntactic theory available at the time of Lees's work on nominalizations. The problem was that the obvious generalizations concerning the
distributional properties of the base and derived forms were expressible, in
that framework, only in terms of grammatical transformations. There was no
other way to express the fact that the contexts in which *refuse* appears as
a verb and *refusal* as a noun are closely related. However, when the lexicon
is separated from the categorial component of the base and its entries are
analyzed in terms of contextual features, this difficulty disappears. We can
enter *refuse* in the lexicon as an item with certain fixed selectional and strict
subcategorization features, which is free with respect to the categorial features
[noun] and [verb]. Fairly idiosyncratic morphological rules will determine
the phonological form of *refuse, destroy*, etc., when these items appear in
the noun position. The fact that *refuse* takes a noun phrase complement or
a reduced sentential complement and *destroy* only a noun phrase complement,
either as a noun or as a verb, is expressed by the feature structure of the
"neutral" lexical entry, as are selectional properties. Details aside, it is clear
that syntactic features provide a great deal of flexibility for the expression
of generalizations regarding distributional similarities. Hence what was a
decisive objection to the lexicalist position no longer has any force.

Let us propose, then, as a tentative hypothesis, that a great many items
appear in the lexicon with fixed selectional and strict subcategorization
features, but with a choice as to the features associated with the lexical
categories noun, verb, adjective. The lexical entry may specify that semantic
features are in part dependent on the choice of one or another of these
categorial features. This is, of course, the typical situation within the lexicon;
in general, lexical entries involve certain Boolean conditions on features,
expressing conditional dependencies of various sorts.[12] Insofar as there are
regularities (cf. Note 11), these can be expressed by redundancy rules in the
lexicon.

Consider now the problem of productivity noted above, specifically, the
fact that we cannot form the derived nominals (8) corresponding to the
sentences (6), although the structures underlying (6) can be transformed to
the gerundive nominals (7), and we can form the derived nominals (9) associated with the gerundive nominals (10).

Consider first the examples *John is easy to please, John is eager to please,* only the second of which is associated with a derived nominal. This consequence follows immediately from the lexicalist hypothesis just formulated, when we take into account certain properties of the items *eager* and *easy.* Thus *eager* must be introduced into the lexicon with a strict subcategorization feature indicating that it can take a sentential complement, as in *John is eager (for us) to please.* In the simplest case, then, it follows that in the noun position, *eager* will appear in the contexts *John's eagerness (for us) to please,* etc., with no further comment necessary. But *easy* (or *difficult*) does not appear in the lexicon with such a feature. There is no structure of the form . . . *easy (difficult) S* generated by base rules. Rather, *easy (difficult)* appears in base phrase-markers as an adjective predicated of propositions as subject [(*for us) to please John is easy,* etc.]; forms such as *it is easy (for us) to please John* are derived by extraposition.[13] Consequently, *easy* (or *difficult*) cannot be introduced by lexical insertion into the noun position with sentential complements, and we cannot derive such forms as (8a), * *John's easiness (difficulty) to please.* No such restriction holds for gerundive nominalization, which, being a transformation, is applicable to transforms as well as to base phrase-markers.

Consider next the examples * *John's certainty to win the prize* [= (8b)], *John's certainty that Bill will win the prize* [= (9b)]. Again, the lexicalist hypothesis provides an explanation for this distinction between the two senses of *certain.* The sentence *John is certain to win the prize* is derived by extraposition and pronoun replacement from a deep structure in which *certain* is predicated of the proposition *John — to win the prize,* as is clear from the meaning.[14] In this sense, *certain* does not permit a propositional complement; it therefore follows from the lexicalist hypothesis that there cannot be a derived nominal *certainty to win the prize,* in this sense. But *John is certain that Bill will win the prize* derives from *John is certain* [$_S$ *Bill will win the prize*]$_S$. In the sense of *certain* in which it is predicated of a person, a propositional complement can be adjoined in the base. Consequently, the lexicalist hypothesis permits the associated derived nominal *John's certainty that Bill will win the prize,* generated by lexical insertion of *certain* in the noun position before a sentential complement.

Consider now examples (6c) through (10c). If derived nominals are formed by transformation, there is no reason why * *John's amusement of the children with his stories* [= (8c)] should not be formed from the proposition that underlies the gerundive nominal *John's amusing the children with his stories,* just as *John's amusement at the children's antics* [= (9c)] would, on these grounds, be derived from the proposition that underlies the gerundive nominal *John's being amused at the children's antics* [= (10c)]. The discrepancy would be accounted for if we were to adopt the lexicalist position and, furthermore, to postulate that such sentences as *John amused the children with his stories* are themselves derived from an underlying structure of a different sort. The latter assumption is not unreasonable. Thus it is well-known that among the properties of verbs of the category of *amuse, interest,* etc., is the fact that there are paired sentences such as (11):

(11)   a. He was amused at the stories.
        b. The stories amused him.

The facts regarding derived nominals suggest that (11b) is derived from a structure that involves (11a); this would account for the similarities in semantic interpretation and distributional properties of (11a) and (11b), and would also, on the lexicalist hypothesis, account for the occurrence and nonoccurrence of derived nominals.[15] Although independent motivation for the assumption that (11a) underlies (11b) is weak, there appears to be no counterevidence suggesting that (11b) underlies (11a). One might, for example, derive (11b) quite plausibly from a "causative" construction with roughly the form of (12):

(12)   The stories [+cause] [$_S$he was amused at the stories]$_S$

I return to such structures briefly below. There is some evidence in support of the assumption that a causative construction exists in English [cf. Chomsky (1965, p. 180); Lakoff (1965, Section 9)],[16] and the operation that erases the repeated noun phrase in the embedded proposition of (12) is of a sort found elsewhere, for example, in the derivation of such sentences as *John used the table to write on, John used the pen to write (with), John used the wall to lean the table against,* etc., from *John used the table* [$_S$*John wrote on the table*]$_S$, and so on.

Other examples for which a causative analysis has been suggested fall into the same pattern, with respect to formation of derived nominals. Consider, for example, the transitive use of *grow* as in *John grows tomatoes,* which might plausibly be derived from a structure such as (12), with *the stories* replaced by *John* in the subject position and the embedded proposition being the intransitive *tomatoes grow.* But consider the nominal phrase *the growth of tomatoes.* This is unambiguous; it has the interpretation of *tomatoes grow* but not of *John grows tomatoes.* If the latter is taken as a base form, there should be an associated derived nominal *the growth of tomatoes* with the same interpretation, just as we have the derived nominal *the rejection of the offer* associated with the transitive verb phrase *reject the offer.* If, on the other hand, the sentence *John grows tomatoes* is derived from a causative construction, the corresponding derived nominal is excluded (though not, of course, the corresponding nominalization *the growing of tomatoes* — we return to nominalizations of this type on p. 214). Hence the lack of ambiguity offers empirical support for a combination of the lexicalist hypothesis with the causative analysis, though not for either of these assumptions taken in isolation.

Summarizing these observations, we see that the lexicalist hypothesis explains a variety of facts of the sort illustrated by examples (6) through (10) [in part, in conjunction with other assumptions about underlying structures, such as (12)]. The transformationalist hypothesis is no doubt consistent with these facts, but it derives no support from them, since it would also be consistent with the discovery, were it a fact, that derived nominals exist in all cases in which we have gerundive nominals. Hence the facts that have been cited give strong empirical support to the lexicalist hypothesis and no support to the transformationalist hypothesis. Other things being equal, then, they would lead us to accept the lexicalist hypothesis, from which these facts follow.

If the lexicalist hypothesis is correct, we should expect that derived nominals will correspond to base structures rather than transforms. I will return to some problems, which may or may not be real, that arise in connection with this consequence of the lexicalist hypothesis. Notice, however, that there is other corroborating evidence. For example, there are many verbs in English that must be listed in the lexicon as verb–particle constructions [*look up* (*the information*), *define away* (*the problem*), etc.]. These forms undergo gerundive nominalization freely (*his looking up the information, his looking the information up, his defining away the problem, his defining the problem away*). The derived nominals, in general, are rather marginal, and hence not very informative. However, it seems to me that the forms of (13) are somewhat preferable to those of (14.)[17]

(13) a.   his looking up of the information
      b.   his defining away of the problem

(14) a. * his looking of the information up
      b. * his defining of the problem away

This consequence follows from the lexicalist assumption, if the forms of (13) are regarded as derived nominals (see Note 17).

Notice also that although gerundive nominalization applies freely to sentences with verb phrase adjuncts, this is not true of the rules for forming derived nominals. Thus we have (15) but not (16):[18]

(15)   his criticizing the book before he read it (because of its failure to go deeply into the matter, etc.)

(16) * his criticism of the book before he read it (because of its failure to go deeply into the matter, etc.)

This too would follow from the lexicalist assumption, since true verb phrase adjuncts such as *before*-clauses and *because*-clauses will not appear as noun complements in base noun phrases.

The examples (15) and (16) raise interesting questions relating to the matter of acceptability and grammaticalness.[19] If the lexicalist hypothesis is correct, then all dialects of English that share the analysis of adjuncts presupposed above should distinguish the expressions of (15), as directly generated by the grammar, from those of (16), as not directly generated by the grammar. Suppose that we discover, however, that some speakers find the expressions of (16) quite acceptable. On the lexicalist hypothesis, these sentences can only be derivatively generated. Therefore we should have to conclude that their acceptability to these speakers results from a failure to take note of a certain distinction of grammaticalness. We might propose that the expressions of (16) are formed by analogy to the gerundive nominals (15), say by a rule that converts *X –ing* to the noun *X nom* (where *nom* is the element that determines the morphological form of the derived nominal) in certain cases. There is no doubt that such processes of derivative generation exist as part of grammar in the most general sense (for some discussion, see *Aspects,* Chapter IV, Section 1, and references cited there). The question is whether in this case it is correct to regard (16) as directly generated or as derivatively generated, for the speakers in question. There is empirical evidence bearing on this matter. Thus if the expressions of (16) are directly generated, we would expect them to show the full range of use and meaning of such derived nominals as *his criticism of the book.* If, on the other hand, they are derivatively generated in the manner just suggested, we would expect them to have only the more restricted range of use and meaning of the expressions of (15) that underlie them. Crucial evidence, then, is provided by the contexts (17) in which the derived nominal *his criticism of the book* can appear, but not the gerundive nominals (15) (with or without the adjunct):

(17)   a. — is to be found on page 15.
      b. I studied — very carefully.

The fact seems to be that speakers who accept (16) do not accept (18) though they do accept (19):

(18)   a. *His criticism of the book before he read it* is to be found on page 15.
      b. I studied *his criticism of the book before he read it* very carefully.

(19)   a. *His criticism of the book* is to be found on page 15.
      b. I studied *his criticism of the book* very carefully.

If correct, this indicates that speakers who fail to distinguish (16) from (15) are not aware of a property of their internalized grammar, namely, that it generates (16) only derivatively, by analogy to the gerundive nominal. It would not be in the least surprising to discover that some speakers fail to notice a distinction of this sort. As we see, it is an empirical issue, and there is relevant factual evidence. This is a general problem that must be borne in mind when acceptability judgments are used, as they must be, to discover the grammar that is internalized. In the present instance, the lexicalist hypothesis receives convincing support if it is true that there are fundamentally two types of acceptability judgment: the first, acceptance of (19) but neither

(16) nor (18); the second, acceptance of (19) and (16) but not (18). It is difficult to see how the transformationalist hypothesis could accommodate either of these cases.

Returning to the main theme, notice that aspect will of course not appear in noun phrases and therefore, on the lexicalist hypothesis, will be absent from derived nominals (though not gerundive nominals).

Consider next the adjectives that appear with derived nominals, as in *John's sudden refusal* or *John's obvious sincerity*. Two sources immediately suggest themselves: one, from relatives (as *John's aged mother* might be derived from *John's mother, who is aged*); another, from adverbial constructions such as *John refused suddenly, John is obviously sincere*. The latter assumption, however, would presuppose that derived nominals can be formed from such structures as *John refused in such-and-such a manner, John was sincere to such-and-such an extent*, etc. This is not the case, however. We cannot have * *John's refusal in that manner* (*in a manner that surprised me*) or * *John's sincerity to that extent*. Furthermore, adjectives that appear with derived nominals often cannot appear (as adverbs) with the associated verbs: for example, we have *John's uncanny* (*amazing, curious, striking*) *resemblance to Bill* but not * *John resembled Bill uncannily* (*amazingly, curiously, strikingly*). We might propose to account for this by deriving *John's uncanny resemblance to Bill* from something like *the degree to which John resembles Bill, which is uncanny*. But this proposal, apart from the difficulty that it provides no way to exclude such phrases as * *their amazing destruction of the city* from *the degree to which they destroyed the city, which was amazing*, also runs into the difficulties of Note 11. Though there remain quite a number of interesting problems concerning adjectives in derived nominal (and many other) constructions, I see nothing that conflicts with the lexicalist hypothesis in this regard.

Evidence in favor of the lexicalist position appears to be fairly substantial. It is important, therefore, to look into the further consequences of this position, and the difficulties that stand in the way of incorporating it into the theory of syntax.

Suppose that such phrases as *eagerness* (*for John*) *to please, refusal of the offer, belief in a supreme being*, etc., are base noun phrases. Clearly, if this approach is to be pursued, then the rules of the categorial component of the base must introduce an extensive range of complements within the noun phrase, as they do within the verb phrase and the adjective phrase. As a first approximation, to be revised later on, we might propose that the rules of the categorial component include the following:

(20)   a. NP → N Comp
       b. VP → V Comp
       c. AP → A Comp

(21)   Comp → NP, S, NP S, NP Prep-P, Prep-P Prep-P, etc.

Is there any independent support, apart from the phenomena of derived nominalization, for such rules? An investigation of noun phrases shows that there is a good deal of support for a system such as this.

Consider such phrases as the following:[20]

(22)   a.   the *weather* in England
       b.   the *weather* in 1965
       c.   the *story* of Bill's exploits
       d.   the *bottom* of the barrel
       e.   the *back* of the room
       f.   the *message* from Bill to Tom about the meeting
       g.   a *war* of aggression against France
       h.   *atrocities* against civilians
       i.   the *author* of the book
       j.   John's *attitude* of defiance towards Bill
       k.   his *advantage* over his rivals
       l.   his *anguish* over his crimes
       m.   his *mercy* toward the victims
       n.   a *man* to do the job
       o.   a *house* in the woods
       p.   his *habit* of interrupting
       q.   the *reason* for his refusal
       r.   the *question* whether John should leave
       s.   the *prospects* for peace
       t.   the *algebra* of revolution
       u.   *prolegomena* to any future metaphysics
       v.   my *candidate* for a trip to the moon
       w.   a *nation* of shopkeepers

In each of these, and many similar forms, it seems to me to make very good sense — in some cases, to be quite necessary — to regard the italicized form as the noun of a determiner–noun–complement construction which constitutes a simple base noun phrase. The only alternative would be to regard the whole expression as a transform with the italicized element being a nominalized verb or adjective, or to take the complement to be a reduced relative clause. In such cases as those of (22), neither alternative seems to be at all motivated, although each has been proposed for certain of these examples. Space prevents a detailed analysis of each case, but a few remarks may be useful.

The analysis of the head noun as a nominalized verb requires that we establish abstract verbs that are automatically subject to nominalization. This requires devices of great descriptive power which should, correspondingly, be very "costly" in terms of a reasonable evaluation measure.[21] Nevertheless, it is an interesting possibility. Perhaps the strongest case for such an approach is the class of examples of which (22i) is an example. It has been argued, quite plausibly, that such phrases as *the owner of the house* derive from underlying structures such as *the one who owns the house;* correspondingly (22i) might be derived from the structure *the one who *auths the book,* *auth* being postulated as a verb that is lexically marked as obligatorily subject to nominalization. However, the plausibility of this approach diminishes when one recognizes that there is no more reason to give this analysis for (22i) than there is for *the general secretary of the party, the assistant vice-chancellor of the university,* and similarly for every function that can be characterized by a nominal phrase. Another fact sometimes put forth in support of the analysis of these phrases as nominalizations is the ambiguity of such expressions as *good dentist* (*dentist who is a good man, man who is good as a dentist*). But this argument is also quite weak. The ambiguity, being characteristic of all expressions that refer to humans by virtue of some function that they fulfill, can be handled by a general principle of semantic interpretation; furthermore, it is hardly plausible that the ambiguity of *good assistant vice-chancellor* should be explained in this way.

For some of the cases of (22), an analysis in terms of reduced relatives is plausible; for example, (22o). But even for such cases there are difficulties in this approach. Notice that there are narrow restrictions on the head noun in (22o). Thus we have the phrase *John's house in the woods* meaning *the house of John's which is in the woods;* but we cannot form *John's book* (*dog, brother, . . .*) *in the woods* (*on the table, . . .*). If John and I each have a house in the woods, I can refer to his, with contrastive stress on *John's,* as *JOHN'S house in the woods;* if we each have a book on the table, I cannot, analogously, refer to his as *JOHN'S book on the table.* Such observations suggest that the surface structure of *John's house in the woods* is *John's — house in the woods,* with *house in the woods* being some sort of nominal expression. On the other hand, in a true reduced relative such as *that book on the table,* there is, presumably, no main constituent break before *book.*

The analysis as a reduced relative is also possible in the case of (22r) and (22s). Thus we have such sentences as (23), with the associated noun phrases of (24):

(23)   a. The question is whether John should leave.
      b. The prospects are for peace.
      c. The plan is for John to leave.
      d. The excuse was that John had left.

(24)   a. the question whether John should leave
      b. the prospects for peace
      c. the plan for John to leave
      d. the excuse that John had left

Despite the unnaturalness of relative clauses formed in the usual way with (23) as the embedded proposition, one might argue that these are the sources of (24), as reduced relatives. Alternatively, one might argue that the sentences of (23) are derived from structures incorporating (24). The latter assumption is far more plausible however. Thus there are no such sentences as (25):

(25) a. * The question whether John should leave is why Bill stayed.
      b. * The prospects for peace are for a long delay.
      c. * The plan for John to leave is that Bill should stay.
      d. * The excuse that John had left was that Bill should stay.

Under the reduced relative assumption, there is no reason why (25) should be ruled out. This would be explained, however, if we assumed that such sentences as (23) are derived from structures incorporating the base noun phrases (24); for example, it might be proposed that (23) derives from (26) by replacement of the unspecified predicate Δ by the complement of the subject noun:

(26) $[_{NP}$ Det N Comp $]_{NP}$ be $[_{Pred} \Delta]_{Pred}$[22]

Under this analysis, the copula serves as a kind of existential operator. Structures such as (26) are motivated by other data as well; for example, as the matrix structure for such sentences as *what John did was hurt himself*, which might be derived from $[_{NP}$ *it that John hurt John*$]_{NP}$ be $[_{Pred} \Delta]_{Pred}$, through a series of operations to which we return below. In any event, there is an argument for taking the forms of (24) to underlie (23), rather than conversely.

The structures (22), and others like them, raise many problems; they do, however, suggest quite strongly that there are base noun phrases of the form determiner–noun–complement, quite apart from nominalizations. In fact, the range of noun complements seems almost as great as the range of verb complements, and the two sets are remarkably similar. There is also a wide range of adjective complements [*eager (for Bill) to leave, proud of John*, etc.]. Therefore, it is quite natural to suppose that the categorial component of the base contains rules with the effect of (20), (21), a conclusion which lends further support to the lexicalist assumption.

These observations, incidentally, considerably weaken the argument that verb and adjective are subcategories of a category "predicator," as has been suggested in recent syntactic work.[23] The argument based on distributional similarities of verbs and adjectives collapses when we recognize that nouns share the same distributional properties; thus the properties are simply properties of lexical categories. A number of other arguments that have appeared in support of this proposal fail for a similar reason. Thus it has been argued that verbs and adjectives can both be categorized as stative–active, so that we have such sentences as (27) in the case of actives, but not (28) in the case of statives:[24]

(27) a. Look at the picture.
      b. Don't be noisy.

      c.   What I'm doing is looking at the picture.
      d.   What I'm doing is being noisy.
      e.   I'm looking at the picture.
      f.   I'm being noisy.

(28)   a. * Know that Bill went there.
      b. * Don't be tall.
      c. * What I'm doing is knowing that Bill went there.
      d. * What I'm doing is being tall.
      e. * I'm knowing that Bill went there.
      f. * I'm being tall.

At best, the logic of this argument is unclear. Suppose it were true that just verbs and adjectives crossclassify with respect to the feature active–stative. It would not follow that verbs and adjectives belong to a single category, predicator, with the feature $[\pm \text{adjectival}]$ distinguishing verbs and adjectives. From the fact that a feature $[\pm F]$ is distinctive in the categories X, Y, it does not follow that there is a feature G such that $X = [+G]$ and $Y = [-G]$, and a category $Z = [\pm G]$. What is more, nouns are subdivided in an exactly parallel way. Thus alongside (27) we have *be a hero, what he's doing is being a hero, he's being a hero;* alongside of (28) we must exclude * *be a person,* * *what he's doing is being a person,* * *he's being a person,* etc. Again, the property in question is a property of lexical categories; the fact that the lexical categories noun, verb, and adjective share this property does not imply that they belong to a super-category. In fact, there is, to my knowledge, no convincing argument for a category including just verbs and adjectives (or, to take another traditional view, nouns and adjectives), although it is not excluded that some such subdivision may be correct. It is quite possible that the categories noun, verb, adjective are the reflection of a deeper feature structure, each being a combination of features of a more abstract sort. In this way, the various relations among these categories might be expressible. For the moment, however, this is hardly clear enough even to be a speculation.

    Returning to the main theme, a good case can be made that the lexical categories noun, adjective, and verb (whatever their further substructure may be) can appear in base forms with complements to form noun phrases, adjective phrases, and verb phrases. If this is correct, then it would be quite reasonable to expect that certain items might appear, with fixed contextual features, in more than one of these categories. The lexicalist analysis of derived nominals proposes that this expectation is fulfilled.

    The lexicalist hypothesis faces additional problems, however. Consider the phrase *John's proof of the theorem,* as a typical illustration. According to the lexicalist hypothesis, the item *prove* appears in the lexicon with certain contexual features that indicate the range of complements it can accept and the choice of items that may appear in these associated phrases. Yet to be accounted for, however, is the possessive noun phrase *John's* and its relation to the head noun *proof.* It might be suggested that the possessive noun phrase derives from a relative clause with *have,* as *John's table* might derive from the structure underlying *the table* [s*John has a table*]s, along lines that have been frequently discussed. Thus the source of *John's proof of the theorem* would be, in this analysis, the structure underlying *the proof of the theorem that John has.* While not implausible in this case, this approach quickly runs into difficulties when extended. Thus to account for *John's refusal to leave, John's invention of a better mousetrap,* and many other forms, it would be necessary to postulate abstract verbs that obligatorily undergo certain transformations, a dubious move at best, as noted earlier.

An alternative would be simply to derive the possessive noun phrase itself as a base form. Suppose, tentatively, that the rules generating determiners in the base component are the following:[25]

(29)   a. Det → (Prearticle of) Article (Postarticle)

   b. Article → $\left\{ \begin{array}{l} \pm\text{def} \\ \text{Poss} \end{array} \right\}$

The noun phrase *several of John's proofs of the theorem,* under this analysis, would have a structure of roughly the following form:

(30)

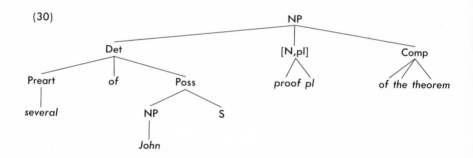

It would be analogous in structure, then, to the phrase *several of those proofs of the theorem.*

If this approach is correct, we would expect to find structures of the form NPs–N even where the N is not a derived nominal, and where the possessive construction in question does not derive from the corresponding structure: *N that NP has.* In fact, there is some evidence in support of this expectation. A number of people have noted that the distinction between alienable and inalienable possession, formally marked in certain languages, has a certain status in English as well. Thus the phrase *John's leg* is ambiguous: it can be used to refer either to the leg that John happens to have in his possession (alienable possession), that he is, say, holding under his arm; or to the leg that is, in fact, part of John's body (inalienable possession). But the phrase *the leg that John has* has only the sense of alienable possession. We cannot say that the leg that John has hurts or that it is weak from the climb, though we can make this statement of John's leg, in the inalienable sense of the phrase *John's leg.*[26] These observations lend plausibility to the view that *John's leg* has another source in addition to the structure underlying *the leg that John has,* from which it can be derived (in the alienable sense) along the same lines as *John's table* from the structure underlying *the table that John has.* The second source, then, might be given by the base rules (29), which are semantically interpreted as specifying inalienable possession. This assumption would account for the facts just noted.

Within the framework that I am here presupposing, grammatical relations are defined by configurations in the deep structure, and selectional features relate the heads of phrases that are associated in specific grammatical relations. Then the words *John* and *proof* are the heads of the related phrases *several of John's* and *proofs of the theorem* in *several of John's proofs of the theorem,* and the same selectional feature that associates subject and verb in *John proved the theorem* will relate these two items, despite the very different syntactic origin of the relationship.[27] We return to this matter later on. For the moment, it is sufficient to point out that by a suitable generalization of the interpretation of selectional features, we can account for the fact that the selectional relation of the possessive noun phrase of the determiner to the "verbal" head of the derived nominal is the same as that of the subject to the verb of the associated verb phrase. Hence in the simplest case, all of the contextual features of the items that appear as verbs in verb phrases and as derived nouns in derived nominals will be common to the two types of context.

It must be noted that only in the *simplest* case will exactly the same contextual (and other) features be associated with an item as a verb and as a noun. In general, lexical entries involve sets of shared features, organized in complex and little understood ways, and we should expect to find the same phenomenon in the case of derived nominals, given the lexicalist hypothesis. Examples such as (31) and (32) illustrate the discrepancy of contextual features that may be found in the case of certain noun–verbs.

(31) a. our election of John (to the presidency)
      b. our belief in God
      c. our consideration of John for the job

(32) a. * our election of John (to be) president
      b. * our belief in God (to be) omnipotent
      c. * our consideration of John (to be) a fool

Reactions to these sentences vary slightly; (31), (32) represent my judgments. Given such data, lexical entries must indicate that embedded sentences are not permitted in the complement to the nouns, although they are permitted in the complement to the associated verbs. Whatever generality there may be to this phenomenon can be extracted from individual lexical entries and presented in redundancy rules. This discrepancy in syntactic features between the noun and verb members of a noun–verb pair corresponds to the semantic discrepancies noted earlier (cf. p. 189) and like them, strengthens the lexicalist hypothesis. The appropriate device to rule out the sentences of (28) [while permitting (27)] is a lexical rule governing contextual features. To formulate such restrictions in the structure indices of transformations would be a rather complex matter.

Consider now some of the transformational rules that apply internally to complex noun phrases. Consider first such phrases as (33) through (36):

(33) a.   that picture of John's
      b.   a picture of John's
      c.   several of those pictures of John's
      d.   several pictures of John's

(34) a.   John's picture, several of John's pictures
      b.   the picture of John's that Bill painted

(35) a. * the picture of John's
      b. * several of the pictures of John's

(36)   * John's picture that Bill painted

The expressions of (35), (36) illustrate a systematic gap in this set. In general, expressions of the form (*prearticle of*) the *N of NPs* and *NPs N that S* are unnatural. The gaps illustrated by (35) and (36) are filled by (34a) and (34b), respectively.

Alongside the examples of (33) there is a superficially similar set in which *John's* is replaced by *John*: thus, *that picture of John,* etc. In this case, the phrases are presumably complex noun phrases with a "relational" head noun, like the examples of (22). The status of the analogues to (35) (namely, *the picture of John, several of the pictures of John*) is unclear. It is clear, however, that such phrases as *John's picture* [= (34a)] are ambiguous, meaning *the picture of John* or *the picture of John's*.

On just the evidence cited so far, one might propose various transformational analyses. Tentatively, let us suppose that there are three transformations, with roughly the effects of (37), (38), (39), applying in the order given:

(37)   *X–the–Y picture that John has* $\Rightarrow$ *X–John's–Y picture*
(38)   *X–John's–Y picture* $\Rightarrow$ *X–the–Y picture of John's*
(39)   *X–the–Y picture of John* $\Rightarrow$ *X–John's–picture*

X and *Y* are pre- and post-article (including the demonstrative element), respectively. There are problems in the formulation of such transformations to which we will return below. To account for the data presented above,

(38) will be obligatory when Y contains a demonstrative element [giving (33a), (33c), for example] or when the phrase contains a relative clause [preventing (36)], and will be blocked when Y is null, thus excluding (35).

Consider now such derived nominals as:

(40)   a. the destruction of the city
       b. the proof of it
       c. the murder of John

Rule (39) will apply, giving such transforms as *the city's destruction, its proof, John's murder.* The applicability of (39) to derived nominals varies in naturalness from case to case and from speaker to speaker, and must therefore be specified in part as an idiosyncratic property of lexical items, along the lines developed in Lakoff (1965). In part, the applicability of (39) is determined by the character of the noun phrase of the complement, there being certain noun phrases that do not possessivize. Whatever the detailed restrictions may be, it seems clear that the operation in question extends to derived nominals as well as to complex noun phrases with "relational" head nouns. For convenience of reference, I will refer to rule (39) as the rule of *NP-preposing.*

Let us suppose, as suggested in the references of Note 2, that the underlying structure for passives is roughly $NP-Aux-V-NP-by$ Δ, where *by* Δ is an agent phrase related, in ways that are still unclear in detail, to adverbials of means and manner. The passive operation, then, is an amalgam of two steps: the first replaces Δ by the subject noun phrase; the second inserts in the position vacated by the subject the noun phrase that is to the right of the verb. Let us refer to the first of these operations as *agent-postposing.* The second bears a close similarity to the operation of NP-preposing just discussed, and perhaps the two fall under a single generalization. If so, then the second component of the passive transformation can apply independently of the first, namely, as operation (39), internally to noun phrases. Whether or not this is so, we may inquire into the possibility that the operation of agent-postposing can apply independently of the second component of the passive transformation.

Pursuing this possibility, we note first that passivizability is a property of verbs — which is natural, given that V is the only lexical category mentioned in the structure index of the transformation. We can indicate this fact, along the lines of the references cited, by associating with certain verbs the contextual feature [— by Δ] either as a lexical property (where it is idiosyncratic) or by a redundancy rule of the lexicon (where it is subject to some regularity). Assuming, as before, that the complements of nouns are the same in principle as those of verbs, we would expect to find in deep structures complex noun phrases of the form $Det-N-NP-by$ Δ, for example, such phrases as *the enemy's-[destroy, $+$N]-the city-by* Δ. The word *destroy* will be spelled out phonologically as *destruction* in this case, and the preposition *of* inserted by a general rule applying to N–NP constructions.[28] Agent-postposing will then apply, as in the passive, giving *the destruction of the city by the enemy.* To provide this result, we need only generalize the operation so that its domain may be a noun phrase as well as a sentence, a modification of the theory of transformations that is implicit in the lexicalist hypothesis; and we must somehow account for the appearance of the definite article in the transform, just as in the case of the transformation (38). A further generalization is required by such phrases as *the offer by John,* which indicate, as is quite natural, that of the two components of the passive transformation, only NP-preposing and not agent-postposing requires the presence of an object (more generally, a noun phrase, as in the "pseudo-passives" *John was laughed at, . . . approved of,* etc.) in the position following the verb.[29]

Notice that a verb which is not passivizable, such as *marry* (in one sense) or *resemble,* will not be subject to this operation as a derived nominal. Thus *John's marriage to Mary, John's resemblance to Bill* will not transform to *the marriage to Mary by John, the resemblance to Bill by John* [though *John's offer* (*of amnesty*) *to the prisoners* does transform to *the offer* (*of amnesty*) *to the prisoners by John*]. For additional related observations, see Lees (1960). This is a confused matter, however, and conclusions cannot be drawn with any confidence.

We have now discussed two transformations that apply to complex noun phrases: agent-postposing, which gives *the destruction of the city by the enemy,* and NP-preposing, which gives *the city's destruction.* Agent-postposing is simply a generalization of one of the components of the passive transformation. NP-preposing is similar to, and may fall under a generalization of, the other component. Suppose now that we have an underlying deep structure of the form *Det–N–Comp,* where the determiner is a noun phrase (ultimately possessive, if it remains in this position) and the complement is a noun phrase followed by the agent phrase *by* Δ; for example, *the enemy–destruction–of the city–by* Δ. Applying agent-postposing, we derive *the–destruction of the city–by the enemy,* as before. If we now extend NP-preposing so that it can apply not only in the cases given before, but also before agent phrases, we derive, from the last-formed structure, the phrase *the city's destruction by the enemy.* It is important to see, then, that the latter phrase is only apparently the nominalization of a passive; if it were really the nominalization of a passive, this fact would refute the lexicalist hypothesis, since, as was emphasized earlier, it follows from this hypothesis that transforms should not undergo the processes that give derived nominals. In fact, one major empirical justification offered for the lexicalist hypothesis was that, in a number of otherwise puzzling cases, it is precisely this state of affairs that we discover. But we now see that the crucial phrases need not be regarded as nominals derived transformationally from the passive (with the auxiliary mysteriously disappearing), but can rather be explained as, in effect, passives of base-generated derived nominals, by independently motivated transformations.

Notice that agent-postposing is obligatory for certain subject noun phrases that do not permit formation of possessives. Since agent-postposing is un-specifiable for gerundive nominals, there are certain derived nominals with no gerundive counterpart, as pointed out in Note 10. Under the transforma-tionalist hypothesis, there would be no more reason to expect agent-postposing in derived than in gerundive nominals. Hence an additional argument in support of the lexicalist hypothesis is that it provides this distinction on independent grounds.

It is possible that such derived nominals as *the necessity for John to leave, the likelihood that John will leave,* and so on might be derived by obligatory agent-postposing from the underlying noun phrases [*for John to leave*]*'s necessity,* [*that John will leave*]*'s likelihood.*

A minor transformational rule will replace *by* by *of* under certain condi-tions, permitting *the refusal to leave of those men* (or *the refusal of those men to leave*) alternating with *the refusal to leave by those men* (or *the refusal by those men to leave*). Presumably, it is this rule that applies in the case of the nominals *the growling of the lion,* etc. Some speakers apparently accept expressions such as *John's likelihood of leaving,* though to me these are entirely unacceptable. Perhaps such expressions can be derived, by an exten-sion of NP-preposing, from *the likelihood of John leaving.* Such expressions as * *John's likelihood to leave* apparently are acceptable to no one, exactly as is predicted by the lexicalist hypothesis.

Implicit in the rules given so far is the possibility that there will be base noun phrases of the form *Det–N–NP by* Δ, where the head noun is not derived from an underlying stem that also appears as a verb, thus a case of the sort illustrated in (22). Of course, such a possibility will be realized as a well-formed surface structure only if the determiner is filled by a phrase which can ultimately appear in the agent position, replacing the symbol Δ, which will otherwise, through the filtering effect of transformations, mark the struc-ture as not well formed. If it is true, as suggested above, that some form of "inalienable possession" is expressed by base rules generating noun phrases in the determiner position, then the possibility just sketched can be realized. That there may be structures of this sort is suggested by a fuller analysis of such phrases as *John's picture,* discussed briefly above. We noted that there are two interpretations of this phrase, one derived from the structure underlying *the picture that John has* by rule (37), and the other derived by NP-preposing, rule (39), from the complex noun phrase that would other-wise be realized as *the picture of John.* There is, however, still a third interpretation, namely, with the same meaning as *the picture that John painted.* Conceivably, this is the interpretation given to the base structure [$_{Det}$ *John's*]$_{Det}$ [$_N$ *picture*]$_N$, with a generalization of the notion "inalienable possession" to a kind of "intrinsic connection." A similar triple ambiguity can be found in other cases, e.g., *John's story*, where John can be the subject of the story (*the story of John*), the writer (intrinsic connection), or an editor proposing the story for publication at a meeting (*the story that John has*). Notice that if *John's picture, John's story*, and so on are generated in the base with the sense of intrinsic connection, they will be subject to rule (38), giving *that picture of John's, those stories of John's, the story of John's that I told you about*, and so on, all with the meaning of intrinsic connection. The latter phrases will thus be two-way ambiguous, meaning *the picture that John has* or *the picture that John painted* (though not *the picture of John*), and so on. This is of course true, and gives some further support for the analysis proposed.

Now consider the base structure *Det–N–NP–by* Δ, where the determiner is realized in the base as the noun phrase *John*, the head noun as *picture*, and the noun phrase complement as *Mary*. Without the agent phrase in the base structure, this will give *John's picture of Mary* (itself of course ambiguous, since another source could have been the structure underlying *the picture of Mary that John has*).[30] With the agent phrase generated in the base, the agent-postposing transformation must apply, giving *the picture of Mary by John*. Had the complement been omitted, we would derive *the picture by John*. Agent-postposing must precede the transformation of NP-preposing that gives *the city's destruction*, or we will derive *the destruction by the city* from *the–destroy–the city*. It therefore follows that *the picture (of Mary) by John* cannot be derived from the phrase *John's picture*, which is derived in turn from *the picture of John*. Hence *the picture of Mary by John* cannot have the latter meaning. Along these lines, a number of facts fall together in what seems a quite natural way.

Consider, finally, a slightly more complicated case, namely, a structure of the form: *Det–N–NP–by* Δ*–that NP has*, where the determiner is a possessivized noun phrase. An example would be (41):

(41)   **Rembrandt's portrait of Aristotle by Δ that the Metropolitan Museum has.**

Applying agent-postposing, we derive *the portrait of Aristotle by Rembrandt that the Metropolitan Museum has*. Rule (37) gives *the Metropolitan Museum's portrait of Aristotle by Rembrandt*. Rule (38) would then give the quite clumsy phrase *the portrait of Aristotle by Rembrandt of the Metropolitan Museum's*. This would be natural if the final phrase, *of the Metropolitan Museum's*, were omitted, in which case rule (39), NP-preposing, would then apply to give *Aristotle's portrait by Rembrandt*. Clearly, the rule of agent-postposing must be permitted to apply before rule (37), which forms *NP's N* from *the N that NP has*. Furthermore, the rule of agent-postposing cannot apply after rule (37). If this ordering were permitted, the underlying structure *the portrait of Aristotle by* Δ *that the Metropolitan has* would become, by (37), *the Metropolitan's portrait of Aristotle by* Δ, and then, by agent-postposing, *the portrait of Aristotle by the Metropolitan.* Therefore the ordering of the transformations we have been discussing must be: agent-postposing, (37), (38), (39).

So far we have been exploring the possibility that complex noun phrases, which ultimately will be possessivized if not removed from the determiner by a transformation, are derived directly by base rules such as (29). We have noted, however, that when the noun phrase is removed from the determiner, an article may appear in the position that it vacated. Thus we can have *the picture of Mary by John, a picture of Mary by John, several pictures of Mary by John, one of the pictures of Mary by John,* etc. These facts suggest that rule (29b) is incorrect, and that it be replaced by something like (42):

(42)   Article → [±def, (NP)]

The article, then, can be either definite or indefinite, or can be a full noun phrase with the associated feature [+ definite] or [− definite]. When the noun phrase is removed from the determiner by a transformation, the feature [±definite] will remain, much as the feature [+PRO] remains in certain positions when a noun phrase is removed. [Continuing with such an analysis, we would have to stipulate that a rule that applies automatically after (37) and after (39) — hence also to NPs generated in the article position by base rules — assigns the possessive formative to the final word of the noun phrase in question.] A similar analysis would hold for derived nominals, giving such phrases as (*several of*) *the proofs of the theorem by John, several proofs of the theorem by John* [which is nondefinite, as we can see from the sentence *there were several proofs of the theorem* (*by John*) *in the most recent issue of the journal*], etc. When the noun phrase constitutes the full determiner in the surface structure, the feature in question must be interpreted as definite, as we can see from the impossibility of * *there were John's proofs of the theorem in the journal,* with the same interpretation.

Rule (42) is not formulable within the framework that we have so far presupposed (cf. Note 2), which takes feature complexes to be associated only with lexical categories, and permits complex symbols to dominate a sequence of elements only within the word [cf. Chomsky (1965, p. 188f.)]. It has been suggested a number of times that this restriction is too heavy and that certain features should also be associated with nonlexical phrase categories.[31] The present considerations lend further support to these proposals.

Such an extension of the theory of syntactic features suggests that the distinction between features and categories is a rather artificial one. In the earliest work in generative grammar it was assumed that the elements of the underlying base grammar are formatives and categories; each category corresponds to a class of strings of formatives. This assumption was carried over from structuralist syntactic theories, which regarded a grammar as a system of classes of elements derived by analytic procedures of segmentation and classification. For reasons discussed in Chomsky (1965, Chapter 2), it was soon found necessary to depart from this assumption in the case of lexical categories. The resulting "mixed theory" had a certain technical artificiality, in that lexical categories were interpreted both as categories of the base (N, V, etc.) and as features in the lexicon ($+$N, $+$V, etc.). In fact, when the reliance on analytic procedures of segmentation and classification is abandoned, there is no reason to retain the notion of category at all, even for the base. We might just as well eliminate the distinction of feature and category, and regard all symbols of the grammar as sets of features. If the elements NP, VP, and so on are treated as certain feature complexes, then there is no incoherence in supposing that there are complex symbols of the form [$+$def, $+$NP]. Of course, it is necessary to stipulate with care the precise conditions under which complex symbols can be formed, at each level, or else the system of grammar becomes so powerful as to lose empirical interest. A number of possible restrictions suggest themselves, but I will not explore this general question any further here.

The reanalysis of phrase categories as features permits the formulation of such base rules as (42) as well as the transformational rules that were introduced in our informal discussion of complex noun phrases. It also opens up other possibilities that should be considered. For example, with this reanalysis it becomes possible, under certain restricted circumstances, to introduce new phrase structure through transformations. To illustrate with a concrete example, consider such sentences as (43), (44):

(43)   A man is in the room.
(44)   There is a man in the room.

It is clear, in (44), that *there* is a noun phrase; (44) is subject to such rules, for example, as the interrogative transformation that presupposes this analysis. At the same time, there is some empirical support for the argument that (44) is derived from (43). However, these conclusions are difficult to reconcile within the theory of transformational grammar, since an item (such as *there*) introduced by a transformation can be assigned phrase structure only when it replaces some string which already has this phrase structure; and it requires some artificiality to generate (44) in this way. However, if [$+$NP] is a feature (or a complex of features) that can be part of a complex symbol introduced by a transformation, the difficulty is easily removed. For example, if we give to the structure underlying (43) the proper analysis (*e, e, a man, is, in the room*)[32] and apply the elementary transformation that replaces the first term by the complex symbol [*there,* $+$NP] (*there* standing for a feature matrix of the usual sort) and the second term by the fourth, which is then deleted, we derive a phrase-marker which is appropriate for further operations.

To take a slightly more complex example, consider such sentences as (45):

(45)   a. **What John did was read a book about himself.**
     b. **What John read was a book about himself.**

As noted earlier (p. 198), we might explain many of the properties of these sentences by deriving them from a base structure of roughly the form (46):

(46)

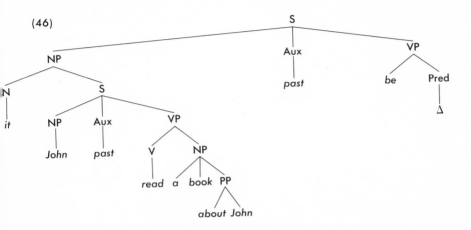

We might then derive (45b) in the following way: Familiar rules apply to the most deeply embedded S to give *John past read a book about himself.* A new substitution transformation replaces the unspecified predicate Δ of (46) by the object of the embedded sentence, *a book about himself,* leaving a "PRO-form" in its place. This gives: *it–John past read it–past be–a book about himself.* Relativization and other familiar rules, supplemented by a rule that replaces *it that* by *what,* give (45b).

But consider now (45a). Again, the most deeply embedded S is converted to *John read a book about himself.* But in this case, the new substitution transformation replaces the unspecified predicate not by the object of the embedded sentence but by its whole verb phrase, which is replaced by a "PRO-form," *do-it,* giving *it–John past do it–past be–read a book about himself.* The remaining rules give (45a). The problem, however, is that the element *do-it* must be specified as a structure of the form V–NP. This is straightforward in the case of the "PRO-verb" *do,* but in the earlier framework there was no way to specify that *it* is a NP in the derived structure. Observe that the embedded VP is replaced by *do-it* even when it contains no NP at all, as in *what John did was read.* The argument that the introduced element *do-it* is actually of the form V–NP is greatly strengthened by other forms, for example, the sentence (47),[33] in which case passivization applies to it:

(47)   **John apologized more meekly than it had ever been done before.**

Once again, if phrase categories are reinterpreted as features, there is no problem in formulating the required rules. The verb of the embedded VP can become *do* by an extension of the rule of *do*-insertion, and the complex symbol [*it*, +NP] is introduced by the transformation in the appropriate position.

In short, there is some motivation for the limited extension of the mechanisms for assigning derived constituent structure that results from a decision to replace categories systematically by features that can enter into complex symbols.

Continuing to explore consequences of the lexicalist hypothesis, let us return to the rules (21) which expand NP, VP, and AP into expressions containing optional complements. The phrase category "complement" seems to play no role in transformations. We can easily abolish this category if we replace the rules (21) by a single schema, with a variable standing for the lexical categories N, A, V. To introduce a more uniform notation, let us use the symbol $\bar{X}$ for a phrase containing X as its head. Then the base rules introducing N, A, and V will be replaced by a schema (48), where in place of . . . there appears the full range of structures that serve as complements and X can be any one of N, A, or V:

(48) $\bar{X} \rightarrow X \ldots$

Continuing with the same notation, the phrases immediately dominating $\bar{N}$, $\bar{A}$ and $\bar{V}$ will be designated $\bar{\bar{N}}$, $\bar{\bar{A}}$, $\bar{\bar{V}}$ respectively. To introduce further terminological uniformity, let us refer to the phrase associated with $\bar{N}$, $\bar{A}$, $\bar{V}$ in the base structure as the "specifier" of these elements. Then the elements $\bar{N}$, $\bar{A}$, $\bar{V}$ might themselves be introduced in the base component by the schema (49):

(49) $\bar{\bar{X}} \rightarrow [\text{Spec}, \bar{X}] \, \bar{X}$

where [Spec, $\bar{N}$] will be analyzed as the determiner, [Spec, $\bar{V}$] as the auxiliary (perhaps with time adverbials associated), and [Spec, $\bar{A}$] perhaps as the system of qualifying elements associated with adjective phrases (comparative structures, *very*, etc.). The initial rule of the base grammar would then be (50) (with possible optional elements added):

(50) $S \rightarrow \bar{\bar{N}} \, \bar{\bar{V}}$.

Thus a skeletal form of the base is induced by the "primitive" categories N, A, V (which, as noted earlier, may themselves be the reflection of an underlying feature structure).

In other respects, the primitive categories might differ, for example, if V is analyzed into a copula–predicate construction. Furthermore, it can be expected that the base rules for any language will contain language-specific modifications of the general pattern. If this line of thought is correct, the

structure of derived nominals would be something like (51), and the structure
of a related sentence, like (52) (omitting much detail):

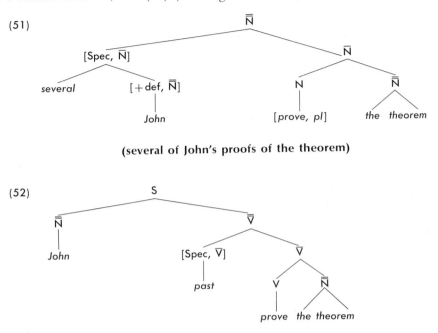

(51)

(several of John's proofs of the theorem)

(52)

(John proved the theorem)

The internal structure of the nominal (51) mirrors that of the sentence (52).
The strict subcategorization features of the lexical item *prove* take account
of the phrases $\overline{V}$ and $\overline{N}$ dominating the category to which it is assigned in
(51), (52), respectively. Its selectional features refer to the heads of the
associated phrases, which are the same in both cases. The category $\overline{\overline{N}}$, like
S, is a recursive element of the base.[34] Correspondingly, it would be natural
to suppose that in the cyclic application of transformations, the phrases of
the form $\overline{\overline{N}}$ play the same role as the phrases of the form S in specifying
the domain of transformations.

A structure of the sort just outlined is reminiscent of the system of phrase
structure analysis developed by Harris in the 1940's.[35] In Harris' system,
statements applying to categories represented in the form X^n (n a numeral)
applied also to categories represented in the form X^m ($m < n$). One might
seek analogous properties of the system just analyzed.

So far, we have surveyed some evidence in support of the lexicalist hypothesis and explored its consequences for grammatical theory and the analysis
of English structure. As was noted, the central objection to any form of the
lexicalist hypothesis in earlier work such as Lees (1960) was eliminated by

later elaborations of syntactic theory to incorporate syntactic features and a separate lexicon. Other objections remain, however. The strongest and most interesting conclusion that follows from the lexicalist hypothesis is that derived nominals should have the form of base sentences, whereas gerundive nominals may in general have the form of transforms. We have indicated that in many cases this conclusion is confirmed, and that at least some apparent counterexamples (e.g., *the city's destruction by the enemy*) can be satisfactorily explained in terms of independently motivated rules. There remain, however, certain more difficult cases. As is well-known, processes of derivational morphology are applicable in sequence — they may even be recursive.[36] But consider such expressions as (53):

(53)   a. The book is readable.
      b. the book's readability
      c. John is self-indulgent.
      d. John's self-indulgence

If the lexicalist hypothesis is accepted for the full range of derived nominals, then (53b) and (53d) must be analyzed in terms of base structures such as (51). Since *readability* and *self-indulgence* are obviously derived from *readable* and *self-indulgent,* it follows that (53a) and (53c) must in effect also be base structures rather than transforms from other structures such as, perhaps (54):

(54)   a. the book is able [$_S$for the book to be read]$_S$
      b. John is indulgent to John.

However, a case can be made for transformational derivation of (53a) and (53c) from something like (54a) and (54b), contradicting the lexicalist hypothesis, in this instance.

The seriousness of this objection to the lexicalist hypothesis depends on the strength of the case for the transformational derivation in question. It seems to me that the case is far from persuasive. Notice, for one thing, that the proposed transformation is not "meaning-preserving" (except in the trivialized sense discussed on p. 188), as Chapin observes. In fact, the remarks of Note 11 can be extended to these cases as well. Thus, *readable* is much more sharply restricted in meaning than *able to be read.* In a wide range of other cases the meaning is restricted or based on a very different subregularity (consider *commendable, abominable, irreplaceable, incomparable, despicable, decidable, laudable, insufferable, noticeable, changeable, pitiable, enviable, preferable, insufferable, inviolable, admirable, deplorable, adorable, irritable, lamentable, quotable, detestable, lovable, admissible, livable, laughable, honorable, valuable,* and so on).[37] It follows that any argument for the transformational analysis that is based on semantic grounds or on grounds of selectional relations will be very weak.

In fact, even in the best of cases such arguments are weak; correspondingly, since the earliest work in transformational generative grammar, the attempt has been made to support them by independent syntactic arguments. The reason is that an alternative, nontransformational approach can be envisaged if the support for transformations is simply meaning equivalence or sameness of selectional relations. Where the grounds are semantic, an alternative is an enrichment of the rules of semantic interpretation;[38] and regularities involving only selectional features might in principle be stated as redundancy rules of the lexicon.[39] For example, insofar as a subregularity exists regarding selectional rules in the case of *–able,* it can be formulated as a lexical rule that assigns the feature $[X —]$ to a lexical item $[V–able]$ where V has the intrinsic selectional feature $[— X]$. It would follow, then, that where the embedded passive in (54a) has as its grammatical subject a noun phrase that is not the underlying object (or, in the case of "pseudo-passives" such as *he can be relied on,* the "pseudo-object"), the corresponding form (53a) will be excluded. In fact, there is evidence in support of this conclusion. Thus we cannot derive *John is believable (imaginable, expectable,* etc.) *to have left* from *NP believes (imagines, expects) John to have left,* although a deep object such as *this claim* can appear in the context — *is believable.* There are many open questions regarding such constructions, but it seems to me that the argument for a transformational analysis of (53a) is not compelling.

What is more, the argument for a transformational analysis of (53b) from (53a) is weak on independent grounds. Thus it is difficult to see how such an analysis could account for the fact that *readability* may refer not to a fact, event, process, etc., but rather to a property; thus the phrase *the readability of the book is its only redeeming feature* does not mean *(the fact) that the book is readable is its only redeeming feature.* Although perhaps such difficulties can be overcome, as matters now stand, examples such as (53a), (53b) do not seem to me to offer a serious argument against the lexicalist hypothesis.

The situation seems to me similar in the case of (53c) and (53d). Examples such as (53c) seem to provide the strongest case for transformational analysis of derived forms, but even here, the matter is far from clear. Consider, for example, the sentences in (55):

(55)   a. John sent a self-addressed envelope.
      b. This is clearly a self-inflicted wound.
      c. The prophecy is self-fulfilling.
      d. Confrontations between students and administration are self-generating.
      e. John is self-educated.
      f. John's remarks are self-congratulatory.
      g. John's actions are self-destructive.

Sentence (55a) does not mean that the envelope was addressed to itself; the phrase *self-addressed envelope* can appear in sentences where there is no syntactic source for *self* at all (*self-addressed envelopes are barred by law from the mails*). The same is true of (55b), (55f), (55g). Sentence (55c) does not, strictly speaking, mean that the prophecy fulfilled the prophecy, which is senseless, but rather that it led to a state of affairs that fulfilled the prophecy. In the case of (55d), what is meant is that certain confrontations generate other confrontations of the same sort; confrontations do not generate themselves. (55e) cannot be derived by a rule analogous to one that purportedly forms (53c) from (54b), since the postulated underlying form, *John was educated by himself,* is ruled out by the principle, whatever it may be, that makes passives incompatible with reflexivization. A similar argument applies to (55g); the postulated underlying form, *John's actions destroy himself,* is ruled out by general conditions on reflexivization. Furthermore, a consideration of forms such as *self-conscious, self-proclaimed* (*enemy*), *self-contained, self-evident, self-esteem, self-explanatory* (i.e., needs no explanation), *self-important, self-seeking,* and so on makes one search for a general transformational analysis of such structures seem ill-conceived. The variety and idiosyncrasy of such items seem to be of the sort that is characteristic of the lexicon; it is difficult to see how they can be accounted for by syntactic rules of any generality. Furthermore, the difficulties in deriving (53b) from (53a) carry over to the pair (53c), (53d).

The discussion so far has been restricted to gerundive and derived nominals, and has barely touched on a third category with some peculiar properties, namely, nominals of the sort illustrated in (56):

(56)   a. John's refusing of the offer
b. John's proving of the theorem
c. the growing of tomatoes

These forms are curious in a number of respects, and it is not at all clear whether the lexicalist hypothesis can be extended to cover them. That it should be so extended is suggested by the fact that these forms, like derived nominals, appear to have the internal structure of noun phrases; thus the possessive subject can be replaced by a determiner, as in (56c). On the other hand, adjective insertion seems quite unnatural in this construction. In fact, there is an artificiality to the whole construction that makes it quite resistant to systematic investigation. Furthermore, the construction is quite limited. Thus we cannot have *the feeling sad, the trying to win, the arguing about money, the leaving,* etc.

In apparent conflict with an extension of the lexicalist hypothesis is the fact that these constructions exist in the case of certain verbs that we have tentatively derived from underlying intransitives, as in the case of (56c), which is structurally ambiguous, as contrasted with the derived nominal (57), discussed on p. 192, which is unambiguous:

(57)   the growth of tomatoes

If the lexicalist hypothesis is extended to the forms (56), then we must suppose that both *tomatoes grow* and *NP grows tomatoes* are base forms. However, to account for the interpretation of (57) as well as for the relation of transitive and intransitive *grow* we were led to regard *NP grows tomatoes* as the causative of the underlying structure *tomatoes grow*.[40] These various assumptions are mutually consistent only if we reject the analysis of the causative discussed on p. 192, which postulated the base structure (58) for *John grows tomatoes*, and assume instead that the base structure is (59):

(58)   John [+cause] [$_S$tomatoes grow]$_S$
(59)   John [+cause, grow] tomatoes

In other words, we postulate that there is a feature [+cause] which can be assigned to certain verbs as a lexical property. Associated with this feature are certain redundancy rules which are, in this case, universal, hence not part of the grammar of English but rather among the principles by which any grammar is interpreted. These principles specify that an intransitive with the feature [+cause] becomes transitive and that its selectional features are systematically revised so that the former subject becomes the object. Similar principles of redundancy apply to the associated rules of semantic interpretation. To account for the distinction between (56c) and (57), we must restrict the feature [+cause] with respect to the feature that distinguishes derived nominals such as *growth* from forms such as *growing*, limiting it to the latter case. Unless there are some general grounds for the hierarchy thus established, the explanation offered earlier for the nonambiguity of (57) is weakened, since it involves an *ad hoc* step. There is, nevertheless, a partial explanation and a natural way of stating a complex of facts.

To summarize, three types of nominalizations have been considered in this discussion: the gerundive nominals such as (60), the derived nominals such as (61), and the "mixed" forms (62), which to me seem rather clumsy, though quite comprehensible, when a derived nominal also exists:

(60)   John's refusing the offer
(61)   John's refusal of the offer
(62)   John's refusing of the offer

On the basis of the evidence surveyed here, it seems that the transformationalist hypothesis is correct for the gerundive nominals and the lexicalist hypothesis for the derived nominals and perhaps, though much less clearly so, for the mixed forms. This conclusion has a variety of consequences for general linguistic theory and for the analysis of English structure. Such material provides a case study of the complex of problems that arise when linguistic theory is elaborated so as to incorporate both grammatical transformations and lexical features.

NOTES

1. This work was supported in part by the U. S. Air Force [ESD Contract AF19(628)-2487] and the National Institutes of Health (Grant MH-13390-01).

2. The presupposed framework is discussed in greater detail in a number of recent publications, specifically, J. Katz and P. Postal (1964); Chomsky (1965); and references cited there.

3. Needless to say, any specific bit of evidence must be interpreted within a fixed framework of assumptions, themselves subject to question. But in this respect the study of language is no different from any other empirical investigation.

4. Henceforth I shall use labeled brackets to indicate structures in phrase-markers; an expression of the form $X[_A Y]_A Z$ signifies that the string Y is assigned to the category A in the string XYZ.

5. There are a number of suggestive remarks on this matter in Kenny (1963).

6. The fullest discussion of this and related topics is in Lees (1960), from which I will draw freely.

7. I follow here the proposal in Chomsky (1965, p. 222) that the base rules give structures of the form NP–Aux–VP, with Aux analyzed as Aux_1 (Aspect), Aux_1 being further analyzed as either Tense (Modal) or as various nominalization elements and Aspect as (perfect) (progressive). Forms such as * *John's being reading the book* (but not *John's having been reading the book*) are blocked by a restriction against certain *–ing –ing* sequences (compare * *John's stopping reading, John's having stopped reading*, etc.). Tense and Modal are thus excluded from the gerundive nominal, but not Aspect. Nothing that follows depends on the exact form of the rules for gerundive nominalization, but I think that a good case can be made for this analysis.

8. The transformationalist position is adopted in much recent work, for example, Lakoff (1965). It is argued in some detail in Chapin (1967). The lexicalist position is proposed in Chomsky (1965, pp. 219–220), but with the analysis of possessive subjects that is rejected here on p. 189; it is implicitly rejected, incorrectly, as I now believe, in Chomsky (1965, p. 184). A compromise position of the sort noted above is developed in detail by Langendoen (1967a). It is also discussed in Annear and Elliot (1965). Langendoen presents an analysis very much like the one that I will propose directly, and cites a good deal of evidence in support of it. He refrains from adopting a full lexicalist position because of such ambiguities as that of *proof* in *John's proof of the theorem* (*took him a long time, is reproduced in the new text*). However, this objection to the full lexicalist hypothesis, for which I am responsible, seems to me very weak. One might just as well suppose that a lexical ambiguity is involved, analogous to the ambiguity of such words as *book, pamphlet*, etc., which can be either concrete or abstract (*the book weighs five pounds, . . . was written in a hurry*), as was noted by Postal (1966b). See Note 12 in this connection.

9. There are certain restrictions. For example, the transformation is inapplicable when the subject is of a type that does not permit possessives (e.g., * *that John was here's surprising me*), and it often is very unnatural with verbs that involve extraposition (* *it's surprising me that John was here*, * *John's happening to be a good friend of mine*), although *it's having surprised me that John was here* and *John's happening to be there* seem tolerable.

10. There is also at least one class of cases where the derived nominals are permitted but not the gerundive nominals, namely, examples where the gerundive is blocked

because the subject does not possessivize (cf. Note 9). Thus the gerundive nominal *his negative attitude toward the proposal's disruption of our plans* is clumsy and *his bringing up of that objection's disrupting our plans* is impossible, but we can form the associated derived nominals: *the disruption of our plans by his negative attitude toward the proposal, . . . by his bringing up of that objection.* We return to these cases directly.

11. The artificiality might be reduced by deriving nominals from underlying nouns with some kind of sentential element included, where the meaning can be expressed in this way: for example, *John's intelligence* from *the fact that John is intelligent* (in *John's intelligence is undeniable*), and from *the extent to which John is intelligent* (in *John's intelligence exceeds his foresight*). It is difficult to find a natural source for the nominal, however, in such sentences as *John's intelligence is his most remarkable quality.* This idea runs into other difficulties. Thus we can say *John's intelligence, which is his most remarkable quality, exceeds his foresight;* but the appositive clause, on this analysis, would have to derive from * *the extent to which John is intelligent is his most remarkable quality,* since in general the identity of structure required for appositive clause formation to take place goes even beyond identity of the given phrase-markers, as was pointed out by Lees (1960, p. 76). Many open questions regarding recoverability of deletion in erasure transformations arise as this problem is pursued. For some discussion, see Chomsky (1965, pp. 145f., 179f.), Ross (1967a); and Chomsky (1968). Ross (1967a) suggests (Chapter 3, *n.* 19) that identity of base structures is required for erasure.

The scope of the existing subregularities, I believe, has been considerably exaggerated in work that takes the transformationalist position. For example, Lakoff (1965) gives what are probably the strongest cases for this position, but even of these very few are acceptable on the semantic grounds that he proposes as justifying them. Thus *John's deeds* does not have the same meaning as *things which John did* (p. IV-2), but rather, *fairly significant things which John did* (we would not say that one of John's first deeds this morning was to brush his teeth). We cannot derive *John's beliefs* from *what John believes* (p. V-23), because of such sentences as *John's beliefs are not mutually consistent, . . . are numerous,* etc., or *John's beliefs, some of which are amazing, . . . ;* nor can we derive it from *the things that John believes,* since the semantic interpretation will then be incorrect in such expressions as *I respect John's beliefs* or *John's beliefs are intense.* It is difficult to see how one can transformationally relate *I read all of John's writings* to *I read all of what John wrote,* in view of such expressions as *I read all of John's critical writings,* etc. And if one is to postulate an abstract verb *poetize* underlying *John's poems,* then what about *John's book reviews, dialogues, sonnets, limericks, Alexandrines,* etc.? In general, there are few cases where problems of this sort do not arise. Correspondingly, the transformationalist position is impossible to support, and difficult even to maintain, on semantic grounds.

12. It is immaterial for present purposes whether a lexical entry is regarded as a Boolean function of specified features or is to be replaced by a set of lexical entries, each of which consists of a set of specified features. It is unclear whether these approaches to problems of range of meaning and range of function are terminological variants, or are empirically distinguishable. Some of the matters touched on in Note 11 may be relevant. Consider, for example, the ambiguity of *book* and *proof* mentioned

in Note 8. Certain conditions on recoverability of deletion would lead to the conclusion that a single lexical entry is involved when two senses of the word can be combined in apposition. Under this assumption, the choice between the alternatives just mentioned in the case of *book* and *proof* would be determined by the status of such sentences as *this book, which weighs five pounds, was written in a hurry* and *John's proof of the theorem, which took him a long time, is reproduced in the new text.*

13. For discussion, see Rosenbaum (1967), and Kiparsky and Kiparsky (1967).

14. See references of Note 13.

15. This solution is proposed by Lakoff (1965, p. A-15f.), but on the transformationalist grounds that he adopts, there is no motivation for it.

16. There are many problems to be explored here. Notice, for example, that *John interested me in his ideas* is very different from *John interested me with his ideas* (both types of prepositional phrases occur in *John interested me in politics with his novel approach*); only the latter is similar in meaning to *John's ideas interested me.* A full analysis of these expressions will have to take into account instrumental phrases, concerning which there are numerous problems that have been discussed in a number of stimulating papers by Fillmore, Lakoff, and others.

The brief mention of causatives in Chomsky (1965) takes the main verb of (12) to be the verb *cause,* but the distinction between direct and indirect causation suggests that this cannot be correct. Lakoff (1966b) argues that the distinction between direct and indirect causation is a matter of use, not underlying structure; thus he argues that *a breeze stiffened John's arm* and *a breeze caused John's arm to stiffen* are generally used to indicate direct causation, while *a breeze brought it about that John's arm stiffened* and *a breeze made John's arm stiffen* are generally used to indicate indirect causation, but that actually either interpretation is possible, from which it would follow that the underlying verb could be taken to be *cause* in causative constructions. However, it does not seem correct to regard this simply as a distinction of use. Thus we can say *John's clumsiness caused the door to open* (*the window to break*) but not *John's clumsiness opened the door* (*broke the window*). For some discussion of this matter, see Barbara Hall (1965).

17. It is not obvious that such forms as *the reading of the book* are ordinary derived nominals. I return to this matter briefly below.

18. This was pointed out to me by M. Kajita. Notice that *his criticism of the book for its failure . . .* is grammatical. Presumably, *for*-phrases of this sort are part of the complement system for verbs and nouns.

19. I refer here to the distinction drawn in Chomsky (1965, p. 11f.). For the distinction between direct and derivative generation, see Chomsky (1965, p. 227, n. 2).

20. Langendoen (1967a) discusses a number of examples of this sort.

21. For example, such a device could be used to establish, say, that all verbs are derived from underlying prepositions. If one wishes to pursue this line of reasoning, he might begin with the traditional view that all verbs contain the copula, then arguing that *John visited England* is of the same form as *John is in England* (i.e., * *John is visit England*), where *visit* is a preposition of the category of *in* that obligatorily transforms to a verb incorporating the copula. Thus we are left with only one "relational" category, prepositions. To rule out such absurdities, it is necessary to exclude the devices that permit them to be formulated or to assign a high cost to the use of such devices.

22. Still another possibility would be to take the underlying form to be $[_{NP}Det\ N]_{NP}$ be $[_{NP}Det\ N\ Comp]_{NP}$ (e.g., *the question is the question whether John should leave*), with the second occurrence of the repeated noun deleted, but this too presupposes that the Det–N–Comp structures are base forms, not reduced relatives.

23. Cf., for example, Lakoff (1966*b*), Appendix A.

24. Examples from Lakoff, (1966*b*).

25. It is immaterial for the present discussion whether the structures to the right of the arrow are, indeed, base structures, or whether certain of them are derived from "deeper" or different structures. It is sufficient, for present purposes, to note that (30), or something sufficiently like it, is the general form of the determiner at some stage of derivation. What is crucial, for the present, is that the possessive noun phrase is being assigned the status of the article $\pm$def, whatever this may be in the base structure.

26. These examples are due to John Ross.

27. If we take the structure in question to be, rather, (*several of* [(*John's*) (*proofs of the theorem*)]), the same conclusion follows, with respect now to the embedded phrase *John's proofs of the theorem*.

28. Alternatively, it has been proposed that the preposition is an obligatory part of the underlying noun phrase, and is deleted in certain contexts, for example, the context: verb — . This seems to me dubious, however. Notice that the preposition is not invariably deleted in the context verb — NP, for example, in such cases as *approve of John*. Hence we would have to postulate an idiosyncratic feature *F* that subdivides verbs into those that do and those that do not undergo *of*-deletion. An arbitrary bifurcation of the lexicon is the worst possible case, of course. No such arbitrary feature is needed if we suppose the *of* to be introduced in the context N — NP. Of course *approve* will be distinguished from *read* by the strict subcategorization features [— PP], [— NP] (or whatever variants of these are employed), exactly as *laugh* (*at John*) is distinguished from *see* (*John*); this, however, is not a new classification, but rather one that is necessary however the matter of *of* is handled. To make matters worse for the theory of *of*-deletion, the new, idiosyncratic feature *F* will have to cut across related senses of a single item, since we have *approve–the proposal* alongside of *approve–of the proposal*. Furthermore, there is a possibility, which should be explored, of combining the proposed rule of *of*-insertion with the rule governing placement of *of* in prenominal constructions such as *lots of work, several of the boys, a group of men*, etc. Such considerations suggest that the preposition is an inherent part of the prepositional phrase, but not of the object.

29. Such an analysis of the phrases in question is proposed by Kinsuke Hasegawa, "The Passive Construction in English," forthcoming in *Language*. Hasegawa suggests, furthermore, that the passive derives from a matrix structure containing the grammatical subject as object: thus *Bill was seen by John* would derive from something like *Bill is: John saw Bill*. Despite his arguments, I am skeptical about this proposal. A serious objection, it seems to me, is that there are phrases which can appear as grammatical subject only in the passive construction. Thus we can have *a man to do the job was found by John* from *John found a man to do the job* [cf. (22n)], but such expressions as *a man to do the job came to see me* seem highly unnatural. Similarly, there are certain idioms that undergo passivization (cf. *Aspects*, p. 190f.) although the phrase that appears as grammatical subject cannot normally appear as a deep subject (*I didn't expect that offense would be taken at that remark, advantage was*

taken of John, etc.). Such facts are difficult to reconcile with the proposal that the passive derives from a matrix proposition with an embedded complement.

30. Notice, then, that the transformation (37) that gives *John's picture* from *the picture that John has* will also give *John's picture of Mary* from *the picture of Mary that John has.* The transformation therefore applies not to a structure of the form *Det-N-that NP has* but rather *Det-N̄-that NP has,* where N̄ represents the expression *picture of Mary* (in *the picture of Mary that John has*) or the expression *picture* (in *the picture that John has*). We return to the status of N̄ below. On p. 197 we noted another situation in which the noun and its complement appear to form a single unit.

31. See Weinreich (1966), and McCawley (1967). Several of the arguments presented in these papers seem to me very weak, however. For example, McCawley argues that indices must be assigned to full noun phrases rather than to nouns, as suggested in *Aspects.* But this argument follows from an assumption which I see no reason to accept, namely, that in the theory outlined by Chomsky (1965), an index must be assigned to the noun *hat* in such sentences as *John bought a red hat and Bill bought a brown one.* This assumption in turn follows from a theory of indices as referents which I find unintelligible, since it provides no interpretation, so far as I can see, for the case in which nouns are used with no specific intended reference, or for plurals of indefinite or infinite reference, and so on. Until these matters are cleared up, I see no force to McCawley's contention.

32. Where *e* is the identity element. To be more precise, the structural description of the transformation would have to provide further information, but this goes beyond the detail necessary to clarify the point at issue. One might extend this operation of *there*-insertion, introducing the complex symbol [*there,* +NP, α *plural*] (α = + or α = −), where the third term in the proper analysis (*a man,* in the cited example) is [α *plural*], plurality now being regarded as a feature that ascends from a head noun to the NP node dominating it. This would make it possible for the rule of *there*-insertion to precede the rule of number agreement. It would also make possible the derivation of *there are believed to be CIA agents in the university* from *it is believed* [*there to be CIA agents in the university*] just as *CIA agents are believed to be in the university* might derive from *it is believed* [*CIA agents to be in the university*], along lines described in Rosenbaum (1967).

33. Brought to my attention by John Ross.

34. The same conclusion is argued on different grounds by Lakoff and Peters (1966). Further evidence that transformations apply to the domain N̄ is provided by the fact (pointed out to me by John Ross) that extraposition from the determiner takes place inside a noun phrase, as in: *one of the boys who are here who is a friend of mine.*

35. Harris (1951, Chapter 16).

36. Some examples are discussed by Chapin (1967), which presents the case for the transformationalist hypothesis on the grounds to which we now briefly turn.

37. There are also, of course, many cases where there is no possible base form such as (54a), e.g., *probable, feasible, (im)practicable, formidable, peaceable, knowledgeable, perishable, appreciable, sociable, flexible, amiable, variable, actionable, amenable, reasonable, seasonable, personable, miserable, venerable, inexorable, favorable, pleasurable, palatable, tractable, delectable, ineluctable, salable, habitable,*

creditable, profitable, hospitable, charitable, comfortable, reputable, irascible, incredible, audible, legible, eligible, negligible, intelligible, indelible, horrible, visible, sensible, responsible, accessible, possible, plausible, compatible.

38. Such an alternative is of course programmatic insofar as semantic interpretation remains obscure. But the necessity for rules that relate deep structures to (absolute) semantic interpretations seems clear, and it is dangerous to base any argument on the fact that we know little about such rules. If we knew nothing about phonology, it would be tempting to try to account for phonetic form by much more elaborate syntactic processes. Knowing something about phonology, we can see why this step is ill-advised.

39. As was pointed out to me by E. Klima.

40. An alternative analysis that derives *tomatoes grow* from *NP grows tomatoes* is implausible, since it would imply that *children grow* derives from * *NP grows children.* See Chomsky (1965, p. 214).

On Declarative Sentences[1]

JOHN ROBERT ROSS

13

1.1 In Austin (1962), the Oxford philosopher J. L. Austin pointed out that there is an important distinction between such sentences as those in (1)

(1) a. Prices slumped.
  b. I like you when you giggle.
  c. Even Rodney's best friends won't tell him.

which can be true or false, and sentences like those in (2)

(2) a. I promise you that I won't squeal.
  b. I sentence you to two weeks in The Bronx.
  c. I christen this ship *The U.S.S. Credibility Gap.*
  d. I pronounce you man and wife.

which have, instead of truth values, various conditions pertaining to appropriateness of use. Thus (2b) may be used appropriately only by a judge, or by one otherwise empowered to impose sentences, and (2d) only by someone with the authority to marry people. (2a) may be uttered by someone who intends to squeal, but it is not false, for all that: the uttering of (2a), whatever the intentions of the utterer, can *constitute* a promise,[2] whereas the action of uttering (1a) does not constitute a slump in prices.

Austin calls sentences like those in (1) *constative* sentences, and ones like those in (2) *performative* sentences. Performative sentences must have first person subjects and usually have second person direct or indirect objects[3] in deep structure.[4] They must be affirmative and nonnegative, they must be in the present tense, and their main verb must be one of the large class of true verbs which includes those in (3).

(3) advise, answer, appoint, ask, authorize, beg, bequeath, beseech, caution, cede, claim, close, command, condemn, counsel, dare, declare, demand,

empower, enquire, entreat, excommunicate, grant, implore, inform, instruct, offer, order, pledge, pronounce, propose, request, require, say, sentence, vow, warn, write[5]

Since the sentences in (4), although their main verbs are [+performative], do not conform to all the above conditions, they are not performative sentences. Therefore, the adverb *hereby*, which is characteristic of performative sentences,[6] produces strangeness or total unacceptability if inserted into these sentences:

(4) a. Bill (* hereby) promises you not to squeal.
     b. I (? hereby) command Tom to pick up that wallet.
     c. * Do I (hereby) promise you to be faithful?
     d. * I don't (hereby) pronounce you man and wife.
     e. I (* hereby) warned you that Bill would be shot.

Austin (1962, p. 32) makes the interesting claim that both sentences in (5) are performative, that the only difference is that in (5a) the performative verb is explicit, while in (5b) it is implicit:

(5) a. I order you to go.
     b. Go!

1.2 It has long been argued by transformational grammarians[7] that imperative sentences like (5b), where no subject need appear in surface structure, but where a second person subject is understood, should be derived from structures which actually contain a noun phrase (NP) *you* as subject. This is but one of the many examples where a part of a sentence which has been called "understood" or "implicit" by traditional grammarians is present in deep structure, the abstract representation which is postulated by generative grammarians as underlying the more superficial constituent structure representations of traditional grammar.[8]

There are a number of facts which suggest that Austin's contention that sentences like (5b) contain implicit performatives is to be captured by postulating deep structures for them which are almost identical to the deep structure which has been assumed to underlie the superficially more complex (5a).[9] I will not discuss these arguments, for they are not central to the main thesis of this present paper.[10] This thesis is that declarative sentences, such as those in (1), must also be analyzed as being implicit performatives, and must be derived from deep structures containing an explicitly represented performative main verb. Thus, for example, the deep structure of (1a) will not be that shown schematically in (6), as has been generally assumed previously [in (6) and throughout this paper I will disregard problems connected with the deep structure representation of tenses and of the English verbal auxiliary, for I have discussed these elsewhere[11]].

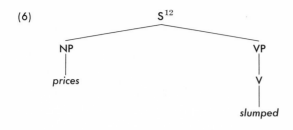

Rather, the deep structure of (1a) must be the more abstract structure shown in (7).[13]

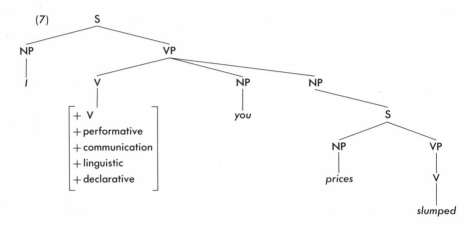

Thus every declarative sentence (but cf. Section 3.4 below) will be derived from a deep structure containing as an embedded clause what ends up in surface structure as an independent clause. Although most of the arguments which I will cite below in support of this analysis are drawn from English, analogs for some of them can be found in many languages, and I know of no evidence which contradicts the assumption that the analysis can be generalized to all languages of the world. Of course, the mere fact that no counterevidence is available in some particular language does not justify the postulation of more abstract deep structures like (7) for that language, unless positive evidence can be found. Nonetheless, the absence of direct counter-evidence is at least encouraging.

1.3 The outline of this paper is as follows: In Section 2, fourteen arguments which support the analysis implicit in (7) are presented. In Section 3, the rule of *performative deletion*, which, among other things, converts (7) to (1a),[14] is stated, and various technical problems in the analysis are discussed. In Section 4, two alternative analyses for the facts presented in Section 2 are proposed, and each is compared with the analysis implicit in (7). Finally, in Section 5, some of the consequences which this analysis has for the theory of languages are examined.

2. The fourteen arguments below for assuming every declarative sentence to be derived from an embedded clause fall into three main groups. In Section 2.1 seven arguments suggesting the existence of a higher subject I are presented. In Section 2.2, I discuss three further arguments which indicate that the main verb of the higher sentences must be a verb like *say*, and in Section 2.3 I discuss the three arguments I know of within English which suggest that the performative verb above must have an indirect object *you*. A final argument falling under none of these categories is discussed in Section 2.4.

2.1.1 In Lees and Klima (1963), it is shown that a large number of the cases in which reflexives cannot appear, such as the sentences in (8)

(8) a. I think that $\left\{ \begin{array}{c} I \\ * \text{ myself} \end{array} \right\}$ will win.

   b. **Have you ever wondered why Jill gave** $\left\{ \begin{array}{c} you \\ * \text{ yourself} \end{array} \right\}$ **that tie?**

   c. **He resented Betty's having seduced** $\left\{ \begin{array}{c} him \\ * \text{ himself} \end{array} \right\}$.

can be accounted for if the reflexive rule is stated (informally) as in (9):

(9) **One NP becomes the anaphoric reflexive pronoun of a preceding coreferential NP only if both NPs are in the same simplex sentence.**[15]

Since (8a) has the deep structure shown in (10),

(10)

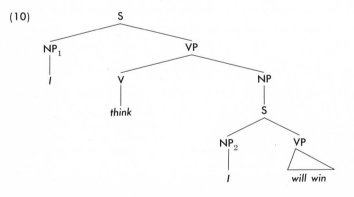

where the two occurrences of I are not in the same simplex sentence (i.e., it is not the case that a node S dominates one occurrence of I if and only if it also dominates the other), (9) will prevent the ungrammatical version of (8a) from arising. The same obtains for (8b) and (8c).

However, as sentence (11b) shows, there are grammatical sentences in which (9) appears to have been violated.[16]

(11)   a. Tom believed that the paper had been written by Ann and him himself.
       b. Tom believed that the paper had been written by Ann and himself.

I have only slight evidence (cf. Note 17) for this, but a plausible source for the reflexive pronoun in (11b) would be (11a), via a rule which deletes an anaphoric pronoun when this pronoun is followed by an emphatic reflexive, under certain further conditions. Whether this analysis is correct, or whether the reflexive in (11b) can be produced by modifying the rule given in Lees and Klima (1963), is of no relevance for the present discussion: I consider the question to be open. Let us assume, however, for the purpose of discussion, that the suggested analysis is correct. Then what are the conditions under which the proposed rule operates?

First of all, note that the pronoun *himself* in (11b) must be anaphoric — it can only refer to Tom. Therefore, sentences like (12), which contain a reflexive pronoun which can have no antecedent in the sentence, are ungrammatical:

(12)   * Tom believed that the letter had been written by Ann and themselves.

Secondly, note that there are conditions on the location of the antecedent of the anaphoric pronoun to be deleted. The pronoun *him* in (11a) can be deleted, for its antecedent (*Tom*) is the subject of a higher sentence. But if the antecedent is embedded in a higher subject, as is the case in (13a), the deletion is impossible: (13b) is ungrammatical.

(13)   a. The girl who Tom spurned believed that the paper had been written by Ann and $\begin{Bmatrix} \text{Tom} \\ \text{him}^{17} \end{Bmatrix}$ himself.
       b. * The girl who Tom spurned believed that the paper had been written by Ann and himself.

Similarly, if the antecedent is in one clause of a coordinate sentence, and the anaphoric pronoun in another, the deletion cannot take place. Thus (14a) cannot be converted into (14b):

(14)   a. Tom was not present, and many of the girls believed that the paper had been written by Ann and him himself.
       b. * Tom was not present, and many of the girls believed that the paper had been written by Ann and himself.

Note that it is not necessary for the NP *Tom* to be a higher subject, nor, in fact, for it to precede the emphatic reflexive. Thus (15a) and (16a) can be converted into (15b) and (16b), respectively:

(15) a. I told Tom that the entries should be designed by Ann and him himself.
      b. I told Tom that the entries should be designed by Ann and himself.

(16) a. That the paper would have to be written by Ann and him himself was obvious to Tom.
      b. That the paper would have to be written by Ann and himself was obvious to Tom.

Note also that the antecedent for the reflexive pronoun need not belong to the next sentence up the tree (in the obvious sense of this expression), as was the case in (11b), (15b), and (16b), for (17a) can be converted into (17b):

(17) a. Tom thinks that I tried to get Mary to make you say that the paper had been written by Ann and him himself.
      b. Tom thinks that I tried to get Mary to make you say that the paper had been written by Ann and himself.

However, it can be seen that in all the cases where the emphatic reflexive is possible [namely, in (11b), (15b), (16b), and (17b)], it is the case that it belongs to a sentence lower than the sentence to which the antecedent NP belongs. This is not an accidental fact about the data, as is shown by the impossibility of converting (18a) to (18b), where this condition is not met:

(18) a. That the paper would have to be written by Ann and Tom was obvious to $\left\{ \begin{matrix} \text{Tom} \\ ? * \text{ him} \end{matrix} \right\}$ himself.
      b. * That the paper would have to be written by Ann and Tom was obvious to himself.

The above facts lead to the formulation stated in (19):

(19) If an anaphoric pronoun precedes an emphatic reflexive, the former may be deleted, if it is commanded by the NP with which it stands in an anaphoric relationship.[18]

Inspection will reveal that (19) is satisfied only by (11b), (15b), (16b), and (17b). It can therefore be used to account for the ungrammaticality of (12), (13b), (14b), and (18b).

The restriction stated in (19) is the major one governing the rule that produces emphatic reflexives, but there are others, which have to do with the internal structure of the sentence to which the reflexive pronoun belongs. That this is so can be seen by the varying degrees of acceptability exhibited by the sentences in (20). [For convenience, I have repeated (11b) as (20a).]

(20) a. Tom believed that the paper had been written by Ann and himself.
      b. ? ? Tom believed that the paper had been written by himself.

    c.   ? Tom believed that Ann and himself had written the paper.
    d.   * Tom believed that himself had written the paper.
    e.   ? Tom believed that the lioness might attack Ann and himself.
    f.   * Tom believed that the lioness might attack himself.

No doubt most readers would assign different degrees of acceptability to the sentences of (20) than I have, especially in the intermediate cases. But this will not concern us here. Nor will we be concerned with stating the rule which produces the sentences of (20) with the spectrum of acceptabilities I have assigned, or some other spectrum — far too little is known of the phrase structure configurations to which such a rule would be sensitive. Cursory inspection of the few facts shown in (20) shows that emphatic reflexives are invariably better if conjoined than if they occur alone, and that such reflexives are more acceptable as agent phrases than as subjects or direct objects. Doubtless there are many other conditions on this rule, which interrelate in a complex manner with those just stated, and which are of some intrinsic interest. But for my present purpose, which is to argue that (7) underlies (1a), they are beside the point. Whatever the rule is that produces the complex spectrum of acceptabilities in (20), it is obvious that the same rule is in operation in the case of such apparently simple sentences as those in (21):

(21)   a.   This paper was written by Ann and myself.
         b.   ? ? This paper was written by myself.
         c.   ? Ann and myself wrote this paper.
         d.   * Myself wrote this paper.
         e.   ? The lioness may attack Ann and myself.
         f.   * The lioness may attack myself.

Notice that it is not the case that just any emphatic reflexive can occur in simple sentences like those of (21): the sentences lose all traces of acceptability if *myself* is replaced by *themselves*,[19] just as (12), whose reflexive pronoun cannot be anaphoric either, is unacceptable. That is, the pronoun *myself* in (21) is an anaphoric pronoun.

These facts are accounted for under my analysis, which assumes that just as (7) underlies (1a), so the deep structures of the sentences in (21) will contain a higher performative clause, which is obliterated by the rule of *performative deletion,* after the application of the rule stated in (19), with whatever additional constraints on this rule are necessary to produce the correct spectrum of acceptabilities in (20). Hereafter, I will refer to this analysis as *the performative analysis,* to distinguish it from the other two alternative analyses I will take up in Section 4.

Whether or not the performative analysis is correct, I submit that as a minimal precondition of adequacy for *any* analysis, the facts of (21) must be accounted for by *the same* rules or principles that account for the facts of (20). That is, it cannot be accidental that the two acceptability spectra match each other so exactly and, more importantly, that the configurations which seem to be producing the variations in acceptability, in both (20) and (21), do not, as far as I know, play a systematic role in any other grammatical phenomenon of English.

I do not want to be thought to be advocating something mystical because of my insistence that (20) and (21) be explained in the same way. Intuitions of similarity between phenomena, while they may prove to be mistaken, are the principal forces behind attempts to find explanations of these phenomena. In linguistics, as in other sciences, if phenomenon A is intuitively felt to be similar to phenomenon B, but if the descriptions of these phenomena do not reflect the intuited similarity, the researcher is dissatisfied with the descriptions; he feels that while they may "work," they do not explain. Thus the fact that imperative sentences like *Kick that damn cat!* are felt to be binary predicates semantically, with a second person argument not being physically expressed, and the fact that the reflexive pronouns that show up in imperatives are second person pronouns (*Kick yourself!* not * *Kick themselves!*) are felt to be the same facts, and no theory of grammar which cannot reflect this sameness (e.g., no theory which provides only one level of syntactic representation) can be considered adequate.

Since the facts of (21) are felt to be the same as the facts of (20), they must be explained in the same way. The rule stated in (19), or its equivalent, must be stated in any adequate grammar of English so that (11b), (15b), (16b), and (17b) will be generated, and not (12), (13b), (14b), and (18b). Moreover, whatever conditions turn out to be appropriate to produce the acceptability spectrum of (20) must also be stated. Given those two pieces of grammatical apparatus, if the performative analysis is adopted, the facts of (21) follow. But it should be noted that the facts of (21) do not force one to accept the performative analysis in all its details: they provide no evidence for the existence of a higher *you,* nor for any higher verb, let alone one with the specific properties attributed to it in (7). Arguments for these stronger claims will be presented below.

2.1.2. The structure of the second argument is identical to that of the first, as are the conclusions that can be drawn from it. It has to do with *like*-phrases, such as the ones in (22).

(22)   a.   Physicists like $\left\{ \begin{array}{l} \text{Albert} \\ \text{him} \end{array} \right\}$ don't often make mistakes.

   b. * Physicists like himself don't often make mistakes.

While full NPs and pronouns can appear freely in *like*-phrases, the ungrammaticality of (22b) shows that this is not the case with reflexive pronouns. However, as the sentences in (23) show, if a pronoun in a *like*-phrase is commanded by the NP to which it refers, it may optionally become a reflexive pronoun:

(23) a. I told Albert that physicists like himself were a godsend.
  b. Albert was never hostile to laymen who couldn't understand what physicists like himself were trying to prove.
  c. That physicists like himself never got invited to horse shows didn't seem to faze Albert.

As (24) suggests, the reflexive pronoun can be indefinitely far away from the commanding NP:

(24) Albert accused me of having tried to get his secretary to tell you that physicists like himself were hard to get along with.

As was the case in Section 2.1.1, it is necessary that the reflexives in *like*-phrases stand in an anaphoric relationship with some other NP in the sentence. Thus if *himself* in the sentences of (23) and (24) is replaced by *themselves*, the sentences become ungrammatical.

The restriction that *like*-phrases containing reflexives be commanded by the NP to which they refer is necessary to exclude the ungrammatical sentences in (25), where this is not the case:

(25) a. * Physicists like himself always claim that Albert was hard to understand.
  b. * That Albert's work wasn't comprehensible to high school science teachers worried physicists like himself.
  c. * Albert was interested in astronomy, and physicists like himself should remember that.

Now note that in simple declarative sentences, the reflexive pronoun that occurs is *myself:*

(26) Physicists like myself were never too happy with the parity principle.

Once again, this fact can be accounted for by assuming a deep structure for all declaratives in which there is an NP *I* which commands what will end up as the main clause, and which will be deleted after the rule introducing reflexives into *like*-phrases has applied. As was the case in Section 2.1.1, the facts of sentences (22) through (26) do not support all facets of the performative analysis, but they are at least consonant with it, and they do support one facet of it.

2.1.3. The third set of facts which support the performative analysis has to do with *as for*-phrases, such as those that start the sentences in (27):

(27) a. As for the students, they're not going to sign.

  b. * As for $\begin{Bmatrix} \text{them} \\ \text{themselves} \end{Bmatrix}$, the students aren't going to sign.

c.   As for the students, adolescents almost never have any sense.

d. * As for the students, hydrogen is the first element in the periodic table.

The requirement in such constructions seems to be that the NP which follows *as for* have some connection with the clause that follows. Thus (27a) is acceptable only if *they* is taken to refer back to *the students*, and (27c) presupposes that all students are adolescents. Since no reasonable connection can be imagined for (27d), it is deviant in some way.[20]

I have no idea as to the deep structure source of these *as for*-phrases, but for my present purposes this is irrelevant. It is sufficient to note that the NP in these phrases cannot be a pronoun which refers to some nonpronominal NP in the following clause, as the ungrammaticality of (27b) shows. In particular, reflexive pronouns are excluded, even if the NP to which they refer is itself a pronoun. Thus, though (28a) is grammatical, (28b) is not:[21]

(28)   a. As for her, she won't be invited.

b. *As for herself, she won't be invited.

However, there are cases where reflexive pronouns can appear in *as for*-phrases, as (29a) shows:

(29)   a.   Glinda knows that as for herself, she won't be invited.

b. * Maxwell knows that as for herself, she won't be invited.

As the ungrammaticality of (29b) shows, it is not the case that just any reflexive pronoun can occur in an *as for*-phrase which has been prefixed to an embedded clause; this is only possible if the pronoun refers back to some NP in the upper clause. Furthermore, as the contrast between (29a) and the ungrammatical sentences of (30) indicates, it is only if the pronoun refers back to a higher subject NP that reflexives can appear in *as for*-phrases.

(30)   a.   Harry told Glinda that as for $\left\{ \begin{array}{l} \text{himself, he} \\ \text{* herself, she} \end{array} \right\}$ wouldn't be invited.

b. * That as for herself, she wouldn't be invited enraged Glinda.

Finally, the ungrammatical sentences in (31) show that the subject NP to which the reflexive pronoun refers must be the subject of the sentence which immediately dominates the clause to which the *as for*-phrase is prefixed.

(31)   Harry believes that the students know that Glinda has been saying that

as for $\left\{ \begin{array}{l} \text{herself, she} \\ \text{* themselves, they} \\ \text{* himself, he} \end{array} \right\}$ won't be be invited.

To sum up, these facts seem to require the postulation of a rule which optionally converts to a reflexive any pronoun appearing in an *as for*-phrase which is prefixed to an embedded clause, just in case this pronoun refers back to the subject of the next higher sentence. But if such a rule must be in the grammar in any event, the fact that *myself* can appear in the *as for*-phrase of an apparently unembedded main clause, as in (32)

(32)   As for myself, I won't be invited.

suggests that in a more abstract representation of (32), it must itself appear as a clause embedded in a sentence whose subject is *I*.

Hence sentence (32) provides stronger evidence for the performative analysis than do the sentences in (21) and (26), which only suggest the existence of an NP *I* which commands all declarative clauses in deep structure. The grammaticality of (32) leads to the conclusion that the *I* cannot be indefinitely far above the embedded clause, but instead must be the next subject up, which is just what is asserted in the performative analysis.

2.1.4. The next argument, which is of the same structure as the one immediately preceding, was discovered by Jeffrey Gruber (1967). He pointed out that reflexive pronouns could be in a clause embedded in the one to which the full NP to which they refer belongs if the embedded clause contains certain constructions with picture-nouns,[22] like *picture, story, tale, photograph*, etc., as is the case in (33):

(33)   a. Tad knew that it would be a story about himself.
        b. Mike will not believe that this is a photograph of himself.
        c. I promised Omar that it would be a poem about himself.

Whether it is possible for the reflexive pronoun to precede the NP to which it refers is not clear to me — the sentences in (34), where this is the case, are perhaps less acceptable than those in (33):

(34)   a. ? That it was a portrait of himself worried Jasper.
        b. ? That this is an article about himself has been emphatically denied by Dieter.

I will not investigate further the many problems related to such constructions, except to point out the obvious fact that these reflexive pronouns are anaphoric (thus if *himself* is replaced by *herself*, the sentences in (33) and (34) become ungrammatical), and the fact that the NP to which the reflexive pronoun bears an anaphoric relationship must belong to the first sentence above the one containing the picture-noun construction.[23] This is borne out by the contrast in grammaticality between the sentences in (33) and those in (35):

(35)   a. * Tad knew that Sheila had claimed that it would be a story about himself.
        b. * Mike will not believe that Jane found out that this is a photograph of himself.
        c. * I promised Omar to tell Betty that it would be a poem about himself.

Of course, these latter sentences become grammatical if *herself* is substituted for *himself,* as is to be expected.

Once again, it is of no relevance to the present discussion whether the reflexives in (33) are to be generated by some extension of the normal reflexive rule, or by an extension of the rule of Section 2.1.1, which deletes an anaphoric pronoun before an emphatic reflexive under various conditions, or by some rule distinct from both of these. Some rule must be inferred to exist, and if the performative analysis is adopted, this rule will account for the fact that *myself* is the reflexive pronoun that appears when such clauses as those embedded in (33) appear as main clauses, as (36) shows:

(36) This is a $\left\{ \begin{array}{l} \text{picture of} \\ \text{story about} \\ \text{description of} \\ \text{joke about} \end{array} \right\}$ myself.

Thus (36) is further evidence for the correctness of the performative analysis.

2.1.5. The next argument is based on an observation made by Zellig Harris,[24] who pointed out that passive sentences with first person agents are generally not fully acceptable [compare (37a) with (37b)]:

(37) a. It was given by him to your sister.[25]
      b. ? ? It was given by me to your sister.

Note, however, that any formulation of the restriction on passives in terms of first person agents will be too narrow, for (38) is also ungrammatical:

(38) ? ? Tom$_i$ thinks that it was given by him$_i$ to your sister.[26]

As the grammaticality of (39) shows, the restriction which is operative here does not exclude all passives in embedded clauses when the pronoun in the agent phrase refers to an NP in the matrix sentence:

(39) That it had been given by him$_i$ to your sister was mentioned by Tom$_i$.

I am unable at present to state any restriction that will mark (38) as being less acceptable then (39), but it seems likely that however the restriction is finally stated, it will be instrumental in excluding (40b) as well as (38):

(40) a. Max$_i$ expected Sue to wash him$_i$.
      b. ? ? Sue was expected by Max$_i$ to wash him$_i$.

As a first approximation to a principle to account for these ungrammaticalities, I suggest (41):

(41) If a deep structure subject NP and some other NP in the same deep structure are coreferential, then the former NP may not become a passive agent.

Rule (41) is obviously too strong, for (39) violates it twice and yet it is perfectly acceptable. But it cannot be assumed that all such double violations will result in grammatical sentences, for (42) is ungrammatical:

(42)   * Sue was expected by Max$_i$ to be washed by him$_i$.

But it does seem reasonable to assume that what is involved in accounting for the ungrammaticality of (38), (40b), and (42) will be some restriction which is like (41) in that it excludes certain types of deep structures *which contain two coreferential NPs* from participation in certain (types of) transformational operations. But if this assumption is correct, then it must be assumed that the deep structure of sentences like (37b) must contain two occurrences of the NP *I*, for it would seem natural to exclude this sentence by the same mechanism that excludes (38). Therefore, the ungrammaticality of (37b) may be taken as weak confirmation for one facet of the performative analysis.

2.1.6. The next argument for the performative analysis was called to my attention by David Perlmutter. He pointed out that the verb *lurk* is awkward with first person subjects, as (43) indicates:

(43)   a. ? * I am lurking in a culvert.[27]
       b. ? * I lurked near your house last night.

However, it is not always the case that *lurk* excludes first person subjects. In embedded clauses, such constructions are perfectly grammatical:

(44)   a. Max believes that I am lurking in a culvert — actually, of course, I'm here with you.
       b. Pat and Mike testified that I lurked near your house last night.

The true nature of the restriction on *lurk* can be seen in the ungrammatical sentences of (45), which differ from those of (44) only in having the subject of *lurk* identical to the subject of the verb in whose object the complement clause is embedded:

(45)   a. ? * Max$_i$ believes that he$_i$'s lurking in a culvert — actually, of course, he$_i$'s here with you.
       b. ? * [Pat and Mike]$_{NP_i}$ testified that they$_i$ lurked near your house last night.

As Perlmutter observed, *lurk* is a verb which one may predicate of others, but not of oneself. This suggests that *lurk* must be constrained to so that it does not appear in deep structures where its subject is identical to the subject of the next higher verb in the tree.[28] It seems to be necessary to state this restriction in terms of subjects of higher clauses, for the sentences of (46), in which the subject of *lurk* is identical to some other NP in the next sentence up, are more acceptable than those in (45):

(46)   a. ? Susan told Max$_i$ that he$_i$ should not lurk near her house any
               longer.
        b. ? Lurking near lakes is easy for Bobby.

Since some restriction on *lurk* must appear in the grammar in any case,
so that sentences such as those in (45) will be blocked, if the performative
analysis is adopted, the same restriction will automatically exclude the sentences of (43). Thus these latter sentences constitute further evidence for
the correctness of this analysis.[29]

2.1.7. The last argument I will adduce to show the existence of a higher
NP *I* in the deep structure of all declarative sentences has to do with sentences
containing *according to,* such as (47):

(47)   According to $\left\{\begin{array}{l} \text{Indira Gandhi} \\ \textit{The Realist} \\ \text{Satchel Paige} \\ \text{you} \\ \text{* me} \end{array}\right\}$, food prices will skyrocket.

As far as I know, there are no restrictions obtaining between the clause
that follows the *according to*-phrase and the NP which appears in that phrase,
but there is a restriction to the effect that first person NPs may not appear
in these phrases in simple declarative sentences. However, as was the case
with *lurk*, first person NPs can appear in these phrases if they occur in an
embedded clause, as (48) shows

(48)   Satchel Paige$_i$ claimed that according to $\left\{\begin{array}{l} \text{Indira Gandhi} \\ \textit{The Realist} \\ \text{* him}_i \\ \text{you} \\ \text{me} \end{array}\right\}$, food
        prices would skyrocket.

It is evident that a situation similar to the case of *lurk* obtains here. But
there, although the restriction that was necessary was not clear in detail, it
seemed fairly certain that the restriction was to be stated in terms of the
deep structure subject of *lurk* and some higher NP. Here, because of the
present lack of knowledge as to the deep structure source of phrases containing
according to, it is not obvious as to whether the necessary restriction should
be stated in terms of deep structure or in terms of some lower level of
structure. I will assume, for the present discussion, that the former is true,
and that phrases containing *according to* are not to be derived from any more
complex source. In the absence of any evidence for or against these assumptions, they seem neutral enough, though I feel sure that the latter assumption
will prove wrong. However, if, for the sake of argument, we make these
assumptions, then the restriction which seems to be necessary to exclude such
sentences as the ungrammatical one in (48) can be stated as in (49):

(49)   No well-formed deep structure may contain an embedded *according
to*-phrase if the NP in that phrase is identical to any NP belonging
to the first sentence above the one containing that phrase.

This condition will exclude the ungrammatical sentence in (48), but it is
also strong enough to exclude the ungrammatical sentences of (50), though
not (51):

(50)   a. * That food prices, according to him$_i$, would skyrocket worried
Satchel Paige$_i$.

b. * Indira Gandhi$_i$ told Satchel Paige$_i$ that according to $\begin{Bmatrix} \text{her}_i \\ \text{him}_i \end{Bmatrix}$,
food prices would skyrocket.

(51)   * Satchel Paige$_i$ stated that it was not true that according to him$_i$
food prices would skyrocket.

Unfortunately, condition (49) is not only too weak to exclude (51), but
also too strong, for it will incorrectly block the grammatical (52):[30]

(52)   Satchel Paige$_i$ drives a truck that gets, according to him$_i$, 37.8 miles
per gallon.

While I am unable, at present, to improve on (49), I suspect that it is
basically correct, for at least it is adequate to the task of excluding the
ungrammatical sentences of (48) and (50). If this suspicion is correct, and
if the performative analysis is adopted, whatever revised version of (49) is
finally arrived at will explain why (47) is ungrammatical if *me* occurs following
according to, for it will be identical to the higher NP *I* which is assumed
in the performative analysis. Thus the sentences of (47) also provide indirect
confirmation for this analysis.

2.1.8. I have avoided many complex issues in my brief discussions of the
seven sets of phenomena above, in an attempt to present the basic evidence
for the existence of a higher *I* as clearly as possible, without invalidating
the arguments by oversimplification. In this section, I would like to mention,
even more fragmentarily, three further constructions which I understand much
too poorly to be able to argue from at present, but which seem to be likely
candidates for future use as evidence for the performative analysis.

The first observation I owe to Joshua Waletzky. In his dialect, such sentences as (53a) are possible, and they are synonymous with sentences like
(53b):

(53)   a. Sid is coming wíth.
b. Sid is coming with me.

However, this stressed *with* is not always synonymous with *with me* —
(54a) is synonymous with (54b), not (54c).

(54)   a. Abe$_i$ mentioned that Sid was coming wíth.

    b. Abe$_i$ mentioned that Sid was coming with him$_i$.
    c. Abe$_i$ mentioned that Sid was coming with me.

The implications of these facts would appear to be the same as those of the other arguments presented above, but there are so many additional idiosyncratic restrictions on this construction that I do not understand that I will not pursue the matter further here.

The second construction was called to my attention by David Perlmutter and, independently, by Charles Elliott. They pointed out that there are relational nouns like *friend* which normally appear followed by an *of*-phrase, as in (55):

(55)   A friend of Tom's is going to drop by.

In simple declarative sentences, however, the *of*-phrase need not be present. If it is not present, as in (56a), the sentence is felt to be synonymous with an otherwise identical sentence which contains the phrase *of mine* after friend [cf. (56b)]:

(56)   a. A friend is going to drop by.
       b. A friend of mine is going to drop by.

Not surprisingly, when sentences like (56a) are embedded, the missing *of*-phrase is not always felt to be *of mine* — (57a) and (57b) are synonymous:

(57)   a. Sheila$_i$ whispered that a friend was in the trunk.
       b. Sheila$_i$ whispered that a friend of hers$_i$ was in the trunk.

Once again, the implications for the performative analysis seem clear — *of*-phrases after nouns like *friend* delete if the NP in the phrase is identical to some higher NP. But there are complications. In (58), the missing *of*-phrase is not *of mine*, but rather something like *of one's*:[31]

(58)   Friends are a great help in times of hardship.

At present, it is not clear to me how the rule which produces (58) is to be generalized so that it will also apply to (57a) and (56a) — if, in fact, it is even the same rule at work. I will leave this question unresolved in the present paper.

Lastly, there are certain types of vocatives which require first person pronouns in them. See, for example, (59):

(59)   Hoboken is a fine city, $\left\{ \begin{array}{l} \text{Peter} \\ \left\{ \begin{array}{l} \text{my} \\ \text{* her} \\ \text{* his} \\ \text{* Bill's} \end{array} \right\} \left\{ \begin{array}{l} \text{darling} \\ \text{boy} \\ \text{friend} \\ \text{son} \\ \text{* lawyer} \\ \text{* rival} \end{array} \right\} \end{array} \right\}$.

At present, I cannot explain why *my* is required in (59), but perhaps it can be shown to relate to the performative analysis somehow.[32]

Although these last three sets of facts are very unclear, it seems to me that those presented in Sections 2.1.1 through 2.1.7 more than amply support one facet of the performative analysis — the claim that deep structures of declarative sentences contain a higher subject NP *I*. The facts discussed in Section 2.1.1 (*by Ann and myself*), Section 2.1.2 (*like myself*), Section 2.1.5(? ? *It was given by me to your sister*), Section 2.1.6 (*lurk*), and Section 2.1.7 (* *according to me*) all show the need for postulating an NP *I* in deep structure which is somewhere above (and which commands) the embedded deep structure clause which will become the main clause in surface structure. The facts discussed in Section 2.1.4 (*a picture of myself*) show that the *I* cannot be indefinitely far away, but must rather belong to the first clause up in deep structure, and the argument in Section 2.1.3 (*as for myself*) indicates that the *I* must in fact be the subject of this first clause up. The remainder of the arguments in Section 2 will be aimed primarily at justifying other facets of the deep structure in (7), but several by-products of these arguments will offer further support for the claim that a higher subject *I* must be postulated to exist in all deep structures for declarative sentences.

2.2.1. The first of the three arguments I will advance in this section to show that the verb of the clause whose subject NP is *I* is a verb like *say* has to do with the verb *believe*. This verb can have a clausal object, but as Robin Lakoff, to whom this argument is due, pointed out, *believe* also can have a pronoun referring back to a human NP as its superficial object, under certain circumstances. Thus if one clause of a sentence contains a verb like *say* whose subject is some NP_a, a later clause can contain *believe* NP_a, as is the case in (60).

(60) Tom$_i$ told her$_j$ that Ann could swim, but nobody believed
a. {* them}
b. {* her$_j$}
c. { him$_i$}.

As the ungrammaticality of (60a) shows, the pronoun that follows *believe* must stand in an anaphoric relationship to some other NP in the sentence. The contrast between (60b) and (60c) shows that the pronoun after *believe* cannot stand in an anaphoric relationship to just *any* NP in the rest of the sentence — in general, it must refer back to a subject of a particular class of verbs, whose precise specification I will now turn to.[33]

Compare the sentences in (61) with those in (62) and (63).

(61) a. Tom_i $\begin{cases} \text{said} \\ \text{declared} \\ \text{asserted} \\ \text{shouted} \\ \text{whispered} \\ \text{told them} \\ \text{explained} \\ \text{wrote} \\ \text{cabled} \\ \text{wigwagged} \\ \text{? groaned} \\ \text{? ? snorted} \\ \text{? ? laughed} \end{cases}$ that Ann could swim, but nobody believed him_i.

   b. Tom_i $\begin{cases} \text{told them} \\ \text{spoke to them} \\ \text{talked to them} \end{cases}$ about $\begin{cases} \text{Ann's being able to swim} \\ \text{Ann's ability to swim} \end{cases}$,
       but nobody believed him_i.

(62) a. * Tom_i frowned his_i displeasure, but nobody believed him_i.
      b. * Tom_i smiled his_i encouragement, but nobody believed him_i.
      c. * Tom_i shrugged his_i resignation, but nobody believed him_i.
      d. * Tom_i roared his_i amusement, but nobody believed him_i.

(63) a. * Tom_i enquired whether Ann could swim, but nobody believed him_i.
      b. * Tom_i commanded them to leave, but nodody believed him_i.
      c. * Tom_i $\begin{cases} \text{knew} \\ \text{believed} \\ \text{felt} \\ \text{doubted} \\ \text{hoped} \end{cases}$ that Ann could swim, but nobody believed him_i.

      d. * Tom_i forced Mary to leave, but nobody believed him_i.

The sentences in (61) all have main verbs denoting linguistic communication, as opposed to those in (62), whose main verbs denote nonverbal communication.[34] The ungrammaticality of the latter suggests that whether the restriction on *believe* is to be stated in terms of deep structure or as some condition on a transformational rule, there is need of some feature [±linguistic], so that (61) and (62) may be distinguished. I use the feature [±linguistic], instead of [±verbal], because of the fact that such verbs as *write*, *cable*, *wigwag*, and possibly *signal*, *buzz*, etc., can appear in sentences like (61a). The crucial feature of these verbs is not that they describe oral communication, but rather a kind of communication which is based on language, or, at least, on some kind of systematic code.

Since the sentences of (63c) and (63d) are ungrammatical, I propose to mark these main verbs with the feature [−communication], to distinguish them from the verbs in (61) and (62).

Presumably, all verbs that are [+linguistic] are redundantly [+communication] (unless verbs like *babble, gibber,* etc., are [+linguistic]), so the verbs *enquire* and *command* would not differ in their feature composition from the verbs of (61), as Mrs. M. A. K. Halliday has pointed out to me. But since the sentences of (61) are (almost) all grammatical, while (63a) and (63b) are not, some feature is necessary to distinguish these sets. I propose the feature [±declarative], to subcategorize verbs that are marked [+communication, +linguistic], and I assume that verbs like *enquire, ask, command, order, exclaim at, beseech,* etc., will be lexically marked [−declarative], while the verbs in (61) will be marked [+declarative].

Paul Kiparsky has pointed out[35] the need for distinguishing syntactically between such verbs as *groan, snort, laugh, quip, grumble,* etc., and verbs like *say, claim,* etc., and it appears that this same class of verbs will produce queer, though perhaps not totally unacceptable, sentences if their subjects serve as the antecedent for a pronominal object of *believe.*

I am at a loss to distinguish in any but an *ad hoc* manner among the verbs in (61b). All these verbs would seem to have the same feature composition, so I cannot explain the differences in their behavior with respect to *believe.* I will leave this question for future research.

To recapitulate briefly, it appears that a human anaphoric pronoun can appear only as the superficial object of *believe* if this NP stands in an anaphoric relationship to another NP which functions as the subject (but see Note 33) of a verb with the feature composition [+communication, +linguistic, +declarative]. No matter where in the grammar such a restriction is to be stated, the existence of such sentences as (64)

(64)   Ann *can* swim; but if you don't believe $\left\{ \begin{matrix} \text{me} \\ \text{* them} \end{matrix} \right\}$, just watch her.

strongly supports two conclusions: 1. in the deep structure of the first clause of (64), the NP *I* appears as the subject of a verb; and 2. this verb shares the features of a large class of verbs like *say, tell, scream, mumble,* etc., i.e., the features [+communication, +linguistic, +declarative]. This is precisely the claim made by postulating (7) as the deep structure of (1a) (see pages 222 and 224). Thus sentences like (64) provide further confirmation for the correctness of the performative analysis.

2.2.2. The second set of facts which indicates that the verb of the higher clause is a verb like *say* has to do with idiomatic expressions like *be damned if,* as exemplified by sentences like (65):

(65) $\left\{\begin{array}{l}\text{I'm}\\\text{I'll be}\end{array}\right\}$ damned if I'll have anything to do with her.

At first glance, it might seem as if this sentence were ambiguous, the first reading being roughly paraphrasable by "I am determined not to have anything to do with her," and the second by "People will damn me if I have anything to do with her." In my own speech, however, the second reading is impossible, because of the presence of the morpheme *will* in the *if*-clause.[36] If the *if*-clause is preposed, the first meaning is also excluded, and the result, (66), is ungrammatical:

(66)   * If I'll have anything to do with her, I'll be damned.

However, it is of no importance whether (65) is ambiguous for other speakers or not — as far as I know, it is grammatical for all speakers in the first meaning, and it is this meaning which the rest of the discussion will be concerned with.

There are a number of peculiarities connected with this idiomatic sense of *be damned if*. Notice first of all that it cannot appear with other modals than *will*, nor with any other sequence of auxiliary verbs; that it cannot appear in the negative or with various kinds of adverbs; and that it cannot be questioned:

(67)   a. * I $\left\{\begin{array}{l}\left\{\begin{array}{l}\text{must}\\\text{may}\\\text{should}\\\text{would}\end{array}\right\}\text{ be}\\\text{am being, etc.}\end{array}\right\}$ damned if I'll have anything to do with her.

b. * I won't be damned if I'll have anything to do with her.

c. * I'll be damned $\left\{\begin{array}{l}\text{tomorrow at 8 A.M.}\\\text{frequently}\\\text{over at your place, etc.}\end{array}\right\}$ if I'll have anything to do with her.

d. * Will I be damned if I'll have anything to do with her?

There are also indications that the embedded clause was a negative sentence in deep structure (in accordance with its meaning). Thus this clause can contain verbs like *budge*, which, as David Perlmutter has pointed out, occur only in negative environments (consider, for example, * *Harry budged*), and idioms like *lift a finger*, which are also restricted to negative environments[37] (for example, * *I'll lift a finger to help you*).

(68)   a. I'll be damned if I'll budge.
b. I'll be damned if I'll lift a finger to help you.

The hypothesis that an originally present negative has been deleted receives further support from the fact that *any* can appear in (65), while this is not possible when the embedded clause appears as an independent sentence, unless it is in the negative:

(69)   I $\left\{ \begin{array}{l} * \text{ will} \\ \text{won't} \end{array} \right\}$ have anything to do with her.

The most important restriction on *be damned if,* however, is that it requires a first person subject when it appears in a simple declarative sentence:

(70)   a. * Somebody will be damned if he'll have anything to do with her.
       b. * Your Uncle Frank will be damned if he'll have anything to do
          with her.[38]

But it is not the case that *be damned if* always requires a first person subject — when it appears in a clause embedded in the object of a verb like *say,* a subject cannot be *I* unless the subject of *say* is [cf. (71)]

(71) $\left\{ \begin{array}{l} \text{I} \\ * \text{ Ed} \end{array} \right\}$ said that I would be damned if I'd have anything to do with her.

The correct generalization becomes obvious upon considering the various sentences in (72).

(72)   a. Ed$_i$ said that Sally. $\left\{ \begin{array}{l} * \text{ I} \\ * \text{ you} \\ \text{he}_i \\ * \text{ Ann} \\ * \text{ we} \\ * \text{ they} \end{array} \right\}$ would be damned if Bill would marry

       b. You said that Sally. $\left\{ \begin{array}{l} * \text{ I} \\ \text{you} \\ * \text{ Ed} \\ * \text{ Ann} \\ * \text{ we} \\ * \text{ they} \end{array} \right\}$ would be damned if Bill would marry

       c. They$_i$ said that Sally. $\left\{ \begin{array}{l} * \text{ I} \\ * \text{ you} \\ * \text{ Ed} \\ * \text{ Ann} \\ * \text{ we} \\ \text{they}_i \end{array} \right\}$ would be damned if Bill would marry

It appears that *be damned if* can appear only in a deep structure [assuming, in the absence of clear counterevidence (but see Note 38), that the restrictions in question are to be stated in terms of deep structure] if its subject is identical to the subject of a higher verb.

Furthermore, examples like (73) show that the higher verb must be the main verb of the first sentence up, in deep structure:

(73) Ed_i said that we had asserted that $Sheila_j$ had screamed that
$\begin{Bmatrix} * \ he_i \\ * \ we \\ she_j \end{Bmatrix}$ would be damned if she_j'd go.

That it is necessary for the subject of *be damned if* to be identical to the subject of the first clause up, rather than to just some NP which belongs to this clause, can be seen by the ungrammaticality of the sentences in (74).[39]

(74)   a. * I told Ed_i that he_i'd be damned if he_i'd have anything to do with her.
       b. * That he_i'd be damned if he_i'd have anything to do with her worried Ed_i.

For some reason that I do not understand, the clause above *be damned if* cannot be passivized — (75b) is ungrammatical.

(75)   a. The Secretary of $State_i$ declared that he_i'd be damned if he_i'd let me travel in France.
       b. * It was declared by the Secretary of $State_i$ that he_i'd be damned if he_i'd let me travel in France.[40]

From the contrast in grammaticality between (76a) and (76b), it can be seen that there is a further restriction on deep structures containing *be damned if*; not only must its subject be identical to the subject of the next higher verb, but that verb must have the features [+ communication, + linguistic, + declarative]:[41]

(76)   a. Ed_i $\begin{Bmatrix} \text{said} \\ \text{stated} \\ \text{asserted} \\ \text{declared} \\ \text{claimed} \\ \text{screamed} \\ \text{whispered} \\ \text{told me} \\ \text{wrote} \\ \text{wigwagged} \\ \text{snorted} \end{Bmatrix}$ that he_i'd be damned if Bill would marry Sally.

       b. * Ed_i $\begin{Bmatrix} \begin{Bmatrix} \text{knew} \\ \text{believed} \\ \text{hoped} \\ \text{expected} \\ \text{doubted} \\ \text{felt} \end{Bmatrix} \text{that} \\ \text{enquired whether} \end{Bmatrix}$ he_i'd be damned if Bill would marry Sally.

Apparently, *be damned if* is impossible with *poss–ing* complementizers,[42] for (77) is ungrammatical, as opposed to the first sentence in (61b).

(77)   * Ed$_i$ told me about being damned if Bill would marry Sally.

The restrictions which so far have been imposed on the occurrence of *be damned if* actually are oversimplified, as the sentences in (78) show.

(78)   a. Ed$_i$ said that it was $\begin{Bmatrix} \text{* likely} \\ \text{? true} \end{Bmatrix}$ that he$_i$'d be damned if he$_i$'d go.

b. Ed$_i$ said that the one thing that he$_i$'d be damned if he$_i$'d sell was this knife.

c. Ed$_i$ claims that Betty $\begin{Bmatrix} \text{* feels} \\ \text{* says} \\ \text{? knows} \end{Bmatrix}$ that he$_i$'ll be damned if he$_i$'ll go.

I have not investigated such constructions as these in detail, but it is my impression that they can be accommodated if the restrictions on *be damned if* are not stated in terms of the subject and verb of the first clause up, but rather in terms of the subject of the first verb of saying above *be damned if* in deep structure. That is, I believe that the eventual restriction on this idiom will be a somewhat less permissive version of (79).[43]

(79)   No deep structure containing the VP *be damned if* S is well-formed unless the subject of this VP is identical to the subject of the first VP up the tree whose head verb has the features [+ communication, + linguistic, + declarative].

If this restriction, despite being inadequate to the task of distinguishing between *likely* and *true* in (78a), or *feel* and *know* in (78c), is basically correct, the grammaticality of such sentences as (65) and (68) provides compelling evidence for the performative analysis. For (79) says, in effect, that whenever the idiom *be damned if* occurs in a surface structure, the associated deep structure must contain a higher verb of saying, and that the subject of this higher verb must be identical to the subject of *be damned if*. Since the subject of the idiom is *I* in (65) and (68), (79) requires the presence of a higher sentence whose subject is *I* and whose verb is a verb like *say*, a requirement entirely in consonance with the performative analysis.

2.2.3. The last set of facts having to do with the nature of the verb in the higher clause was discovered by Michael Brame. In Arabic, there are three complementizers, which all start with highly similar phonetic sequences: *ʔan,* which is used after verbs like *ʔuriidu* "(I) want," *ʔaʔmuru* "(I) command," and other verbs denoting expectation, command, or request; *ʔinna,* which is used *only* after the verb *ʔaquulu* "(I) say"; and *ʔanna,* which is used after all other verbs [e.g., after *waswastu* "(I) whispered"]. Such a strange distribution would suggest an analysis which recognized only two basic complementizers, *ʔan* and *ʔanna,* whose distribution could hopefully be predicted largely on semantic grounds, and which postulated a low-level morphological (or even phonological) rule which replaced the expected *ʔanna* by *ʔinna* after the verb *ʔaquulu.*

However, if this rather plausible analysis is to be adopted, a rule deleting the verb *ʔaquulu* must be added to the grammar, and this rule must be ordered so as to follow the rule converting *ʔanna* to *ʔinna,* because of the rather startling fact that *ʔinna* occurs not only in sentences which contain forms of the verb *ʔaquulu* explicitly, but also optionally at the beginning of almost all declarative sentences. Thus the three sentences of (80) (*the boy left the house*) are synonymous and in free variation:

(80)   a. *ʔaquulu*   *ʔinna lwalada*   *qad*   *taraka lbayta*
            I say (indic.) that   the boy (acc.) (past)   leave   the house (acc.)

   b. *ʔinna lwalada qad taraka lbayta.*

   c. *ʔal   walad u   qad   taraka lbayta.*
       the   boy   (nom.) (past) leave   the house (acc.)[44]

The consequences of these facts for the performative analysis need not be belabored. Even if no other evidence were available in Arabic,[45] one would be tempted to propose an analysis along the general lines of the performative analysis to account for them.[46] I might point out that Arabic is the only language I know of where strong evidence points to a rule deleting a particular verb, instead of a pro-verb specified only by an abstract bundle of features.[47] In English, it does not seem possible to identify the verb as being one particular member of the class of verbs designated by the feature bundle [+ communication, + linguistic, + declarative].

2.3.1. The first of the three arguments I know of within English for claiming that the deep structure for all declaratives contains an indirect object *you* was pointed out to me by David Perlmutter.

In sentences like those in (81), a possessive adjective referring back to the subject of the main verb must modify an NP in the object:

(81)   a. I craned $\left\{ {\begin{array}{c} my \\ * \text{ Suzie's} \end{array}} \right\}$ neck.

   b. You hold $\left\{ {\begin{array}{c} your \\ * \text{ Bob's} \end{array}} \right\}$ breath well.

   c. Ootek$_i$ went on $\left\{ {\begin{array}{c} his_i \\ * \text{ Farley's} \end{array}} \right\}$ way.

When the verbal idiom *to hold one's breath* is embedded in the object of such verbs as *want, need, would like,* etc., as it is in (82)

(82)   a.   I want you to hold your breath for 2 minutes.
       b.   I want Tom$_i$ to hold his$_i$ breath for 2 minutes.

an optional rule can operate on the complements to convert (82a) to (83a):

(83)   a.   I want your breath (to be) held for 2 minutes.
       b. * I want Tom's breath (to be) held for 2 minutes.[48]

As the strangeness of (83b) indicates, this rule would appear to be restricted to cases where the idiom has a second person subject.

I have suggested converting (82a) directly to (83a), instead of postulating a prior application of the passive on an earlier cycle, because the sentences in (84), which would result from such a derivation in isolation, are ungrammatical, for me at least:

(84)   a. * Your breath was held by you for 2 minutes.
       b. * Tom's$_i$ breath was held by him$_i$ for 2 minutes.

The ungrammaticality of the sentences in (85) shows that it is not the case that whatever rule effects the conversion of (82a) to (83a) works in the objects of all verbs:

(85)   a.   ?? I expect your breath to be held for 2 minutes.

       b.   * I $\begin{Bmatrix} \text{believe} \\ \text{know} \\ \text{etc.} \end{Bmatrix}$ your breath to have been held for 2 minutes.

Let us now return to the restriction as to the deep subject of the idiom in such sentences as those in (83). That it is wrong to insist that this subject must be second person can be seen from the sentences in (86):

(86)   a.   I told Max$_i$ that I wanted $\begin{Bmatrix} \text{his}_i \\ * \text{ your} \end{Bmatrix}$ breath (to be) held for 2 minutes.

       b.   They said to us$_i$ that they wanted $\begin{Bmatrix} \text{our}_i \text{ breath} \\ * \text{ Max's breath} \end{Bmatrix}$ (to be) held for 2 minutes.

       c.   We informed them$_i$ that we wanted $\begin{Bmatrix} \text{their}_i \\ * \text{ your} \end{Bmatrix}$ breath (to be) held for 4 minutes.

It is easy to see that the more general restriction to which this construction is subject is that the deep subject of the idiom must be identical to the indirect object of the second sentence up. Since any grammar must contain this restriction, so that the facts of (86) can be accounted for, if the performative analysis is adopted, the fact that only *your* is possible in (83) becomes a consequence of this independently motivated restriction.

2.3.2. The second argument for postulating a higher indirect object *you* was pointed out to me by Ray Jackendoff. He observed that the ungrammaticality of such sentences as those in (87)

(87)   * You feel $\left\{ \begin{array}{l} \text{tired} \\ \text{bored} \\ \text{jaded} \\ \text{etc.} \end{array} \right\}$.

is to be attributed to the more general restriction which must be postulated so that the ungrammatical sentences of (88) can be blocked:

(88)   a. I told Mr. Feuerstein$_i$ that $\left\{ \begin{array}{l} \text{I} \\ \text{you} \\ \text{* he}_i \end{array} \right\}$ felt tired.

b. Blondie announced to Dagwood$_i$ that $\left\{ \begin{array}{l} \text{I} \\ \text{you} \\ \text{they} \\ \text{* he}_i \end{array} \right\}$ felt bored.

c. Jerry told Joyce$_i$ that $\left\{ \begin{array}{l} \text{Sam} \\ \text{Petrarca} \\ \text{we} \\ \text{* she}_i \end{array} \right\}$ felt jaded.

That is, the subject of such subjective predicates as *be tired, be bored, love,* etc., cannot be identical to the indirect object of the first verb up. In conjunction with the performative analysis, this restriction explains the ungrammaticality of (87), for this analysis postulates an indirect object *you* in the sentence which dominates all declarative sentences. Put in another way, (87) provides evidence for this facet of the performative analysis.

2.3.3. In addition to the fairly strong support for postulating a higher indirect object *you* which is provided by the arguments in Sections 2.3.1 and 2.3.2, there is some support from those dialects of English in which sentences like (89) are possible:

(89)   ?? This paper was written by Ann and yourself.

To me, this sentence is highly dubious, but there are speakers who find no difference between it and (21a), while they would totally reject (89) with *themselves* in the place of *yourself.*

I have not investigated such dialects in detail, but it is my belief that in just those cases where *yourself* is possible in "simple" declaratives like (89), anaphoric reflexives like *himself* will be possible in sentences like (90):

(90)   ? ? **Ted told Sarah$_i$ that the paper had been written by Ann and herself$_i$.**

If this prediction holds true, then sentences like (89) will constitute further evidence for the performative analysis, by an argument exactly paralleling that in Section 2.3.1.

2.4. There is one final argument for the performative analysis which does not lend itself to grouping under Sections 2.1 through 2.3. It is based on such sentences as (91), which were called to my attention by Thomas Bever and, independently, by Edward Klima.

(91)   **Jenny$_i$ isn't here, for I don't see her$_i$.**

It is clear that the *for*-clause in (91) does not provide a reason for Jenny's absence (indeed, Jenny may not in fact *be* absent), but rather a reason for the speaker to assert that she is absent. It is not clear to me how such a reading could be derived in a non-*ad hoc* way from any analysis of the sentence *Jenny isn't here* which did not derive it from a deep structure containing the main clause in surface structure as an object clause of some verb of saying.

2.5. To summarize briefly, in the fourteen arguments above, I have attempted to justify all facets of the performative analysis, which postulates (7) as the deep structure of (1a). Paradoxically, the one facet for which I have the least support is the claim that the verb of the deleted higher clause has the feature [+performative] and is in fact a performative in (7). Aside from the rather weak argument which is mentioned in Section 3.4 below, I have no syntactic justification for this claim. Nevertheless, the fact that the uttering of (1a) constitutes an assertion, just as the uttering of (2a) constitutes a promise, suggests that their deep structures should not differ markedly, so that there will be a uniform deep structural configuration on which to base the semantic notion *speech act*. And as Lakoff and I argue elsewhere [Lakoff and Ross (in preparation)], it is likely that all types of sentences have exactly one performative as their highest clause in deep structure, so the deep structures of declaratives should not differ from this general scheme. It should be quite clear, however, that this claim is highly speculative at present, so the facet of the performative analysis from which its name derives must for the time being be recognized as the most tentative claim of the whole analysis.

Finally, I would like to make two points which are perhaps too obvious to need emphasis. Firstly, the facts on which I have based the arguments given in Sections 2.1 through 2.4 are not logical truths. There is no reason why they should be consistent with one another. That is, it is logically possible that *myself* could appear in sentences like (21), but *himself* in sentences like (32), and that it could be only *Baxter* that was impossible in sentences like (47). Or *believe* [+human, +PRO]$_{NP}$ might require a verb of saying, while *be damned if* could only occur after a verb denoting fear. That these facts all *do* cohere requires an explanation, therefore, and the performative analysis is an attempt at one.

Secondly, the performative analysis makes a claim which transcends the fourteen sets of facts I have used in the arguments above. The claim is that if, in any language, other constructions are discovered in which there are restrictions on first or second person NPs, then these restrictions will prove to be special cases of more general restrictions which will be formulated in terms of properties of higher subjects and indirect objects, respectively.[49] And if peculiarities having to do with the allowable constructions in the objects of verbs of saying should turn up, then just these peculiarities should be observable in simple declaratives. Whether this strong claim is correct or not can only be decided by future research.

3.1. The rule which effects the conversion of (7) into (6) is stated in (92).[50]

(92) **Performative Deletion**

$$[I]_{NP} \quad \begin{bmatrix} +V \\ +\text{performative} \\ +\text{communication} \\ +\text{linguistic} \\ +\text{declarative} \end{bmatrix} \quad [you]_{NP} \quad S_{VP}$$

1	2	3	4	⟹
0	0	0	4	

There are a number of problems with this rule. First of all, as was mentioned in Section 2.5, it appears that (92) must be made more general, so that not only verbs of saying will be deleted in generating declaratives, but also verbs of commanding, in generating imperatives. It also seems likely that it will be necessary to delete other types of verbs, so that exclamatory sentences, and optative sentences, and other sentence types, will arise from the same rule. At present, it is not clear to me how this rule is to be generalized sufficiently to handle this class of cases but still kept specific enough so that performative verbs like *authorize* and *grant* will not be deleted. Perhaps no general condition is statable, and verbs must be lexically marked as to whether or not they undergo this rule.

3.2. Secondly, is rule (92) optional or obligatory? McCawley (1968) has pointed out that while (93a) is possible, (93b) is not

(93)   a.   I tell you that prices slumped.
        b. * I hereby tell you that prices slumped.

and has suggested that rule (92) be made sensitive to the presence of *hereby*, obligatorily converting (93b) into (la). This proposal seems highly plausible, and I will adopt it, in the hope that the (probably minor) difficulties mentioned in Note 47 can be avoided.

3.3. McCawley (1968) and Postal (1967*a*) have suggested that the pronouns *I* and *you* should be derived from underlying third person NPs. Under this proposal, the deep structure of (94)

(94)   You nauseate me.

would be that shown in (95):

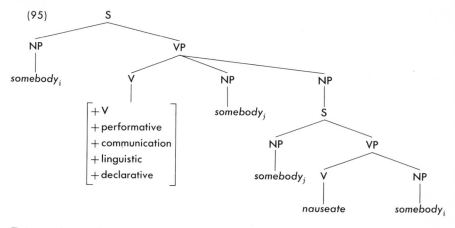

Prior to the application of rule (92), a rule of pronominalization would convert all NPs which were subjects of performative clauses, and all NPs identical to these subjects, to first person definite pronouns, and all indirect objects of performative clauses (but see Note 3), and NPs identical to these indirect objects, to second person pronouns.[51]

This proposal of McCawley's and Postal's also strikes me as correct. There are a number of facts which suggest that first and second person pronouns really derive from deeper third person NPs. Note, for instance, the possibility of using third person NPs to refer to the utterer, as in (96):

(96)   a.   The court is not amused, Mr. Nizer.

        b. $\begin{Bmatrix} \text{The king} \\ \text{Your president} \end{Bmatrix}$ will announce his decision as soon as possible.

        c.   Yours truly better get himself a seven.[52]
        d.   Mrs. Ross's little boy needs to win himself a fat one.

Also, in German, appositive clauses which modify first or second person pronouns can either have the verb of the clause inflected for first person, as in (97a), or for third person, as in (97b), if the relativized NP is the subject of the appositive clause (*I, who am responsible*):

(97)   a. *ich,   der   ich   verantwortlich   bin*
        I   (rel. pron.) I   responsible   be (1st pers. sg. pres.)

       b. *ich,   der   verantwortlich   ist* (3rd pers. sg. pres.)

Finally, this proposal may provide a starting point for an explanation of the extremely puzzling facts of (98) and (99).

(98)   a. It is I who $\left\{ \begin{matrix} \text{am} \\ \text{* is} \end{matrix} \right\}$ responsible.

       b. It is me who $\left\{ \begin{matrix} \text{* am} \\ \text{is} \end{matrix} \right\}$ responsible.

       c. It is you who $\left\{ \begin{matrix} \text{are} \\ \text{is} \end{matrix} \right\}$ responsible.

       d. The one who $\left\{ \begin{matrix} \text{* am} \\ \text{* are} \\ \text{is} \end{matrix} \right\}$ responsible is $\left\{ \begin{matrix} \text{I} \\ \text{me} \\ \text{you} \end{matrix} \right\}$.

(99)   a. I am the one who will have to protect $\left\{ \begin{matrix} \text{myself} \\ \text{himself} \end{matrix} \right\}$.[53]

       b. The one who will have to protect $\left\{ \begin{matrix} \text{* myself} \\ \text{himself} \end{matrix} \right\}$ is $\left\{ \begin{matrix} \text{I} \\ \text{me} \end{matrix} \right\}$.

While I agree with both of these proposals — that is, that rule (92) should be made to depend on the presence of *hereby*, and that *I* and *you* are to be derived from underlying third person NPs — I have postponed revising rule (92) until I understand better what other consequences the proposals will have. Thus (92) must be regarded as a very preliminary formulation.

3.4. A third problem connected with the operation of rule (92) is the following: if some syntactic rules can apply to their own output, as would seem necessary,[54] why can rule (92) not apply to its own output and produce infinite ambiguity? That is, why can (7) not be embedded again in the object of a higher performative verb of saying? Or doubly embedded? Or embedded an indefinitely large number of times?

The answer to this question is that there is an independently necessary constraint that prohibits any verb from having a performative interpretation when it is embedded as the complement of another verb. Thus while (100a), said in isolation, constitutes an admission, and (100b) a promise,

(100)   a. I admit that I'll be late.
         b. I (hereby) promise that I'll be late.

when (100b) appears as the object of *admit,* as in (101)

(101)   I admit that I (* hereby) promise that I'll be late.

the result is an admission of having made frequent promises, but it is not a promise. This fact is also reflected in the inability of the adverb *hereby* to precede *promise* in (101). Thus, since performative verbs cannot be used performatively in complements, rule (92) will not produce infinitely ambiguous surface structures. This point provides some nonsemantic evidence for including the feature [+performative] in (7) and in (92).

3.5. One final point about the operation of rule (92): even granting that this rule operates in the derivation of sentences like (21), (26), (32), (64), (65), etc., where the superordinate sentence leaves traces in the surface structure, it might be argued that there is no superordinate sentence in the deep structure of sentences where no trace can be found of this higher clause. Thus (1a) would have (6), instead of (7), as its deep structure.

It seems to me that this line of argument is not tenable, for it would make the claim that while sentences like (21) are unambiguous (they can be derived only from deep structures containing a higher performative), sentences like (1a) are ambiguous, in that they can be derived from (6) *or from* (7). Since rule (92) must be in the grammar, it will convert (7) to (6) and then to (1a). But it is false that sentences like (1a) are ambiguous, so one of the two structures, (6) and (7), which were postulated to underlie (1a), must in fact not be a well-formed deep structure. It is obvious that (7) must be retained, and not (6), unless some non-*ad hoc* way can be found to block the conversion from (7) to (6). The only thing that suggests itself to me is some vastly more powerful convention on recoverability of deletion than is now available.[55] In the absence of such a convention, however, I will for the present assume that the only deep structure for (1a) is (7), or, more generally, that every declarative sentence has one and only one performative sentence as its highest clause, and that this highest clause is deleted by the rule of *performative deletion.*[56]

There is a class of true counterexamples to this claim, as was pointed out to me by Paul Kiparsky. The sentences which appear in an instruction manual, or in a newspaper article without a byline, obviously are not to be derived from a deep structure containing a superordinate clause. In fact, it is precisely in impersonal contexts like this that first person pronouns cannot occur. So my claim must be weakened somewhat, as has been done in (102).

(102)   All declarative sentences occurring in contexts where first person pronouns can appear derive from deep structures containing one and only one superordinate performative clause whose main verb is a verb of saying.

At present, I do not know of any reason to assume a more abstract underlying structure than (6) for (1a), if it is used in a newspaper article. Nor, more importantly, do I know how to give formal content to such terms as "occur" and "context," which Kiparsky's observation has forced me to use in stating (102). They seem to be definable only within a systematic theory of pragmatics, an area which up to now has been largely disregarded by generative grammarians. I will return to this topic, briefly, in Section 4.2 and in Section 5 below.

4. In this section, I will propose two alternative analyses of the facts in Section 2. While the first of these appears clearly inferior to the performative analysis, the second does seem to be equally satisfactory, and possibly superior.

4.1. The first alternative analysis I will refer to as *the quotative analysis*. The explanation it provides for the facts in Section 2 is the reverse of the explanation I have given. That is, while I have tried to account for the occurrence of *myself* in the *as for*-phrase of (32), which I repeat here for convenience

(32) As for myself, I won't be invited.

by assuming a rule that optionally reflexivizes a pronoun in an *as for*-phrase if the pronoun refers back to the subject of the next higher verb, the quotative analysis assumes that (32) is basic — that an optional rule allows the *me* in an *as for*-phrase which starts an independent clause to become *myself*. Given this rule, and another, which converts direct quotes to indirect quotes, the fact that in embedded sentences other reflexives appear in *as for*-phrases is explained by the rule which changes pronouns in forming indirect quotations. That is, just as (103a) would be converted into (103b), so (104b), which has resulted from (104a) by the operation of the *as for* reflexivization rule, would be converted into (104c)

(103) a. Harpo said to Greta, "I'll never forget you."
       b. Harpo said to Greta that he'd never forget her.

(104) a. Harpo said to Greta, "As for me, I'll never forget you."
       b. Harpo said to Greta, "As for myself, I'll never forget you."
       c. Harpo said to Greta that as for himself, he'd never forget her.

It seems to me that there are insuperable difficulties with this analysis. First of all, since *as for*-phrases containing reflexives can appear after such verbs as *believe*, as in (105a), the objects of such verbs would have to be derived from direct quotes, as in (105b), which is hardly a plausible structure for semantic rules to work on:

(105) a. Ed_i believed that as for $himself_i$, he_i'd be spared.
       b. * Ed_i believed, "As for me, I'll be spared."

Further, since (105b) is ungrammatical, the indirect discourse rule would have to convert it to (105a) obligatorily.

Secondly, although it can perhaps be plausibly maintained that first person pronouns become third person pronouns which refer back to the subject of the matrix verb, by the operation of the indirect discourse rule, there is a problem concerning what should happen to second person pronouns. It might seem that they should become third person pronouns which refer back to the indirect object, but this proposal cannot be maintained, because there are verbs, like *determine,* which have no indirect objects for the second person pronouns to refer back to. So while (106a) could be converted to (106b), no "indirect quote" can be provided for (107a).

(106)   a. * Tom determined, "As for myself, I won't eat anything Sarah cooks."
    b.   Tom determined that as for himself, he wouldn't eat anything that Sarah cooked.

(107)   a. * Tom determined, "As for myself, I won't eat anything you cook."
    b.   Tom determined that as for himself, he wouldn't eat anything ? ? cooked.

Finally, if *I* and *you* are obligatorily converted to third person anaphoric pronouns by the rule which produces indirect discourse, what is the source for the *I*'s and *you*'s which can appear in indirect discourse, as in (108)?

(108)   Philip$_i$ said to Mabel$_j$ that he$_i$ and I would go out with you and her$_j$ sometime.

Until these objections can be answered, the quotative analysis must be rejected as a possible explanation for the facts in Section 2.

4.2. The second alternative to the performative analysis I will refer to as *the pragmatic analysis.*

In this analysis, it is accepted that sentences like (32) are to be explained on the basis of sentences like (29a) by the same rule of optional reflexivization of the NP in the *as for*-phrase as was proposed for the performative analysis. What is different about the two analyses is that the pragmatic analysis postulates (6), and not (7), as the deep structure for (1a), and claims that certain elements are present in the context of a speech act, and that syntactic processes can refer to such elements. Thus, since the context provides an *I* which is "in the air," so to speak, and since the rule which produces reflexives in *as for*-phrases would be stated in such a way that the antecedents to the reflexive pronouns could either actually be present in deep structure or be "in the air," this rule would correctly produce the *myself* of such sentences as those in (21), (26), (32) and (36). Similarly, however, if the constraint preliminarily stated in (41) is to be revised, it would be stated in such a way as to take into consideration elements "in the air," so sentences like (37b) would be blocked. Furthermore, deep structure constraints would not only specify what interrelationships among elements of deep structure were permitted, but also what interrelationships were possible between elements of deep structure and elements "in the air." Thus the ungrammatical sentences in (43) and (47) would be blocked by the same mechanisms used to block the ungrammatical sentences in (45) and (48).

Note that in order to account for the facts in Sections 2.2 and 2.3 under the pragmatic analysis, it would have to be assumed not only that there was also a verb of saying and an NP *you* "in the air," but also that the *you* functioned as the indirect object of this verb [to account for the sentences of (83) and (87)]. Furthermore, the *I* that is "in the air" would have to function as the subject of this verb, for it will be recalled that the restrictions on *as for*-phrases and idioms like *be damned if* make use of the relation *subject of* in their formulations. Thus the elements that would have to be assumed to be "in the air" under the pragmatic analysis do not merely form an unstructured set. Rather, they must be assumed to be hierarchically grouped to form a structure which is exactly the same as that of a normal clause in deep structure.

Given this isomorphism, it may well be asked how the pragmatic analysis differs from the performative analysis: why are they not merely notational variants? Where the latter analysis has more abstract deep structures than the former, and needs a rule like (92), the former presupposes richer notions of analyzability [cf. Chomsky (1955)] and deep structure constraint, so there would not appear to be much to motivate a choice on the grounds of simplicity or elegance. Presumably, the two analyses would make different psychological claims, but exactly how these would differ is obscure to me.

The only argument I know of for distinguishing between these two analyses has to do with sentences like (109), which were called to my attention by François Dell:

(109)   As for myself, I promise you that I'll be there.

The problem is, how can the pronoun *myself* be generated? Since (109) can be a performative sentence, it cannot be argued that there is a higher performative verb of saying, for performative verbs cannot be embedded, as was pointed out in connection with (101). Furthermore, it is simply incorrect to claim that (109) is both a promise and an assertion, as the ungrammaticality of (110) shows:

(110)   * Fritz said to Ken, "As for myself, I promise you that I'll be there," which was a lie.

Thus sentence (109) poses real problems for the performative analysis.

In the pragmatic analysis, however, since there would presumably be elements "in the air" for promises, as well as for assertions, the regular rule which produces reflexives in *as for*-phrases could refer to the *I* "in the air," and *myself* would be generated in such sentences as (109). This type of sentence, therefore, seems to constitute evidence for rejecting the performative analysis in favor of the pragmatic analysis.

However, there may still be a way to account for (109) in terms of the performative analysis. Paul Kiparsky has suggested to me that the *as for*-phrase which starts (109) may not modify *promise* in deep structure, but rather that it may be a constituent of the embedded clause. That is, (109) would be derived from (111), by means of a rule which preposes the embedded *as for*-phrase:

(111)   I promise that, as for myself, I'll be there.

In support of this derivation, Kiparsky points out that the strangeness of (112) is preserved when it is embedded in the object of *promise*, as shown by the contrast in acceptability between (113a) and (113b):

(112)   * ? ? As for me, Tom will be there.

(113)   a.   I promise you that Tom will be there.
           * b.   ? ? I promise you that, as for me, Tom will be there.

If the normal rule which produces reflexives in *as for*-phrases applies to (113b), and then Kiparsky's proposed rule preposes this phrase, the resulting sentence, (114), retains the strangeness of (113b):

(114)   ? ? As for myself, I promise you that Tom will be there.

Thus, Kiparsky proposes to explain the strangeness of (114) on the basis of the strangeness of (112).

It is obvious that the pragmatic analysis cannot explain the difference between (109) and (114), for if the *I* "in the air" can occasion the conversion of *as for me* to *as for myself* in the former sentence, it should also be able to do so in the latter.

There is an assumption in the pragmatic analysis account of (109) that I have not challenged till now, namely, that *as for*-phrases can occur as constituents of performative clauses. That is, even if *myself* cannot occur in *as for*-phrases in sentences like (114), *me* should be able to, according to this analysis. However, I find (115) only slightly less strange than (114):

(115)   ? As for me, I promise that Tom will be there.

If (115) must be excluded, as well as (114), it is clear that only Kiparsky's account of (109) can be correct. However, my intuitions about (115) are not sharp enough to decide the issue.

If Kiparsky's proposal regarding the embedded origin of the *as for*-phrase in performative sentences is correct, we would predict that there could be no such *as for*-phrases in performative sentences containing no clause embedded as a direct object. The performative sentences in (116), which have this property, are certainly strange, but I am not sure enough in my judgments to state categorically that no such sentence would be grammatical.

(116)   As for myself,
$$\begin{cases} \text{? * I authorize the purchase of a rodent.} \\ \text{? ? I sentence you to two years of TV dinners.} \\ \text{*   I christen this ship } \textit{The U.S.S. Intervention.} \\ \text{*   I pronounce you man and wife.} \\ \text{*   I grant you your freedom.} \\ \text{? * I dare you to leave.} \\ \text{? ? I condemn your intransigence.} \end{cases}$$

If even one such sentence is grammatical, the performative analysis must be rejected. However, even if they are all ungrammatical, the pragmatic analysis can be maintained, for their ungrammaticality would only confirm the correctness of Kiparsky's proposed rule to prepose embedded *as for*-phrases. Since such a rule is compatible with both analyses, performative sentences which start with *as for myself* do not provide crucial evidence for choosing either the performative analysis or the pragmatic analysis. However, if (115) is ungrammatical, this fact, in conjunction with the grammaticality of (109), does constitute counterevidence to the pragmatic analysis.

In conclusion, I must emphasize that neither the quotative analysis nor the pragmatic analysis has ever been worked out in detail. I have discussed them here merely as foils to the performative analysis.

However, even if they are only foils, certain qualitative differences between them remain. At present, the quotative analysis seems to be totally out of the question — not only would it occasion violent and otherwise unmotivated disruptions in fairly well established analyses, but it has a number of internal difficulties, which, as far as I can see, are irremediable.

The pragmatic analysis, by contrast, seems to me to be far less of a straw man. Since there are valid statements like (102) which seem to be linguistically significant, in an admittedly broad sense of "linguistic," somehow an extended theory of language, or a related theory of language use, must incorporate them. But it is clear that such a theory will have to be given a precise formulation, and that stylistic devices such as making use of colorful terms like "in the air" do not ensure that such a theory exists. A precise theory would have to specify formally what features of the infinite set of possible contexts can be of linguistic relevance. Furthermore, these features would have to be described with the same primes which are used for the description of syntactic elements, so that rules which range over syntactic elements will also range over them. While such a theory can be envisioned, and may even eventually prove to be necessary, it is obvious that it does not exist at present.

In fact, it seems to me that the only concrete information about the structure of contexts at present is that which can be inferred from the facts discussed in Section 2. These facts show that if the pragmatic analysis is to be carried through, contexts must be assumed to have the structure of clauses: They must have elements which share properties with subject NPs, elements which share properties with indirect object NPs, and elements which share properties with verbs of saying. Furthermore, if Lakoff and I are correct in our claim that questions are to be derived from structures roughly paraphrasable by *I request of you that you tell me S* (cf. Note 19), then contexts also exhibit properties of syntactic constructions with embedded clauses. However, while such observations may be interesting, they only serve to illustrate the enormous gap between what can now be said about contexts in fairly precise terms and what would have to be said in any theory which could provide a detailed understanding of language use.

Since no such theory exists, the pragmatic analysis does not exist. The performative analysis, on the other hand, can be said to exist: it fits naturally into a theoretical framework whose broad outlines are relatively clear, and it is for this reason that I have argued for its adoption in this paper. However, while the pragmatic theory, in the absence of a detailed theory of language use, is too vague to be testable, it does not seem to me to be impossible in principle, as the quotative analysis does. Therefore, while I would urge that the performative analysis be adopted now, given the vanishingly small amount of precise present knowledge about the interrelationship between context and language, I consider open the question as to whether the theory of language can be distinguished from the theory of language use. A pragmatic analysis implicitly claims that they cannot be distinguished, whereas the performative analysis makes the more conservative claim that they can be.

5. What consequences do the facts of Section 2 have for the theory of grammar?

First of all, regardless of whether the performative analysis, or the pragmatic analysis, or some third possibility I have not envisioned, turns out to be correct, it is obvious that English syntax in particular, but all syntax in general, will become more abstract than has previously been realized. If the performative analysis is chosen, the relationship between deep and surface structures will become slightly less direct than it formerly was. While rules which delete various grammatical morphemes or designated elements are well-known within generative grammar, I know of no rule which operates like rule (92) to delete a whole clause of deep structure. While no formal constraint precluded the existence of such a rule, no evidence had ever been discovered which suggested such rules might be necessary.

If, on the other hand, a precise theory of language use is developed, and the pragmatic analysis is chosen, the relationship between deep and surface structures will remain the same, but there will be an increase in the abstractness of the structures which must be assumed to be being manipulated by transformational rules. Thus, whether or not the superordinate *I, you,* and verb of saying are conceived of as being generated by the base rules, the constructs which must be postulated within generative grammar to explain features of surface structures will become even further removed from observable behavior than is now the case. Whatever analysis of the facts of Section 2 is finally decided upon, they will make generative grammar more mentalistic.

With this increase in the abstractness of the syntax of particular languages comes the possibility of making far stronger claims about universal grammar than have previously been tenable. It has often been observed that languages differ far less in their deep structures than they do in their surface structures. And as deep structures become more and more abstract, and get closer and closer to semantic representation,[57] it appears that differences between deep structural representations of widely disparate languages get smaller and smaller, which would follow, if semantic representations can be assumed to be universal.

As a case in point, it now seems likely that no matter whether the performative or the pragmatic analysis is adopted for English, the same analysis will hold universally. I would expect that arguments cognate to those in Sections 2.1.5 through 2.1.7, 2.2.1 and 2.2.2, and 2.3.2 will be discoverable in virtually all languages, so that rule (92), if it is a rule of English, will be a universal rule, when given a formulation abstract enough to allow for automatic reordering of its terms.[58]

But if it is correct to claim that this analysis is universal, not only will the deep structures of declaratives in all languages resemble each other in having a performative clause containing a verb of saying as their highest clause, but other apparent discrepancies in the base rules of various languages can be disposed of. Thus if we say, for the sake of argument, that one of the base rules for English is that given in (117)

(117) S → NP   VP

then the base rules of Arabic would differ from those of English, without the performative or the pragmatic analysis, for one of the base rules for Arabic would presumably be (118):[59]

(118) S → (ʔinna) NP   VP

If we adopt the performative or the pragmatic analysis for Arabic, however, this apparent difference in deep structures disappears.

It might be argued that the ʔinna at the beginning of (80b) need not be introduced in deep structure, but could be attached by a transformation. This appears to be possible for the Arabic example, but it would not be for the following facts from Thai.[60]

In this language, every sentence must end with the particle *khráp* or *kâ.*

The first particle signifies that a male has spoken the sentence; the second, that it was spoken by a female. Thus there are two sentences which translate the English sentence *he is coming* — both are given in (119):

(119)   *khaw maa* $\begin{Bmatrix} khráp \\ k\hat{a} \end{Bmatrix}$.

       he   come

Since these utterer agreement particles (UAP) have meaning, and can be the cause of semantically anomalous sentences, I assume that they must appear in deep structure. That is, the base component for Thai would have to contain either the rule in (120) or those in (121):

(120)   S → NP   VP $\begin{Bmatrix} khráp \\ k\hat{a} \end{Bmatrix}$

(121)   a. S → NP   VP   UAP

       b. UAP → $\begin{Bmatrix} khráp \\ k\hat{a} \end{Bmatrix}$

But here once again the putative differences vanish if the performative or the pragmatic analysis is adopted — both English and Thai have rule (117) in their base components. The only difference will be that Thai will have a copying rule which precedes (92) and which places a morpheme which agrees in semantic gender with the superordinate *I* at the right end of the sentence.[61]

Rudolf de Rijk has informed me of a similar phenomenon in Basque. In this language, a morpheme in the verbal complex agrees with the semantic gender of the addressee. Once again, since this morpheme has semantic significance, it must find some reflection in the deep structures of Basque. However, Basque need not have a language-particular base rule introducing this morpheme, if the performative or the pragmatic analysis can be motivated for this language. A rule adjoining a copy of the semantic gender of the superordinate *you* in the appropriate place in the verbal complex can instead be used to account for the facts.

These three examples of the effects of more abstract syntactic representations on the theory of universal grammar are not atypical. Not only will the performative or the pragmatic analysis, if it can be internally motivated in Arabic, Thai, and Basque, *reduce* differences in the deep structure representations chosen for these languages, in this case it will *eliminate* them. This suggests that the hypothesis stated in (122) may be tenable:

(122)   THE UNIVERSAL BASE HYPOTHESIS
        The deep structures of all languages are identical, up to the ordering
        of constituents immediately dominated by the same node.

In Lakoff and Ross (in preparation), George Lakoff and I investigate a number of constructions in detail, attempting to show for each that underlying structures of far greater abstractness than have been proposed up to now must be assumed to underlie them. These abstract deep structures lead us to propose a concrete, albeit highly tentative, set of rules that generate an infinite set of deep structures that we hope may prove to be universal.

In conclusion, I want to emphasize that this investigation of declarative sentences cannot be viewed in isolation. The performative analysis of declaratives is only one fragment of a far more inclusive analysis which postulates that every deep structure contains one and only one performative sentence as its highest clause. The pragmatic analysis would have to be broadened in a similar way. Until an analysis with a scope broad enough to encompass all sentence types has been carried out, the conclusions I have reached in this paper must remain extremely tentative. In such a broader study, the interconnections between syntax and pragmatics should be investigated in detail. Possibly when they have been clarified, a reason for choosing either a performative analysis or a pragmatic analysis of all sentence types will emerge.

NOTES

1. This work was supported by the National Institute of Health (Grant MH-13390-01).
I would like to thank Stephen Anderson, Michael Brame, Charles Fillmore, Bruce Fraser, Morris Halle, Ray Jackendoff, Paul and Carol Kiparsky, Edward Klima, Robin Lakoff, James McCawley, David Perlmutter, and Carlota Smith for many stimulating discussions and much criticism, which have greatly influenced the final shape of this paper. Far more than thanks goes to George Lakoff, with whom I am collaborating on a larger work on syntax and semantics, and to Paul Postal, whose ideas we are elaborating. Without their insights, the work would not have been possible.

2. I say "can constitute," because (2a), like all the sentences in (2), is ambiguous. It can be either a promise or a description of a habitual action of the utterer, as in *I make promise after promise to you that I won't squeal.* In this latter sense, the sentences in (2) are declaratives and do not differ in any significant way from those in (1). Henceforth I will disregard this sense of sentences like (2), and will concentrate instead on the usage which Austin was concerned with.

3. There are some performatives (I will use this term to refer to verbs which may appear in performative sentences), such as *move, question,* and *second,* and possibly *proclaim,* which exclude indirect objects, and some, such as *christen* and *name,* whose direct object can be second person, but need not be [cf. sentence (2c)]. For some performatives, such as *demand, order* and *promise,* the second person object need not appear in surface structure (cf. *I promise that I won't squeal*), but for others, it must (cf. * *I appoint captain,* * *I sentence to death,* ? *I warn that the trip will be difficult*). I assume that there is a rule which operates to delete the second person object in the former class of verbs, but I have no evidence to support this assumption.

4. This qualification is necessary because of the existence of passive performative sentences, such as *you are hereby authorized to commandeer sufficient bubblegum to supply a battalion for a week,* etc.

5. I will assume that such verbs as these are lexically marked with the feature [+performative], which will mean that they can be, but need not always be, used in performative sentences. They are thus distinct from such verbs as *divorce, insult, jump,* etc., which cannot be used as the main verb of a performative sentence, and will be marked [−performative].

6. At present it is not clear what the source for this adverb is. It would seem desirable to generate it and its related adverb *thereby* by the processes which produce such words as *thereafter, thereupon,* and possibly *therefore,* as well as other uses of *thereby.* I assume that the following sentences are all to be derived from the same underlying structure, by a sequence of optional rules:

Mort fell down, and he broke his leg by falling down.
Mort fell down, and by it (OBL thereby) he broke his leg.
$\Rightarrow$
Mort fell down, thereby breaking his leg.

Hereby might be derived from *by uttering this,* in a parallel fashion, but at present, such suggestions are only speculation. I am not aware of any research on such sentences as the above.

7. Cf., for example, Chomsky (1955, pp. 691–694).

8. For a discussion of this distinction, cf. Chomsky (1965).

9. A detailed analysis of a wide range of English complement constructions can be found in Rosenbaum (1967). In an important recent study [Kiparsky and Kiparsky (1967)], it is shown that semantic considerations play a much larger role in the grammar of these constructions than had previously been realized. Cf. also Robin Lakoff (in press).

10. A discussion of all the relevant evidence will be presented in Lakoff and Ross (in preparation).

11. Cf. Ross (1967*b*). A fuller treatment of this highly complex matter will appear in Lakoff and Ross (in preparation).

12. In (6), as elsewhere in the paper, I have drastically simplified the constituent structure representations, both deep and superficial, of the examples discussed, as long as the point at issue was not materially affected by such simplification.

13. The bundle of syntactic features [cf. Chomsky (1965, Chapter 2)] dominated by the highest V of (7) would appear in the lexical representation of such actually existing verbs as *assert, declare, say, state, tell,* etc.; but it need not be assumed that any of these occurs in the deep structure of (1a). The more abstract feature representation, which all these verbs have in common, is sufficient for my present purposes (but cf. Section 2.2.6). For some arguments that the stronger claim that a particular member of this class of verbs must be singled out as the performative verb for all English declarative sentences, cf. McCawley (1968). I assume that the preposition *to* which appears in surface structure before the indirect objects of most such verbs will be introduced transformationally, though nothing below depends on this assumption.

14. I will often use the locution "sentence *A* is transformed (converted, etc.) into sentence *B*" for the more correct but awkward phrase "the structure underlying sentence *A* is converted into one which more immediately underlies sentence *B*." No theoretical significance should be attached to this abbreviation.

15. For some suggestions as to the way Lees and Klima's notion "simplex sentence" should be captured within the theory of grammar, cf. Ross (1967a, Chapter 5).

16. I say "appears," because it is doubtful whether the reflexive pronoun in (11b) is produced by the same rule as the one that Lees and Klima were discussing. The reflexives in (11) are felt to be emphatic, as in the sentence *I myself thought I could vote against Goldwater.* This matter will be taken up again shortly.

Ray Jackendoff has recently called attention to a large number of interesting cases which seem to be true exceptions to the formulation proposed by Lees and Klima [cf. Jackendoff (1967)].

17. I am not sure whether (13a) can even have a pronoun replace *Tom* before *himself,* hence the question mark before *him.* When I wish to distinguish between more than two degrees of acceptability, I will use the following notation: if a sentence has no prefix, it is (for me) completely acceptable. If it is preceded by a single question mark, it is doubtful; by a double question mark, very doubtful; by an asterisk, completely unacceptable; and if it is preceded by a sequence of question mark and asterisk, it is very bad, but maybe not completely out: some vestiges of grammaticality may remain. It is to be expected that when such fine distinctions are drawn, disagreements as to the choice of prefix will be frequent. However, none of the arguments below depends crucially upon such fine distinctions, and only large differences will be critical.

It is of course totally irrelevant to the point at hand as to whether (13a) is possible at all with *him* referring back to Tom; if it is impossible, then some constraint must be imposed upon the pronominalization rule that produces *him.* In fact, if *him* is impossible, that fact would provide support for the analysis I have proposed, for it is only anaphoric pronouns that can be deleted by the rule I suggested, and if *him* cannot replace the second *Tom* in (13a), the ungrammaticality of (13b) is explained.

However, all this is beside the point under discussion, which is that emphatic reflexives, such as I assume the reflexive in (11b) to be, cannot occur in all environments (unless, of course, an NP immediately precedes). Exactly what rule accounts for the ungrammaticality of the bad cases is immaterial.

18. The important notion of *command* is defined and discussed in detail in Langacker (1966). Briefly, node *A* commands node *B* if neither dominates the other, and if the first S node above *A* dominates *B.* Or, in the informal usage of the text, *A* commands *B* if *A* "belongs to" a sentence which dominates *B.*

19. The attentive reader will have noticed that *yourself* appears, with the same spectrum of acceptabilities, in questions related to the sentences in (21). I suggest that this should be accounted for by deriving questions from deep structures whose two highest sentences are, roughly, *I request of you that you tell me S',* where S' eventually becomes the main clause of the question. This suggestion is explored at some length in Lakoff and Ross (in preparation).

20. I might remark in passing that it is not at all clear to me that sentences like (27d) can be excluded on purely linguistic grounds — I suspect that the requirement that there be some connection between the NP of the *as for*-phrase and the following clause can be satisfied if there is a real-world connection. Thus while the sentence *as for Paris, the Eiffel Tower is really spectacular* is acceptable, it becomes unacceptable if *Albuquerque* is substituted for *Paris.* And since the knowledge that the Eiffel Tower is not in Albuquerque is not represented in the semantics of English, I conclude that this unacceptability is not linguistic.

21. This fact, and its implications for the performative analysis, were pointed out to me by Edward S. Klima.

22. This terminology was suggested by Florence Warshawsky Harris in two extremely interesting unpublished papers, Warshawsky (1964a, 1964b).

23. This statement is adequate for my purposes, but it is an oversimplification, as can be seen from the grammaticality of such sentences as *Tad concedes that it is probable that it was not known that it would be a story about himself.* What differentiates this sentence from the ungrammatical ones in (35) is the fact that the sentences which separate the NP *Tad* and its anaphoric reflexive pronoun here do not contain any occurrences of other human NP. Some consequences of this difference, which was first noted by Ray Jackendoff, are discussed in Jackendoff (1967).

24. In a class at the University of Pennsylvania in the fall of 1962.

25. David Perlmutter has brought to my attention the fact that most passive sentences with definite pronouns as agents are somewhat unacceptable. Thus, though the sentence *the final exam was passed by everybody in my class* is unobjectionable, the sentence *?? the final exam was passed by them* is decidedly odd. However, in line with Harris's observation, the sentence *? * The final exam was passed by me* is even worse. I suspect that the explanation for the phenomenon noted by Perlmutter will be connected to the solution of problems in the area of what the Prague linguist Vilem Mathesius called "functional sentence perspective" (*aktuální členění větné*). Mathesius's basic idea was that, normally, the order of constituents in a sentence was determined by the amount of new information they conveyed to the listener. Already known constituents would tend to come at the beginning of the sentence, and constituents conveying new information at the end. Thus definite noun phrases of all kinds, but definite pronouns in particular, would tend to occur early in a sentence, which could explain the fact noted by Perlmutter.

An excellent introductory exposition to these problems, and a review of work done on them by Czech linguists, can be found in Garvin (1963). For an attempt to deal with functional sentence perspective within the framework of generative grammar, cf. Heidelph (1965).

26. Of course, I mean the pronoun *him* in (38) to refer back to the subject NP *Tom.* I will use the device of subscripting nouns which are intended to be coreferential with the same index.

27. Some speakers appear not to find sentences like those in (43) at all out of the ordinary, but for me they are beyond redemption. Robert Wall has suggested the verb *purport* as a substitute for *lurk*, for it exhibits all the properties of *lurk*, but with clearer ungrammaticalities for most speakers. Thus while *he purports to be with it* is grammatical, * *I purport to be with it* is not.

28. This restriction is actually not stated correctly, for in addition to such sentences as those in (43), sentences with factive verbs [cf. Kiparsky and Kiparsky (1967)] like *know, find out,* etc., cannot embed as objects sentences with *lurk* and a first person subject (cf. ? * *Did Merv find out that I am lurking in his car?*), and some intransitive adjectives, like *likely*, are also transparent to this restriction (cf. ? * *it's not likely that I'll lurk here much more than 40 hours a week now*). These last two examples suggest the complexity of the necessary revisions to the restriction stated above, which I will not attempt to specify more fully here, as the stated version is adequate to prove the point at hand.

For a detailed examination of various kinds of deep structure constraints, cf. Perlmutter (1968).

29. It has been called to my attention by Izumi Ushijima that a situation paralleling that with *lurk* exists in Japanese. The bound morpheme *–garu*, when added to any of a lexically designated set of adjectives, converts the adjective to a verb. Thus, *omosiroi* "interesting": *omorosirogaru* "to feel interested (in something)." These verbs in *–garu* differ from other verbs in that they may not occur with first person subjects — the following sentence (*I feel interested in this*) is ungrammatical:

* *watakusi*	*wa*	*kore*	*o*	*omosirogaru*
I	(part.)	this	(part.)	feel interested.

As was the case with *lurk*, when such sentences as the above are embedded, it turns out that first person subjects are possible, as long as the first verb up does not have a first person subject. The general restriction, then, is that the subject of verbs in *–garu* not be identical to the subject of the first verb up. Thus, while the first two versions of the sentence below are grammatical, the third, where the subject was identical in deep structure and has been deleted by the general rule which deletes unstressed pronouns, is ungrammatical:

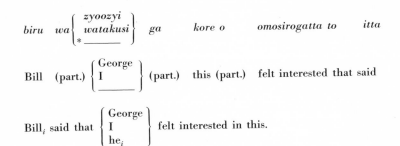

I have no reason to believe that when a more precise restriction on *lurk* can be formulated (See Note 28), it will differ in any way from the restriction that is necessary for verbs in *–garu*. Thus, just as the facts of (43) support the performative analysis for English, those with *–garu* support it for Japanese. Together, these arguments suggest that it may be universally valid.

I wish to thank Agnes Niyekawa Howard and Susumu Kuno for their help in clarifying the above facts.

30. Sentence (52) will be blocked by (49) only if relative clauses are deep structure constituents of the NP whose head noun they modify in surface structure, an assumption which has been widely assumed to be correct. However, recent studies by Postal (1967*b*) and Brame (1968) indicate the untenability of this hypothesis, and suggest that relative clauses are to be analyzed as deriving from conjoined clauses in deep structure. If this analysis is correct, (52) will not constitute counterevidence to (49).

31. I assume, of course, that the ungrammatical phrase * *friends of one's* would be obligatorily converted into *one's friends* by the normally optional rule which changes phrases like *a friend of mine* into *my friend*.

32. Note that there are some titles which require *my* when used as vocatives, and some that require *your;* compare, for example, the following:

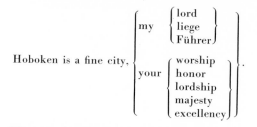

Why this should be is a total mystery.

33. There is one verb, *hear,* whose indirect object can serve as an antecedent to a pronominal object of *believe* — cf. *they heard from Tom$_i$ that Ann could swim, but nobody believed him$_i$.* As far as I know, *hear (from)* is the only verb which can appear in sentences like this — near synonyms like *learn (from), find out (from)* cannot. This suggests that *hear (from)* may be derived from *say (to)* by an optional rule which interchanges the subject and object of certain verbs, adjoining prepositions like *from* to the deep subject in the process. This rule, which was first proposed by Postal [cf. Rosenbaum (1967), where it was called *subject–object inversion*], relates such sentences as *your advice benefited me* and *I benefited from your advice.* One indication that *hear (from)* is not basic is the fact that its indirect object cannot be a reflexive pronoun, whereas this is possible in the case of *say (to), tell,* and other verbs whose subjects can be antecedents for a pronominal object of *believe.* (Compare *I said to myself that she couldn't hurt me* with * *I heard from myself that she couldn't hurt me,* paralleling *I taught myself that she couldn't hurt me* but * *I learned from myself that she couldn't hurt me.*) The restriction which appears to be operative here is a very general condition on all transformational rules which prevents moving one NP in such a way that it crosses over a coreferential NP, under various complicated conditions. One of the effects of this condition is to exclude passives of reflexives (e.g., *they understand themselves* but not * *they are understood by themselves*). Hopefully, this restriction, which is studied in great detail in Postal (1968), can be generalized to include (41) as a subcase.

34. Sentences like those in (62) have never been studied by generative grammarians, to the best of my knowledge. There are some strange restrictions on whatever rule it is that produces such sentences. First of all, note that the possessive pronoun modifying the abstract noun in the object must refer back to the subject (cf. * *Tom frowned $\left\{ \begin{matrix} Ann's \\ my \end{matrix} \right\}$ displeasure*). Secondly, there appear to be restrictions between the main verb and the abstract noun in the object; such sentences as

$$? * \text{Tom}_i \text{ scowled his}_i \left\{ \begin{matrix} \text{mirth} \\ \text{gaiety} \\ \text{willingness} \\ \text{eagerness} \\ \text{bonhomie} \end{matrix} \right\}.$$

are certainly odd, though probably only for semantic, if not extralinguistic reasons.

A stronger restriction on the abstract noun is that it denotes a certain kind of mental state. Thus the following sentences are all unacceptable:

$$* \text{Tom}_i \text{ frowned his}_i \left\{ \begin{array}{l} \text{departure} \\ \text{perusal of the text} \\ \text{height} \\ \text{construction of a counterexample} \end{array} \right\}.$$

Interestingly, it appears not to be the case that all nouns which denote mental states can appear in such constructions: only those nouns which denote mental states which can be behaviorally manifested can, it would seem. For me, at least, there are clear differences between the sentences below.

Tom_i frowned his$_i$ disbelief of the witness's story.

$$? * \text{Tom}_i \left\{ \begin{array}{l} \text{nodded} \\ \text{smiled} \\ \text{grinned} \\ \text{etc.} \end{array} \right\} \text{his}_i \text{ belief in the witness's story.}$$

Other abstract nouns which cannot appear in this construction are: *recklessness, prejudice, greed, hope, kindness,* and many more.

Such considerations suggest a derivation like the following

$$\text{Tom}_i \text{ registered (his}_i\text{) displeasure by} \left\{ \begin{array}{l} \text{frowning} \\ \text{scowling} \\ \text{roaring} \\ \text{etc.} \end{array} \right\} \rightarrow$$

$$\text{Tom}_i \left\{ \begin{array}{l} \text{frowned} \\ \text{scowled} \\ \text{roared} \\ \text{etc.} \end{array} \right\} \text{(his}_i\text{) displeasure.}$$

for it is only those abstract nouns which can follow such verbs as *register* that can appear in sentences like those in (62). The proposed rule, which would substitute such basically intransitive verbs as *frown, scowl,* etc., for a pro-verb of the class of *register,* closely parallels the derivation of sentences like *Max beat his wife into submission* from a deeper *Max got his wife to submit by beating her,* which was suggested in Lakoff (1965). It seems not unlikely that the same rule is involved.

One final note on this construction: the transformational rule which copies the subject NP as a possessive pronoun on the abstract noun in the object must follow the very general rule which nominalizes such sentences as those in (62), for these possessive pronouns do not appear in the associated nominalizations. Thus,

$$\text{He} \left\{ \begin{array}{l} \text{grimaced disgust} \\ \text{shrugged resignation} \\ \text{nodded approval} \end{array} \right\} \rightarrow \text{his} \left\{ \begin{array}{l} \text{grimace of (* his) disgust} \\ \text{shrug of (* his) resignation} \\ \text{nod of (* his) approval} \end{array} \right\}$$

$$\downarrow$$

$$\text{He} \left\{ \begin{array}{l} \text{grimaced his disgust} \\ \text{shrugged his resignation} \\ \text{nodded (his) approval} \end{array} \right\}.$$

The productivity of this nominalization (* *his beam of pleasure* is the only counterexample I know of) would appear to constitute one counterexample to Chomsky's proposal [cf. Chomsky (1967*b*)] that all constructions he refers to as derived nominals should be lexically derived.

35. In several lectures at MIT in the spring of 1967. Cf. also Dean (1967).

36. Barbara Hall Partee has made a plausible case for postulating the existence of a rule which deletes *will* in all *if*-clauses which superficially resemble present tense clauses [cf. Hall (1964)]. Two facts support such an analysis: firstly, future tense adverbs, like *tomorrow*, can occur in *if*-clauses, but not in certain of the corresponding present tense clauses (cf. *if he knows the answer tomorrow, he should raise his hand*, but not * *he knows the answer tomorrow*); and secondly, the only cases where *will* can occur at all in *if*-clauses are cases where it means "persist in" or "agree to" (cf. *if your son will stay up tóo late, slip him a Mickey Finn* and *if you will meet me in Tokyo, we can conclude the deal there*). Thus sentences where such a meaning is impossible (e.g., *there will be an explosion tomorrow*) are decidedly strange in *if*-clauses (cf. ? **only if there will be an explosion tomorrow should you stay here*). Probably such sentences are only acceptable with a sense parallel to that of *if you're so smart, why aren't you rich?*, which, as Paul Kiparsky has observed, mean "If what you say is right, ..."

It can be seen that the matter is too complex to pursue further here, but it should be clear, nonetheless, that it is not normal for *will* to appear in *if*-clauses. Therefore, the *if*-clause in sentence (65) is not a normal one.

37. This fact was noted in Kiparsky and Kiparsky (1967).

38. Sentence (70b) is ungrammatical if it is uttered as an observation about the subject, as would be the case in a sentence like *your Uncle Frank will be 39 next year*. There are certain contexts, however, where (70b) can be uttered as a report of a speech act, so that it would be paraphrased by the sentence *your Uncle Frank says that he'll be damned if he'll have anything to do with her*. Although I have none at present, I would hope that evidence will be forthcoming which would support the derivation of the grammatical reading of (70b) from this latter sentence. I would suppose this rule to be responsible for the well-known phenomenon of stream-of-consciousness prose (or *discours indirect libre*), which is typical of the novels of Virginia Woolf, for instance. I would hope that the rule involved could be combined with rule (92), which is discussed in Section 3.1. I am grateful to Morris Halle for calling my attention to this phenomenon in connection with the performative analysis.

39. If my intuition that the following sentence is grammatical is correct,

? I heard from Ed$_i$ that he$_i$'d be damned if he$_i$'d go.

then this would further support an analysis under which this sentence is derived from something like the following:

Ed$_i$ told me that he$_i$'d be damned if he$_i$'d go.

40. The contrast in grammaticality between (75a) and (75b) seems to indicate that, counter to my previous assumption, the restrictions on *be damned if* cannot be stated in terms of deep structure, at least not if previous conceptions of the passive as an optional rule are correct. Of course, if the passive is not optional, but instead triggered by some element in deep structure, like the one suggested in Chomsky

(1965), or by some other property of deep structure, then it would be possible to make reference to this element or this property in stating the restriction on *be damned if*. But such a complication in an otherwise fairly straightforward restriction is highly unsatisfying, and I hope that some alternative to this solution will turn up, for it seems impossible to state the necessary restriction on *be damned if* in surface structure, for a number of reasons too complex to go into here.

Ray Jackendoff has suggested to me that pronominalization should be constrained so that the agent phrase in a passive sentence may never enter into an anaphoric relationship with any other NP. Such a constraint would then render (41) unnecessary, as well as explaining the ungrammaticality of (75b). However, it would also rule out such acceptable sentences as (39) and *that Sheriff Clarkson$_i$ has ever taken any bribes has been repeatedly denied by him$_i$*, both of which are acceptable to me. Therefore, I see no way out of the *ad hoc* "solution" sketched above at present, although Jackendoff's suggestion should certainly not be dismissed without further study.

41. William Watt has pointed out to me that there are at least three verbs, *be resolved (that)*, *decide (that)*, and *make up one's mind (that)*, but not, for some unknown reason, such a near synonym as *be determined (that)*, which can occur with *be damned if* but not with *believe*. Compare the following sentences;

$$\text{Ed}_i \left\{\begin{matrix} \text{is resolved} \\ \text{has} \left\{\begin{matrix}\text{decided} \\ \text{made up his}_i \text{ mind}\end{matrix}\right\} \end{matrix}\right\} \text{ that he}_i\text{'ll be damned if Bill will marry Sally.}$$

$$\text{* Ed}_i \left\{\begin{matrix} \text{is resolved} \\ \text{has} \left\{\begin{matrix}\text{decided} \\ \text{made up his}_i \text{ mind}\end{matrix}\right\} \end{matrix}\right\} \text{ that Bill will marry Sally, but nobody believes him}_i.$$

I have no explanation for this fact.

42. Cf. Rosenbaum (1967) for an explanation of this term, which is roughly equivalent to the traditional term "gerund."

43. I have not mentioned the various restrictions on negatives, auxiliaries, adverbs, and questions in (79), for the sake of simplicity.

44. The phonetic sequence [ʔa] which begins this sentence is inserted by an automatic phonological rule which applies to prevent certain sequences from starting with two consonants. I will not be concerned here with this rule, nor with the regular rule accounting for the automatic alternation between nominative and accusative case markings on the subject NP of the embedded clause.

45. I should point out that there is an unsolved problem concerning the specification of which declarative sentences can start with *ʔinna*. Brame informs me, for example, that (80b) becomes less acceptable if the particle *qad* is not present. But the argument has force if there are any sentences at all which can start with *ʔinna*. Furthermore, in Brame (1967), several other arguments are discussed, and it would not surprise me if an argument cognate to the one in Section 2.2.1 (*believe me*) could be constructed in Arabic, or if verbs with the properties of *lurk* and *be damned if* could be found. It is my belief that such arguments will be discovered in a wide variety of languages.

46. James Harris has called my attention to a similar, but weaker, argument in Spanish. There, both of the following sentences are possible:

Que	*mi*	*gato*	*se*	*en*	*raton*	*ó.*
that	my	cat	itself	(pref.)	mouse	(3rd pers. sg. pret. indic.)

Mi *gato* *se enratonó.*
My cat got sick from eating too many mice.

However, the complement structure *que* + indicative is not unique to *decir* "say," and furthermore, the sentences appear to differ slightly in meaning — the sentence with *que* is more emphatic and more insistent than the one without it.

47. In McCawley (1968), it is argued that the particular verb *tell* is deleted by the rule of *performative deletion*, on the basis of the fact that while *hereby* can appear with performatives like those in (2), it is odd to say:

? * *I hereby tell you that prices will skyrocket.*

I agree that it is odd, but this sentence seems equally odd with *say* (*to*) in the place of *tell*. Therefore, while McCawley's argument is suggestive, I do not regard it to be as compelling a one as exists in Arabic.

48. Sentence (83b) is perhaps grammatical if construed as a request to ask or force Tom to hold his breath. This interpretation is impossible, however, if an adverbial modifier such as *starting now* is appended. In the sense which this modifier forces, the sentence is totally impossible, and it is with this sense in mind that I have starred it.

49. This may not always be true, for a rather trivial reason. For example, although sentences like those below must be restricted to first person subjects

$$
\text{(Well,)} \left\{ \begin{array}{l} \text{I'll} \\ \text{* you'll} \\ \text{* Blake'll} \\ \text{* Mr. Wonton'll} \\ \text{etc.} \end{array} \right\} \text{be} \left\{ \begin{array}{l} \text{a monkey's uncle} \\ \text{hornswoggled} \\ \text{blowed} \\ \text{goldurned} \\ \text{etc.} \end{array} \right\} .
$$

this restriction cannot be stated in terms of higher subjects, for the simple reason that such sentences cannot be embedded, as the ungrammaticality of the following sentence shows:

* *Blake said he'd be hornswoggled.*

Barring special circumstances like this, however, the claim should hold true.

50. I disregard here a number of minor problems, such as how the nodes VP and NP which dominate the embedded S in (7) are to be pruned [cf. Ross (1967b)], and how the complementizer *that*, which would presumably have been inserted by the time rule (92) applies, is to be deleted (in English).

51. This analysis thus *explains* why *I*, *you*, and *we* are pronouns (note that they must be analyzed as such in English to account for the fact that they behave like the anaphoric pronouns *he*, *she*, *it*, and *they* in not following particles in verb-particle constructions — * *I egged on you* is as bad as * *I egged on them*).

52. Edward S. Klima first called such sentences as (96c) to my attention.

53. Ray Jackendoff has pointed out that the two sentences of (99a) answer different questions. With *myself*, the sentence answers the question "Who will have to protect you?" while with *himself*, it answers the question "Who will have to protect himself?"

Correct though this observation is, it merely adds to my bafflement concerning the analysis of (98) and (99).

54. In phonology, the convention which appears to be necessary is that no rules apply to their own output within the same cycle [cf. Chomsky and Halle (1968)]. In syntax, however, it appears that while cyclic rules may not apply to their own output, post-cyclic rules must be able to. One clear case of a cyclic syntactic rule which must not be allowed to apply to its own output is the rule of *there-insertion*. As William Grossman has pointed out to me, if this constraint were not imposed, an infinite number of derivations of the form

> A man was standing in the surf.
> There was a man standing in the surf.
> * There was there a man standing in the surf.
> * There was there there a man standing in the surf.

would ensue, unless an otherwise unnecessary restriction were imposed on this rule. Similarly, if the *dative rule* converts (i) to (ii)

> (i) I gave John a book.
> (ii) I gave a book to John.

then unless cyclic rules cannot apply to their own output, or some *ad hoc* restriction is imposed on the *dative rule*, (ii) will be converted to (iii):

> (iii) * I gave to John to a book.

That post-cyclic rules must be able to apply to their own output can be seen by examining sentences (iv) through (vi):

> (iv) They all must have left.
> (v) They must all have left.
> (vi) They must have all left.

If, as seems likely, (vi) is to be derived not directly from (iv), but rather *via* (v), and if the same rule converts (iv) to (v), and (v) to (vi), then obviously some rules must be able to apply to their own output. I know of no argument against claiming that the rule in question is a post-cyclic one.

And if there is a post-cyclic rule that freely permutes elements of the same clause in free word-order languages like Latin, then this rule, which I have called *scrambling* [cf. Ross (1967a, Section 3.1.2)], must be able to apply to its own output, as long as only adjacent constituents can be permuted, for (vii) must somehow become (viii), and no single permutation of adjacent constituents can effect such a change:

> "The good man loves the beautiful girl."

(vii)	*Homō*	*bonus*	*amat*	*puellam*	*pulchram.*
	man	good	loves	girl	beautiful

> (viii) *Pulchram homō amat bonus puellam.*

Finally, G. H. Matthews (1965) has proposed a late rule reordering nominal affixes in Hidatsa, and this rule must be able to apply to its own output.

Thus it seems likely that post-cyclic rules can apply to their own output, and since *performative deletion* is such a rule, some way must be found to block it from applying in this manner, if infinite ambiguity is to be avoided.

55. For some discussion of this notion, cf. Chomsky (1964) and Chomsky (1965, Chapter 4, Section 2).

56. There are some apparent counterexamples to this claim. Deictic sentences such as the following, which were pointed out to me by Paul Postal

There's Judy, behind that boar.

although they have the superficial form of declaratives, are really not declaratives. Note that such sentences cannot be negated, embedded, or put in the past tense. More importantly, they cannot appear in such contexts as the one below:

* *Mike said, "There's Judy, behind that boar," which was a lie.*

Nor can such sentences as those mentioned in Note 49:

* *Hiram said, "I'll be hornswoggled!" which was a lie.*

Since it seems to be possible for all other declaratives to be followed by the sentential relative clause *which* $\begin{Bmatrix} is \\ was \end{Bmatrix}$ *a lie*, I tentatively conclude that the sentences in direct quotes are not declaratives, despite their surface form, and that they therefore are not embedded in the object of a performative verb of saying (though they may be, and probably are, embedded as objects of some other performative verb).

57. That increases in the abstractness of syntactic representations decrease the distance between these representations and semantic representations is a fact which needs explanation, since it is not a logical necessity. One possible explanation, which Lakoff and I and others are now exploring, is that there may be no level of syntactic representation which is distinct from semantic representation, and which could be called "deep structure."

58. For some discussion of the notion of a convention for automatically reordering the terms of certain types of transformational rules, cf. Ross (1967a, Section 4.1).

59. I disregard here the differences between Arabic and English in the order of the main constituents of S.

60. I am grateful to Mr. Udom Warotamisikkhadit for furnishing the Thai examples.

61. A further bit of evidence for the correctness of this rule, which I am grateful to Samuel E. Martin for bringing to my attention, is the fact that among the twenty-six words Thai has for the first person singular pronoun, there are some for male speakers (e.g., *pôm*) and others for females (e.g., *chân*).

Bibliography

ANDERSON, STEPHEN, 1968. "Pro-sentential Forms and Their Implications for Sentence Structure," in Harvard Computation Laboratory Report to the National Science Foundation on Mathematical Linguistics and Automatic Translation, Number NSF-20, Cambridge, Massachusetts.

ANNEAR, SANDRA and D. ELLIOT, 1965. "Derivational Morphology in Generative Grammar," paper delivered at the meeting of the Linguistic Society of America, Chicago: December 1965.

AUSTIN, JOHN L., 1962. *How to Do Things with Words.* Cambridge, Massachusetts: Harvard University Press.

BACH, EMMON, 1968. "Nouns and Noun Phrases," in Bach and Harms (1968).

————, and ROBERT T. HARMS (eds.), 1968. *Universals in Linguistic Theory.* New York: Holt, Rinehart and Winston.

BIERWISCH, MANFRED, 1967. "Some Semantic Universals in German Adjectivals," *Foundations of Language, 3:*1–36.

BOOLE, GEORGE, 1854. *Laws of Thought.*

BRAME, MICHAEL, 1967. "Evidence for Performatives from Arabic," unpublished paper, M.I.T.

————, 1968. "On the Nature of Relative Clauses," unpublished paper, M.I.T.

CHAPIN, P., 1967. *On the Syntax of Word Derivation in English,* unpublished doctoral dissertation, M.I.T. Also in MITRE Technical Paper #68, Bedford, Massachusetts: MITRE Corporation, September 1967.

CHOMSKY, NOAM, 1955. *The Logical Structure of Linguistic Theory,* on microfilm at the reference department, M.I.T. Library.

————, 1957. *Syntactic Structures.* The Hague: Mouton and Company.

————, 1962. "The Logical Basis of Linguistic Theory," *Preprints of the IXth International Congress of Linguistics,* Halle (ed.), 509–575. Reprinted in Fodor and Katz as "Current Issues in Linguistic Theory."

————, 1964. *Current Issues in Linguistic Theory.* The Hague: Mouton and Company. This is a revised version of Chomsky (1962).

————, 1965. *Aspects of the Theory of Syntax.* Cambridge, Massachusetts: M.I.T. Press.

————, 1966. *Cartesian Linguistics.* New York: Harper and Row.

————, 1967a. "The Formal Nature of Language," in E. H. Lenneberg (ed.), *Biological Foundations of Language.* New York: Wiley and Sons, 397–442.

————, 1967b. "Remarks on Nominalization." Appears in this volume.

————, 1968. "Problems of Explanation in Linguistics," in R. Borger and F. Cioffi (eds.), *Explanations in the Behavioural Sciences*, Cambridge, Massachusetts.

————, and MORRIS HALLE, 1968. *The Sound Pattern of English*. New York: Harper and Row.

————, 1969. "Deep Structure, Surface Structure, and Semantic Interpretation," in L. Jakobovits and D. Steinberg (eds.), *Semantics: An Interdisciplinary Reader*. Urbana, Illinois: University of Illinois Press.

CURME, GEORGE O., 1931. *A Grammar of the English Language*, Vol. III. Boston: D. C. Heath.

DEAN, JANET, 1967. "Noun Phrase Complementation in English and German," unpublished paper, M.I.T.

FILLMORE, CHARLES J., 1963. "The Position of Embedding Transformations in a Grammar," *Word, 19,* 208–231.

————, 1966. "A Proposal Concerning English Prepositions," unpublished paper, Ohio State University.

————, 1968. "The Case for Case," in Emmon Bach and Robert Harms (eds.), *Universals in Linguistic Theory*. New York: Holt, Rinehart and Winston.

FODOR, J. A., and J. J. KATZ, (eds.), 1964. *The Structure of Language: Readings in the Philosophy of Language*. Englewood Cliffs, New Jersey: Prentice-Hall.

FRASER, BRUCE, 1965. *An Examination of the Verb Particle Construction in English*, unpublished doctoral dissertation, M.I.T.

GARCIA, E., 1967. "Auxiliaries and the Criterion of Simplicity," *Language, 43:*853–870.

GARVIN, PAUL, 1963. "Linguistics in Czechoslovakia," in Thomas Sebeok (ed.), *Current Trends in Soviet and East European Linguistics*. The Hague: Mouton and Company.

GRUBER, JEFFREY, 1965. *Studies in Lexical Relations*, unpublished doctoral dissertation, M.I.T.

————, 1967. Unpublished, untitled paper on child language, M.I.T.

HALE, E. AUSTIN, 1966. *"Review of Studia Grammatica," I, II,* and *III, Foundations of Language 2:*295–316.

HALL, BARBARA, 1964. "Adverbial Subordinate Clauses," working paper W-07241. Bedford, Massachusetts: MITRE Corporation.

————, 1965. *Subject and Object in Modern English*, unpublished M.I.T. doctoral dissertation.

HALLE, MORRIS, 1959. *The Sound Pattern of Russian*. The Hague: Mouton and Company.

HARRIS, ZELLIG, 1951. *Methods in Structural Linguistics*. Chicago: University of Chicago Press.

HEIDOLPH, KARL ERICH, 1965. "Kontextbeziehungen zwischen Sätzen in einer generativen Grammatik," unpublished mimeograph, East Berlin: Deutsche Akademie der Wissenschaften.

HOFMANN, T. RONALD, 1966. "Past Tense Replacement and the Modal System," in Harvard Computation Laboratory Report to the National Science Foundation on Mathematical Linguistics and Automatic Translation, Number NSF-17, Cambridge, Massachusetts.

HUDDLESTON, R., 1967. "More on the English Comparative," *Journal of Linguistics 3:*91–102.

JACKENDOFF, RAY, 1967. "An Interpretive Theory of Pronouns and Reflexives," unpublished paper, M.I.T.

JACOBS, RODERICK A., and PETER S. ROSENBAUM, 1968. *English Transformational Grammar.* Waltham, Mass.: Ginn.

————, 1970. *An Introduction to Transformational Grammar, Grammars I–IV* (4 vols.). Boston: Ginn.

————, forthcoming. *Transformational Grammar and Style.* Waltham, Mass.: Ginn.

JAKOBSON, ROMAN, 1941. *Kindersprache, Aphasie, und Allgemeine laut Gesetze,* Sällskapets i Uppsala, Förhandlingar: Spraakweten skapliga. Translated into English by A. R. Keiler, *Child Language, Aphasia and Phonological Universals.* The Hague: Mouton and Company, 1968.

JESPERSEN, OTTO, 1954 (reprinted). *A Modern English Grammar,* Part VII. London: Bradford & Dickens, Draynton House.

KATZ, J. J. and J. A. FODOR, 1963. "Structure of a Semantic Theory," in *The Structure of Language: Readings in the Philosophy of Language,* J. A. Fodor and J. J. Katz (eds.), Englewood Cliffs, New Jersey: Prentice-Hall. Also in *Language 39*:120–210.

————, and P. M., POSTAL, 1964. *An Integrated Theory of Linguistic Descriptions,* Cambridge, Massachusetts: M.I.T. Press.

KENNY, ANTHONY, 1963. *Action, Emotion, and Will.* London: Routledge and Kegan Paul.

KIPARSKY, CAROL, and PAUL KIPARSKY, 1967. "Fact," unpublished paper, M.I.T. A version of this paper will appear in Manfred Bierwisch and Karl Erich Heidolph (eds.), *Recent Developments in Linguistics.* The Hague: Mouton and Company, (in press).

KLIMA, EDWARD, 1964. "Negation in English," in J. A. Fodor and J. J. Katz (eds.), *The Structure of Language: Readings in the Philosophy of Language.* Englewood Cliffs, New Jersey: Prentice-Hall.

LAKOFF, GEORGE, 1966a. "Deep and Surface Grammar," unpublished paper, Harvard University. Later published in the *Linguistic Institute Packet of Papers,* University of Illinois, Summer 1968.

————, 1966b. "Some Verbs of Change and Causation," in Harvard Computation Laboratory Report to the National Science Foundation on Mathematical Linguistics and Automatic Translation, Number NSF-20, Cambridge, Massachusetts.

————, 1967. Remarks delivered at the *Texas Conference on Language Universals.*

————, 1968a. "Instrumental Adverbs," in *Foundations of Language 4.* 1:4–29.

————, 1968b. "Pronouns and Reference," Harvard Mimeo.

————, and STANLEY PETERS, 1966. "Phrasal Conjunction and Symmetric Predicates," in Harvard Computation Laboratory Report to the National Science Foundation on Mathematical Linguistics and Automatic Translation, Number NSF-17, Cambridge, Massachusetts.

————, and JOHN ROBERT ROSS, 1966. "Criterion for Verb Phrase Constituency," in Harvard Computation Laboratory Report to the National Science Foundation on *Mathematical Linguistics and Automatic Translation,* Number NSF-17, Cambridge, Massachusetts.

————, and JOHN ROBERT ROSS, 1967. "Is Deep Structure Necessary?" unpublished paper, M.I.T.

————, and JOHN ROBERT ROSS. *Abstract Syntax,* in preparation.

LAKOFF, ROBIN T., 1969a. *Abstract Syntax and Latin Complementation,* Cambridge, Massachusetts: M.I.T. Press

————, 1969b. "A Syntactic Argument for Negative Transportation," Proceedings of the Chicago Linguistic Society.

LANGACKER, RONALD, 1966. "Pronominalization and the Chain of Command," to appear in David Reibel and Sanford Schane (eds.), *Modern Studies in English,* Englewood Cliffs, New Jersey: Prentice-Hall. Already published in *Linguistic Institute Packet of Papers,* University of Illinois, Summer 1968.

LANGENDOEN, D. TERENCE, 1967a. "The Syntax of the English Expletive *It,*" *Georgetown University Monographs on Languages and Linguistics,* No. 19, Washington, D. C.

————, 1967b. "Selection, Projection, Meaning, and Semantic Content," Ohio State University Research Foundation Working Papers in Linguistics.

LEES, ROBERT B., 1960. *The Grammar of English Nominalizations.* The Hague: Mouton and Company. Also supplement to *IJAL, 12,* of the Research Center in Anthropology, Folklore, and Linguistics, reissued, 1963.

————, 1961. "Grammatical Analysis of the English Comparative Construction," *Word, 17:*171–185.

————, and EDWARD KLIMA, 1963. "Rules for English Pronominalization," *Language, 39:*17–29.

LONG, R. B., 1961. *The Sentence and Its Parts.* Chicago: University of Chicago Press.

MATTHEWS, G. HUBERT, 1965. *Hidatsa Syntax.* The Hague: Mouton and Company.

McCAWLEY, JAMES D., 1964. "Quantitative and Qualitative Comparison in English," paper presented at the meeting of the Linguistic Society of America, New York, December 29.

————, 1967. "How to Find Semantic Universals in the Event that There Are Any," paper presented at the *Texas Conference on Language Universals,* April. Also in the *Linguistic Institute Packet of Papers,* University of Illinois, Summer 1968.

————, 1968. "The Role of Semantics in Grammar," in Emmon Bach and Robert Harms (eds.), *Universals in Linguistic Theory.* New York: Holt, Rinehart and Winston.

MILLER, GEORGE, 1967. "A Psycholinguistic Approach to the Study of Communication," in David L. Arm (ed.), *Journeys in Science: Small Steps—Great Strides.* Albuquerque: University of New Mexico Press, 39–73.

PERLMUTTER, DAVID M., 1968. *Deep and Surface Structure Constraints in Syntax,* unpublished doctoral dissertation, M.I.T.

PILCH, H., 1965. "Comparative Constructions in English," in *Language, 41:* 37–58.

POSTAL, PAUL M., 1966a. "A Note on 'Understood Transitively,'" *IJAL, 32.1:* 90–93.

————, 1966b. "Review of R. M. W. Dixon, *Linguistic Science and Logic, Language 42.*1:84–93 (Footnote 16).

————, 1967a. "Performatives and Person," unpublished paper, Yorktown Heights, New York: Thomas J. Watson Research Center, IBM.

————, 1967b. "Crazy Notes on Restrictive Relatives and Other Matters," unpublished paper, Yorktown Heights, New York: Thomas J. Watson Research Center, IBM.

———, 1968. *Crossover Phenomena: A Study in the Grammar of Coreference,* unpublished monograph, Yorktown Heights, New York: Thomas J. Watson Research Center, IBM. Also in the *Linguistic Institute Packet of Papers,* University of Illinois, Summer 1968.

ROBERTS, PAUL, 1964. *English Syntax.* New York: Harcourt, Brace & World.

ROSENBAUM, PETER S., 1967. *The Grammar of English Predicate Complement Constructions.* Cambridge, Massachusetts: M.I.T. Press.

ROSS, JOHN R., 1966a. "A Proposed Rule of Tree-pruning," in Harvard Computation Laboratory Report to the National Science Foundation on Mathematical Linguistics and Automatic Translation, Number NSF-17, Cambridge, Massachusetts.

———, 1966b. "Relativization in Extraposed Clauses," in Harvard Computation Laboratory Report to the National Science Foundation on Mathematical Linguistics and Automatic Translation, Number NSF-17, Cambridge, Massachusetts.

———, 1966c. "On the Cyclic Nature of Pronominalization," in *To Honor Roman Jakobson:* Essays on the Occasion of His Seventieth Birthday, *III.* The Hague: Mouton and Company, 1669–1682. Also in the *Linguistic Institute Packet of Papers,* University of Illinois, Summer 1968.

———, 1967a. *Constraints on Variables in Syntax,* unpublished doctoral dissertation M.I.T. Also in the *Linguistic Institute Packet of Papers,* University of Illinois, Summer 1968.

———, 1967b. "Auxiliaries as Main Verbs," unpublished paper, M.I.T. Also in *Linguistic Institute Packet of Papers,* University of Illinois, Summer 1968.

SMITH, CARLOTA S., 1961. "A Class of Complex Modifiers in English," *Language,* 37:342–365.

———, 1964. "Determiners and Relative Clauses in a Generative Grammar of English," *Language, 40:*48–49.

VETTER, DAVID, 1967. *Need,* Honors Thesis, M.I.T.

WARSHAWSKY, FLORENCE, 1964a. Unpublished, untitled paper on English reflexives, M.I.T.

———, 1964b. Unpublished, untitled paper on English reflexives, M.I.T.

WEINREICH, U., 1966. "Explorations in Semantic Theory," in T. A. Sebeok (ed.), *Current Trends in Linguistics,* Vol. III, "Theoretical Foundations." The Hague: Mouton and Company.